CHATGPT HACKS FOR TEACHERS

A Comprehensive ChatGPT Guide for Educators for Teaching and Learning with Step-by-Step Instructions, Practical Demonstrations, Examples, Prompts, and Video Outputs

Dedicated to 85 Million Teachers Worldwide

COPYRIGHT

info@maxlifepublishing.com

Printed by Maxlife Publishing

Edited by Judith Rooney

Cover Design by Keshav Jha

Photos Pixabay

Printed in Australia

First Printing Edition, 2023

Ebook - ISBN 978-1-922580-02-3

Printed: ISBN 978-1-922580-03-0

NATIONAL LIBRARY OF AUSTRALIA

A catalogue record for this book is available from the National Library of Australia

MAXLIFE PUBLISHING
KNOWLEDGE & WISDOM

www.MaxLifePublishing.com

AUTHOR - KESHAV JHA

FOREWORD BY – DR. JOHN DEMARTINI

DISCLAIMER

The information contained in this non-fiction book is based on the author's research, personal experiences, and opinions. Although every effort has been made to ensure the accuracy and completeness of the information presented, the author and publisher do not assume any liability for any errors, inaccuracies, or omissions in the content.

The material in this book is intended for informational purposes and should not be considered professional advice. Readers are advised to seek the advice of qualified professionals in the relevant field for their specific needs and circumstances.

The author and publisher also do not endorse any products, services, or organisations mentioned in this book. The inclusion of any information or reference to any product, service, or organisation does not constitute an endorsement or recommendation by the author or publisher.

All company logos, images, and trademarks displayed in this book are the property of their respective owners. These images and logos are used for illustrative purposes only. No association, endorsement, or affiliation is implied or intended by the use of these images. All rights reserved by the respective copyright holders.

Readers should use their own discretion and judgement when applying the information presented in this book. The author and publisher shall not be held liable for any losses, damages, or injuries arising from the use or application of the information presented in this book.

DEDICATION

This book is dedicated to the **85 million teachers worldwide** who assiduously and relentlessly work daily towards shaping the minds and futures of individuals, nations, and the world at large.

Writing this book is a humble attempt to honour the legacy of teachers and educators worldwide and aims to help the teachers of today and tomorrow to be well-equipped with the knowledge of "How to use Artificial Intelligence for Teaching and Learning".

I sincerely hope that the book serves as a beacon, guiding teachers to harness the power of AI for imparting education.

May you continue to inspire and be inspired, evolving as the teachers of tomorrow, equipped with the knowledge of Artificial Intelligence, ready to contribute even more profoundly to the brighter future of our world.

"The art of teaching is the art of assisting discovery."

- Mark Van Doren

"One book, one pen, one child, and one teacher can change the world."

- Malala Yousafzai

"The dream begins, most of the time, with a teacher who believes in you, who tugs and pushes and leads you on to the next plateau, sometimes poking you with a sharp stick called truth."

- Dan Rather

QUOTES

"I am in the camp that is concerned about superintelligence. Once humans develop artificial general intelligence, it will take off on its own and redesign itself at an ever-increasing rate. Humans, who are limited by slow biological evolution, couldn't compete and would be superseded."

-- **by Stephen Hawking**

"Artificial intelligence will reach human levels by around 2029. Follow that out further to, say, 2045, we will have multiplied the intelligence, the human biological machine intelligence of our a billion-fold."

-- **by Ray Kurzweil**

"Artificial intelligence is not the end of the journey, but the beginning of a new kind of art, a new kind of culture, a new kind of consciousness."

-- by Benoit Mandelbrot

THREE BONUS INCLUDED

BONUS 1 – PDF DOWNLOAD OF 1165 CHATGPT PROMPTS

Weblink and QR code for downloading 1165 ChatGPT Prompts in **PDF format**. These prompts are specifically written for using ChatGPT to complete common teaching, learning, and professional development tasks. The included ChatGPT prompts are organised into 24 different categories for easy access, enabling readers to copy the prompts directly into ChatGPT and customise them further as deemed necessary for their own teaching and learning tasks.

BONUS 2 – 100+ VIDEOS FOR MORE IMMERSIVE LEARNING

Gain access to more than 100 video outputs of ChatGPT prompts via **weblinks or QR codes** included throughout the book. Videos potentially can make it easier for readers to understand and comprehend "how ChatGPT produces output in real-time," making it simple to follow along, especially for beginners. Each video is quick to watch, lasting around 1-3 minutes, and offers valuable learning insights.

BONUS 3 – COMPLIMENTARY AFFIRMATION APP

An Android app designed for developing a **positive mindset**. The app has built-in brainwave sounds and white noise, which can be used to cultivate a positive mindset. This app can help you stay focused on your core values and achieve your goals.

Upcoming Books – Visit www.MaxlifePublishing.com

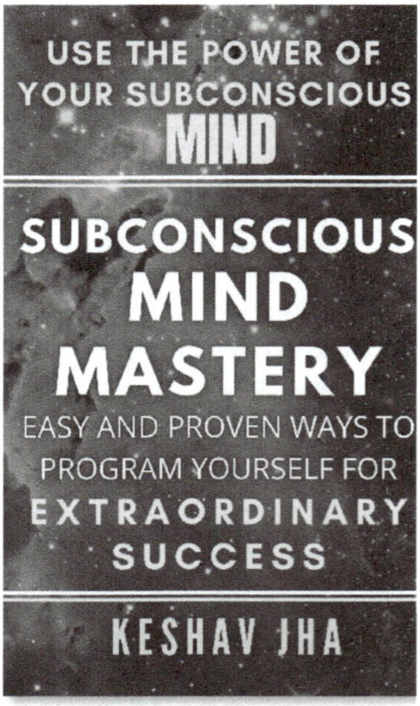

Upcoming Books – Visit www.MaxlifePublishing.com

PRAISE FOR THE BOOK

" 'ChatGPT Hacks for Teachers' is a practical book that will serve teachers in multiple ways. What sets this book apart is its pragmatic approach. It's not merely another theoretical discourse on the potential of AI in education. Instead, it's a comprehensive guide designed to help you harness the power of ChatGPT, featuring step-by-step instructions, demonstrations, examples, prompts, and video outputs.".

Houston, Texas, United States

-- Dr John Demartini, world-renowned Human Behaviour Specialist, researcher, global educator and international best-selling author of "The Values Factor", who featured in "The Secret", a documentary film released in 2006, which transformed millions of lives

" 'ChatGPT Hacks for Teachers' is a helpful resource for educators seeking to explore the use of generative AI in their classrooms and assist with teaching preparation. The book provides practical tips and clear instructions on how to effectively utilise ChatGPT for different purposes - including examples of how we can upskill students in using these advancements in technology to support their learning. It is a valuable tool for educators looking to enhance their teaching with AI technology and for those seeking to better understand the utility of generative AI in learning and teaching."

Port Macquarie, NSW, AUSTRALIA

-- Jess Macer-Wright PhD, Lecturer, University of New South Wales

"If you are new to experimenting with ChatGPT or more experienced, either way, this resource is a must have. Consulting with 'ChatGPT Hacks for Teachers' means that searching is streamlined as the book is meticulously organised, making it easy to jump to sections that are most relevant to your needs. Creating, customising and differentiating quizzes, lesson plans, activities and flashcards is easy. Save yourself some time and embrace the future of teaching with this book as this is the ultimate partner in crime when reducing our time as teachers and creating engaging and effective learning resources."

Mermaid Beach, Queensland, AUSTRALIA

-- Kerianne Williams, Teacher, Librarian, M.Lib., MEd., BAEd(Hons)

"The book is a useful instruction manual that caters for both beginner and experienced users. On top of the well written instructions, the easy to follow practical examples provide a clear and concise picture of the instructions put into action in a real-world scenario. This goes a long way in alleviating a user's apprehension and hesitation in using ChatGPT during their everyday routine. Overall, 'ChatGPT Hacks for Teachers' is a powerful toolkit for assisting teachers & learners alike to maximise their teaching and learning experience."

Sydney, NSW, AUSTRALIA

-- Adel Omer, Coordinator & Teacher – UOW (University of Wollongong) College, PhD Candidate –UTS (University of Technology Sydney)

“ ’ChatGPT Hacks for Teachers’ is a comprehensive guide that equips educators with a clear and accessible approach to integrating ChatGPT into their teaching practices with practical examples of clear and concise prompts covering a variety of topics; this book is a must-read for teachers eager to harness the potential of AI in their day to day work and for their student's learning journey.”

Melbourne, Victoria, AUSTRALIA | Isfahan, IRAN

-- Sheida Toomani, Educator & Coordinator - Kangan Institute, Former Director - Sheida English Language Institute

“This book compiles a variety of ChatGPT tools and applications well worth exploring for the pursuit of creative learning experiences in the educational field. A must read for the consummate teaching professional. One of the strengths of this book is its reliance on research and case studies to substantiate its points. This adds a layer of credibility that is often missing in tech-oriented educational guides. As a teacher, I often find myself overwhelmed with administrative tasks. This book offers practical solutions that have already saved me hours of work. The author uses anecdotes and real-world examples to illustrate points, making it engaging from start to finish."

Sydney, NSW, AUSTRALIA

-- Walter Alvarez, Teacher – TAFE NSW, Former IT Consultant, Business Manager, IT Officer – Department of Defence of Australia

"Reading 'ChatGPT Hacks for Teachers' has broadened my perspective on the acceptance and integration of AI (Artificial Intelligence) as a valuable tool for teaching, learning, and research. It is truly a remarkable innovation that deserves recognition. Even if you're not a tech expert, this book makes the subject approachable. It demystifies the use of ChatGPT in a teaching environment, making it accessible for educators of all levels. Congratulations to the author!"

Pasig City, Manilla, PHILIPPINES

-- Zeneca I. Joseph, Educator - Our Lady of Perpetual Help School

"As teachers and students, it has become increasingly clear that our futures now entail a new, and somewhat intimidating, relationship.. one with AI. Since the release of ChatGPT, the question for teachers has been – how can we use ChatGPT to improve our own teaching and better support student learning? In this easy-to-use guide, Keshav Jha outlines a range of creative and effective ways to do just that. Exploring topics such as summarising and comprehending difficult texts, language development, presentations, developing personalised study tools, stimulating new assessment ideas, coding and more, this practical ChatGPT-user-manual helps guide teachers through each topic with a range of ideas for pedagogical applications and copyable prompt commands. Even those of us who feel anxious about ChatGPT can now relax and get the most out of this powerful new technology."

Wollongong, NSW, AUSTRALIA

-- Anthony Spinks, Coordinator & Teacher – UOW (University of Wollongong) College

"Innovative and timely, 'ChatGPT Hacks For Teachers' offers a fresh look into the potential of AI in education. Keshav Jha skillfully combines theory with practical tips, providing teachers with actionable steps to integrate ChatGPT into their teaching methods. Highly recommended for educators wanting to stay ahead of the tech curve. What I appreciate most about this book is its practicality. It offers actionable steps and hacks that can be easily implemented in the classroom, making it a must-have for any teacher who wants to save time."

Mississauga, Ontario, CANADA

-- Deepti Nair, Solutions Analyst - Wawanesa Insurance

"This book has great potential to support educators by offering a range of 'ChatGPT Hacks for teaching and learning'. It provides practical easy-to-follow tips on differentiation for personalising learning experiences to enhance student engagement in classrooms. The practicality of examples and templates provided by the author provides a treasure trove to educators and will assist in closing the gap between AI and education. Whether you teach primary, tertiary or university, the strategies outlined can be adapted to suit various educational levels and subjects. A versatile guide for any educator."

Sydney, NSW, AUSTRALIA | New Delhi, INDIA

-- Pritipal Baweja, Manager – UNSW (University of New South Wales), Former Senior Manager - Packaging Company

"Keshav Jha's book is a game-changer for educators globally. In an era where teachers grapple with the complexities of AI in schools, this text presents a refreshing viewpoint and empowers them with essential time-saving tools. Chapter 5 & 6 stands out, offering insights on boosting student engagement and simplifying intricate concepts. Overall, this practical guide is indispensable for teachers, delivering crucial daily assistance."

Boonah, Queensland, AUSTRALIA

-- Anne Artesi, Head Of Department Senior Schooling, Queensland Department of Education

"It is a very descriptive and instructive book for ChatGPT. What sets this book apart is its holistic approach. It not only discusses how ChatGPT can be used for teaching and learning but also explores ChatGPT's potential in performing professional development related tasks such as preparing for job interviews, writing and updating resumes and even generating cover letters. The chapters are logically sequenced, making it easy to implement these practical and time saving hacks progressively. "ChatGPT Hacks For Teachers" equips teachers with the knowledge and skills they need to navigate the evolving landscape of education and start using AI for teaching and learning."

Sydney, NSW, AUSTRALIA | Izmir, TURKEY

-- Mert Can Karabulut, Freelance Geriatric Physiotherapist, Former Physiotherapist - Studio Altay Tekin Pilates

"If you've ever wondered how AI could fit into your teaching practices, look no further. This book elucidates the 'Artificial Intelligence powered Chatbot' and shows you how it can make your life easier and your teaching more effective. The book is not just informative but also immensely practical. Keshav Jha does an excellent job of breaking down how ChatGPT can be used to enhance student engagement, create teaching and learning activities, improve language skills, develop and optimise teaching resources and provide feedback to learners. Teachers new to AI can find this book as a gateway to revolutionising their teaching practices by integrating AI within the teaching practices."

Sydney and Melbourne, AUSTRALIA | Kathmandu, NEPAL

-- Bhim Kharel, CEO – KII (Kingsford International Institute), Director - Kingsford Academy Australia,

"This book will prove invaluable for teachers of all subjects, including sciences, humanities, and both natural (human) and programming languages, at all levels. It offers myriad teaching ideas, with clear instructions that even the least tech-savvy among us can follow, along with advice about the limitations of ChatGPT and the need to check the content it produces for errors. As an English teacher who has just begun to dabble in this technology, I can already see that some of Keshav's hacks are going to save me a lot of time and effort."

San Jose, COSTA RICA | Sydney, NSW, AUSTRALIA

-- Peter Tonkin, Freelance English Teacher, Former Academic Manager – STEPS Sunshine Coast International College

"The resources and information within this book are helpful and very straightforward. A teacher can pick this up and, with the prompts and explanations, easily create lessons, PowerPoints and create and check code. Overall a great resource."

Knoxfield, Victoria, AUSTRALIA

-- Ben Eilenberg, STEM and ICT Teacher – St Joseph College, Microsoft Innovative Educator, Former Generalist Primary Teacher and Robotic Co-ordinator – Department of Education and Early Childhood Learning, Victoria, Silverton Primary School, Head of ICT – Adass Israel School

"Keshav Jha's book is well-researched and filled with insights that help educators understand the potential of ChatGPT in educational settings. It's a compelling read that offers new perspectives on teaching and learning. It's particularly beneficial for those struggling with time management. The book takes a novel approach by integrating ChatGPT into teaching methodologies. It offers step-by-step guides that make it easy for even the least tech-savvy teachers to get on board. This book covers a lot of ground but does so in a concise manner. It's not overwhelming making it a practical choice for time-crunched educators. A must-read for those looking to modernise their teaching."

Sydney, NSW, AUSTRALIA | Zurich, SWITZERLAND | Toronto, CANADA | Amsterdam, NETHERLANDS | Denver, USA

-- Prashant Kumar, Principal Consultant - INFOSYS, Former Business Consulting - Capgemini, Solutions Consultant - Accenture, Business Analyst – CMC Ltd.

"It is heartening to know that the initiative for writing this book is based on the author's rich and long experience as a teacher. This is combined with his profound understanding of, and passionate desire to address, the many challenges faced by teachers and learners. It is commendable how Keshav Jha explores the endless possibilities that the new technology of artificial intelligence offers to help guide both teachers and learners.

He aptly defines his objectives in the subtitle of the book itself: 'A Comprehensive ChatGPT Guide for Teaching and Learning with Step-by-Step Instructions, Practical Demonstrations, Examples, Prompts, and Video Outputs.' His distilled experiential wisdom, shared in the book, serves as an excellent and indispensable resource for charting new paths for educators and trainers.

I am certain of the exposure and future possibilities that ChatGPT offers for professional development, thereby enhancing the quality of education at all levels. I take this opportunity to congratulate Keshav Jha for achieving excellence in his chosen career as an educationist.

This book sheds considerable light on the future possibilities that ChatGPT offers for the professional development of educators, as well as in enhancing the quality of education. I congratulate Keshav, one of our own Notre Dame alumni from India, on his achievements in the field of education. I am proud that he continues to share this knowledge of ChatGPT - an emerging technology - to benefit the community of educators."

Munger, Jamalpur, New Delhi, INDIA | Arusha, TANZANIA

-- Sister Lalita (Sisters of Notre Dame), Former Education Coordinator for Notre Dame Schools, India, Manager Counsellor - Notre Dame School

"In the hype surrounding ChatGPT and its use in education, we often marvel at the instantly available output which may have taken us sometimes hours or longer to generate. What I marvel at more than this development of 'our' ability to procure a result is the development of the 'art and science of asking a good question' to get useful and well targeted responses. 'ChatGPT Hacks For Teachers" contains hundreds of clever prompts of many kinds that have certainly stimulated my desire to use ChatGPT as an incredibly fast, resourceful, capable but sometimes equally daft 'teaching buddy'. I can't implicitly trust, nor forgive, this mechanical buddy as one would like to perhaps trust a machine (calculator anyone?) - but strangely that's a very human thing. Thank you Keshav for this stimulating and diverse collection of prompts for teaching and learning."

Padbury, Greater Perth, WESTERN AUSTRALIA

-- Tomaz Lasic, Graduate Teacher Consultant – Western Australia Department of Education, Humanities and Social Science Teacher – Yule Brook College, Former PhD Candidate and Researcher – Murdoch University

HOW TO USE THIS BOOK

As a teacher of over 20 years, I've experienced firsthand the **major challenges** that teachers face in their **daily work**.

These include **not having enough time** to create **high-quality** teaching and learning **resources**, **marking assessments**, providing **detailed feedback**, and **creating lesson plans** for learners with special needs.

To help tackle these challenges and more, this book acts as a **practical guide** that teaches about using artificial intelligence powered **chatbot ChatGPT**, to **empower educators and trainers** to complete their routine tasks **more efficiently**.

The book provides step-by-step instructions and guidance supported by over **100+ videos** showcasing ChatGPT outputs for various tasks, such as creating **lesson plans**, designing **assessments**, providing **student feedback**, generating **programming** language codes, and more.

You can access the **videos using the QR code** provided in the **book** or use the **provided links** as an alternative way to access the videos. In order to make the **videos more accessible and non-distracting,** minimal audio has be used.

The book also includes over **1,500+ ChatGPT prompts** that can be **used to quickly** complete tasks with **little customisation**. **Resources** can be **accessed** in a **non-sequential manner**, allowing readers to **navigate directly to sections or topics of interest** to produce **desired documents** using ChatGPT.

By **harnessing the power of ChatGPT**, teachers and educators can potentially save **hundreds of hours** every year while improving the **overall quality of generated content**, increasing **productivity, creativity, and efficiency**.

For instance, the book introduces **innovative ways** to use **educational videos** available on platforms like YouTube to create **quizzes and assessments in just a few minutes**.

Finally, this book has a humble goal of **helping teachers** to become **more valuable** to their current and future organisations by being equipped with **knowledge and skills** to use ChatGPT to help their **school, university, training organisation or workplace** and **deliver high-quality teaching** without sweat.

SPECIAL BONUS INCLUDED IN THE BOOK

- **Download 1165 ChatGPT Prompts in PDF format** for teaching, learning, and professional development.
- **Gain access to over 100 video outputs of ChatGPT prompts** tailored for teaching, learning, and professional development. These videos are readily available via weblinks or QR codes for your convenience.
- **Android App for developing a positive mindset**. The app has built-in brainwave sounds and white noise, which can be used to cultivate a positive mindset. This app can help you stay focused on your core values and achieve your goals.

CONTENT

ACKNOWLEDGEMENT

Writing this book has been an internally challenging yet immensely fulfilling experience.

I must begin by thanking Henry Lee, Academic Program Manager at UOW (University of Wollongong) College, who invited me to share my views on the "Use of Artificial Intelligence(AI) in Education" at the UOW College's "Curriculum Development Day", attended by academic staff.

The presentation was well-received and was shared among other faculties within UOW College, leading to further interest and requests to present it again to other faculties.

The heightened interest in how to use ChatGPT for teaching and learning led me to contemplate writing a book that can serve as a comprehensive manual covering practical instructions and strategies about using ChatGPT for teaching and learning thereby saving teachers time and also enhancing the quality of various teaching and learning resources.

This book would never have come to fruition if not for Henry, to whom I am deeply grateful for his encouraging words and guidance.

A very special thanks to my friend Bhim Kharel from whom I came to learn about ChatGPT for the first time. I would also like to thank my friends Anuraj Gambhir, Najla Turk, Adel Omar, Nikesh Lalchandani and Bigyan Kharki for their valuable feedback along the way. Their friendship has made a positive difference to the quality of my life.

I am eternally grateful to my late grandfather Bindeshwari Prasad Misra who taught me about the seven core human values essential for a meaningful life - love, passion, courage, dedication, discipline, punctuality and forgiveness.

I am immensely grateful to my father Rabindra Kumar Mishra and my mother Kiran Devi for blessing me with their unconditional love and nurturing from the moment I was born.

A heartfelt thanks to my Uncle Dr. Lakshmishwar Jha for teaching me the importance of good education and for having a curious mind.

I sincerely thank my sister Nina for believing in me and my ability to make a positive difference in this world.

ABOUT AUTHOR

Keshav Jha has worked as a teacher at multiple Australian Colleges and Universities. A teacher, technologist, and researcher by training, Keshav is also a contributing writer to leading Australian magazines and an avid yoga, meditation, and NLP practitioner.

Keshav was fortunate to escape death in Nov 2011 when he drowned in a community swimming pool on a sunny Sunday afternoon, whilst enjoying cool water splashes with his daughter. Luckily, he was rescued by an off-duty police officer attending a family barbeque next to the pool, separated by a fence.

Instant Channel 7 media personality – for two minutes! Thankful for this second chance to live and enjoy seeing his two daughters grow up, Keshav is committed to living a life of gratitude and is determined to help people live more inspiring, purposeful and productive lives.

He is a passionate learner, researcher and curious person by nature, and holds qualifications in information technology, hospitality management, sustainability, finance and mortgage broking, real estate and property management. He has received numerous educational, vocational, and entrepreneurial awards.

He lives in Sydney, Australia with his wife and two daughters.

He is reachable on **LinkedIn** for educational training and consulting in the field of Artificial Intelligence.

https://tinyurl.com/LinkedinKeshav

FOREWORD

As a specialist in human behaviour, as well as a professional speaker, author, researcher, and business consultant, I'm fortunate to mentor and coach a wide range of individuals worldwide. This includes Wall Street executives, professionals in various fields, celebrity actors, healthcare providers, and sports personalities. I offer guidance in areas such as relationships, wealth, education, and business.

I first met Keshav and his wonderful family in 2013 when they attended one of my live events in Sydney, Australia. Through our interactions, I've discovered that Keshav is deeply committed to a mission of continual learning. He is inspired and dedicated to acquiring new knowledge and skills, and he applies them effectively to enhance productivity.

In an era where technology shapes and reshapes the fabric of education, the need for teachers to stay ahead of the curve has never been more pressing. As you leaf through the pages of this easy to read book, 'Chatgpt Hacks for Teachers' you'll find yourself immersed in a timely exploration of how artificial intelligence can revolutionise teaching and learning and save time in doing tasks such as developing lesson plans, creating assessment activities, grading assessments, providing student feedbacks, doing brainstorming session, improving language skills, summarising resources for greater comprehension, proofreading, writing essays, sentiment analysis, developing program codes, simplifying teaching resources, professional developing tasks such as resume writing and updating, preparing for interviews and more.

The timing of this book's arrival could not be more fortuitous. As we navigate the complexities of 21st-century teaching, grappling with remote learning, diverse student needs, and ever-changing curricula, this book serves as a compass pointing us toward the future.

What sets this book apart is its pragmatic approach. It's not just another theoretical discourse on the potential of AI in education. Instead, it's a comprehensive guide designed to help you, the educator, harness the power of ChatGPT for tangible classroom results. With step-by-step instructions, practical demonstrations, examples, prompts, and video outputs, this book is a one-stop shop for transforming your teaching methods.

The book has the potential to empower teachers to transcend traditional boundaries, enabling them to create a more engaging, interactive, and personalised learning experience for the students. Whether you are a seasoned educator or a new entrant into this noble profession, this book has something for everyone.

The future of education augmented by Artificial Intelligence technologies is knocking on our doors, and this book hands you the key. As you delve into its contents, may you find inspiration, practical solutions, and, above all, a renewed sense of purpose in your teaching journey.

About Dr. John Demartini

Dr. John Demartini is a world-renowned specialist in human behaviour, a polymath, a best-selling author and a global educator. He has addressed audiences of up to 11,000 people at a time across the world and shared the stage with some of the world's most influential people such as Sir Richard Branson, Stephen Covey, Steve Wozniak, Robert Kiyosaki, Tony Fernandes, Wayne Dyer, Deepak Chopra and many more.

He has been a welcomed guest on Larry King Live, a contributor to Oprah Magazine, and has been featured in the international phenomenon "The Secret", a documentary film that swept the world in 2006, transforming millions of lives.

Dr. Demartini is the author of over 40 self-development books and manuscripts such as the acclaimed 'The Breakthrough Experience®' which has been translated into over 40 languages and has been delivered in person and online globally to over 125,000 students to date.

He has produced 100+ audio and video online courses and products covering subjects such as Building Wealth, Mind-Body Connection, Accessing Your 7 Greatest Powers, Conscious Intention, Powerful Business Insights and many more. He has worked with entrepreneurs, board members, CEOs, managers, teams and employees for over 50 years in over 190 countries such as India, Iran, USA, SA, UK, Australia, New Zealand, Botswana, Canada, Japan, Singapore and Malaysia, to name a few.

Dr. Demartini has appeared in over 50 documentaries, including The Secret, The Opus, The Compass and Oh My God, alongside celebrities such as Hugh Jackman, Seal, Ringo Star and Bob Geldof. He has been interviewed by thousands of newspaper and magazine publications, and radio and television talk shows across the globe (www.DrDemartini.com/media) and his work has been referenced in over 740 books.

'The magnificence of who you are far exceeds any fantasy you will ever impose upon yourself.'

-- Quote by Dr. John Demartini

CHAPTER 1

INTRODUCTION TO AI CHATBOT CHATGPT

1. Introduction to AI Chatbot ChatGPT

Chatbots and artificial intelligence have been **rapidly advancing in recent years**, transforming industries such as healthcare, finance, and customer service.

In the **education sector**, there is a growing interest in **exploring** the potential of chatbots for **enhancing teaching and learning**. One such chatbot that has **gained a lot of attention** is ChatGPT.

ChatGPT is an **artificial intelligence language model** developed by OpenAI (2022) that is designed to respond to a wide range of prompts and questions in a **conversation style**.

Its programming is based on **deep learning algorithms** that have been trained on **massive amounts of text data from the internet**.

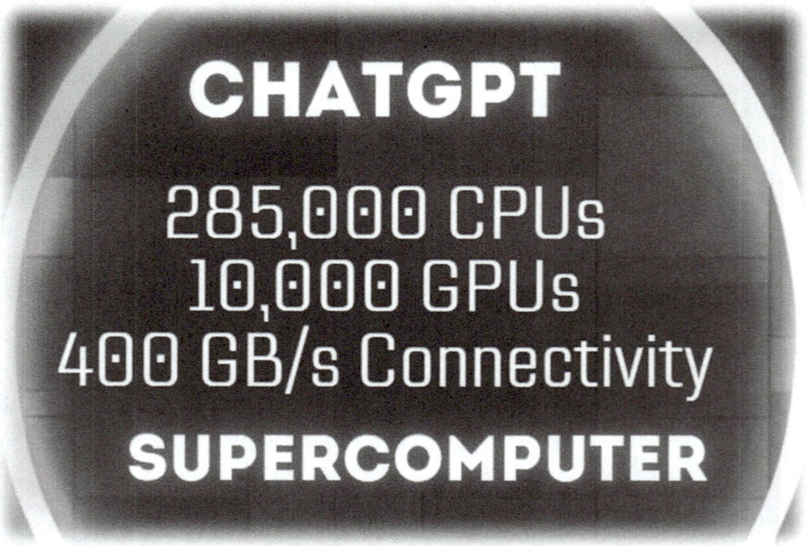

This allows ChatGPT to understand natural language and **generate responses that are contextually relevant and coherent.**

Pre-trained language models such as ChatGPT and others are designed to **understand** and **generate human-like language**.

ChatGPT uses a **supercomputer** which at the time of writing this book is using around **285,000 CPUs, and 10,000 GPUs** and has **400GB/s** connectivity. It has been trained on **300 billion words.**

Here is a **comparison** of some of the **most popular pre-trained language models** including their **number of parameters**.

Language Model	Developer	Number of Parameters	Notable Features
GPT-4	OpenAI	1.76 trillion	1000 times larger than GPT-3
GPT-3	OpenAI	175 billion	Strong language generation capabilities
T5	Google	11 billion	Trained on a diverse set of language tasks
BERT-base	Google	110 million	Strong performance on various language tasks
BERT-large	Google	340 million	Strong performance on various language tasks
RoBERTa	Facebook AI	355 million	Strong performance on various language tasks

Multiple Ways ChatGPT Can Be Used in Education

ChatGPT has **enormous potential** for enhancing teaching and learning in many **ways**.

Here are some of the ways in which ChatGPT can be **leveraged to improve the educational experience**:

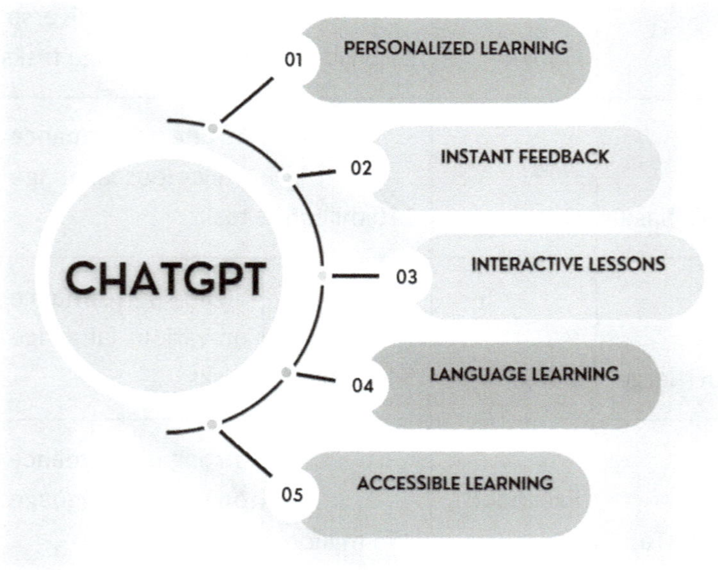

1. **Personalised Learning:** ChatGPT can be used to create personalised learning experiences for students. By analyzing each student's learning style and adapting the curriculum to

their individual needs, ChatGPT can help students learn more effectively and efficiently.

2. **Instant Feedback:** ChatGPT can provide instant feedback to students, allowing them to gauge their progress and adjust their approach accordingly. This feedback can be in the form of quizzes, assessments, or even conversational interactions.

3. **Interactive Lessons:** ChatGPT can be used to create interactive lessons that engage students and make learning more fun. By using conversational prompts, quizzes, and interactive activities, ChatGPT can help students stay engaged and interested in content.

4. **Language Learning:** ChatGPT can be used to facilitate language learning by providing conversational practice and feedback. By practising conversations with ChatGPT, students can improve their language skills in an immersive way.

5. **Accessible Learning:** ChatGPT can help make education more accessible by providing resources and support to students who may not have access to traditional educational materials. By using conversational interfaces, ChatGPT can help bridge the gap between students and educational resources, regardless of location or background.

Setting Up Your ChatGPT Account

Step 1 – Visiting the Website: You can Visit ChatGPT's page at https://chat.openai.com/chat and click "Try ChatGPT" to create a new account.

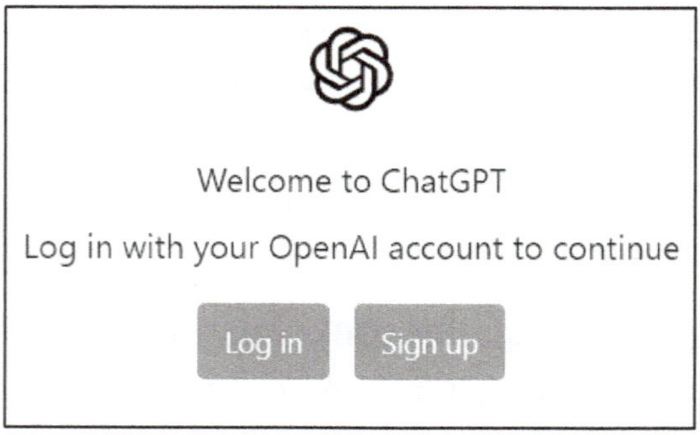

Step 2 – Registration: Use the **"Create your account"** to sign up for a ChatGPT account.

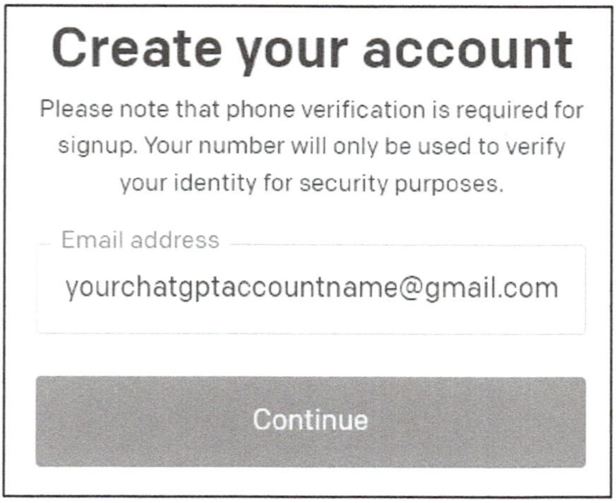

Tip: Please use your generic email such as Yahoo, Gmail or Hotmail rather than organisational email as you need an email that you can access over a long time.

Step 3 – Verification: You will need to **verify the email address** by opening the email that you used earlier for the Chatgpt sign-up and verifying by clicking on **"Verify email address"** in the email message sent to you by OpenAI company.

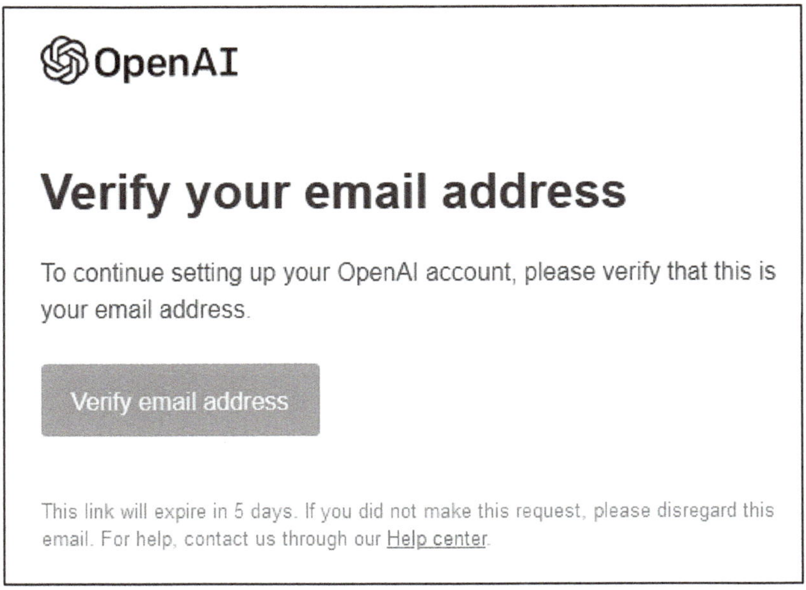

You can use the free account now and later will have the option to upgrade it to a paid account if you want faster and uninterrupted high bandwidth performance from ChatGPT.

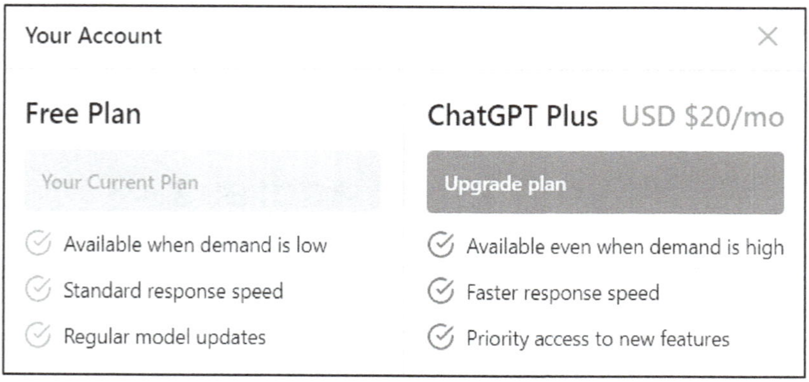

Step 4 – User Interface: Once you're logged into ChatGPT, you'll see a **user interface like the one pictured below**.

On the left, you'll find the **menu and activity log** where you can store your conversations with the bot for later. The **new chat** button is also located there.

Step 4 – Interaction: When you first log in, the log will be empty, and the bot will be **ready and waiting to start a new conversation**. Your messages and the **bot's replies will appear in the middle section** of the page.

Finally, the text box at the bottom is where you'll **type in your questions and prompts**. Click on the **new chat or empty box to try a conversation**.

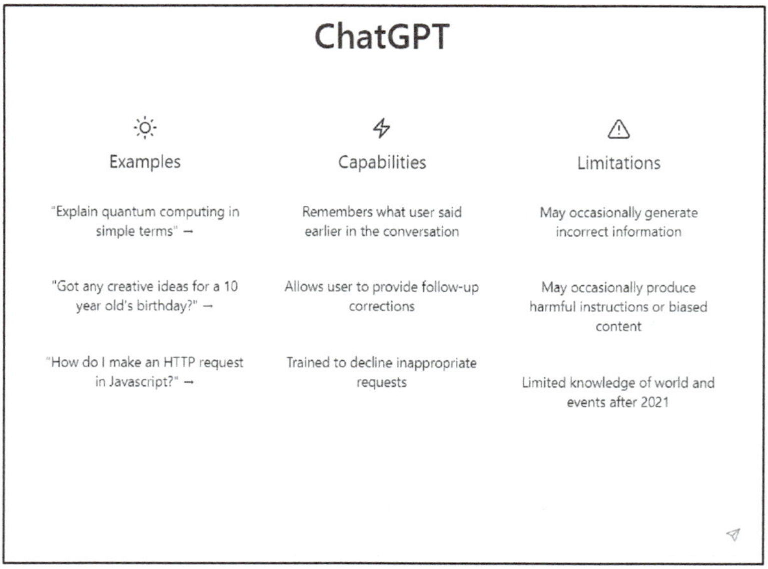

Step 5 – Asking Questions: You can try asking **"Tell me about yourself"** to learn more about ChatGPT from ChatGPT.

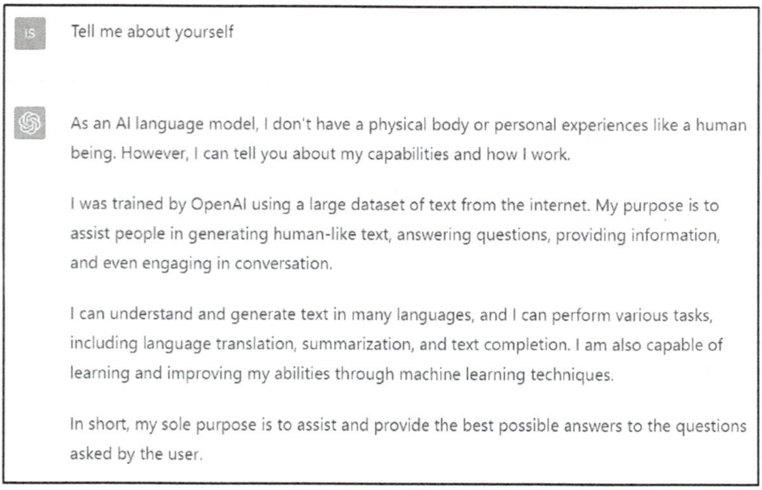

Step 6 – Quick Tips for Asking Questions: When you're ready to start your conversation with ChatGPT, just type your question or request in the text box.

Unlike standard chatbots and search engines, **ChatGPT can understand natural language** and conversational language.

The more precise your prompts are, the more precise the responses will be from ChatGPT. You can start with a general question or request, and then further refine it in a subsequent question, just like you would with a human.

Eight Proven Strategies to Make Prompts More Effective

Prompting or **"the way of asking questions"** from ChatGPT is a critical component of ChatGPT conversations.

A prompt is a **piece of text** that is used to **initiate a conversation with ChatGPT**. The **quality of the prompt** can have a **significant**

impact on the quality of the response generated by ChatGPT. Here are some tips for creating good prompts:

1. Be Specific: The more specific your prompt is, the more likely you are to get a relevant response from ChatGPT. For example, instead of asking **"Can you tell me about physics?"** try asking **"What are the basic principles of Newton's laws of motion?"**

> IS What are the basic principles of Newton's laws of motion?
>
> Newton's laws of motion are the foundation of classical mechanics, and describe the behavior of objects in motion. The three laws are:
>
> 1. First Law: The law of inertia - An object at rest will remain at rest, and an object in motion will remain in motion at a constant velocity, unless acted upon by an external force. This law describes the concept of inertia, which is the resistance of an object to a change in its motion.
> 2. Second Law: The law of acceleration - The acceleration of an object is directly proportional to the net force applied to it, and inversely proportional to its mass. This law is often expressed mathematically as F = ma, where F is the net force applied to an object, m is its mass, and a is its acceleration.
> 3. Third Law: The law of action and reaction - For every action, there is an equal and opposite reaction. This law describes how forces occur in pairs, with one force acting on one object and the other force acting on another object.

2. Use Keywords: Including relevant keywords in your prompt can help ChatGPT understand what you are looking for. For example, if you are **looking for information on a specific topic**, include the topic name in your prompt.

A prompt like "**Tell me about the human genome with 3 specific examples**" will generate a more focused response.

The human genome is the complete set of DNA that contains all of the genetic information necessary to build and maintain a human being. It is composed of approximately 3 billion nucleotide base pairs and is organized into 23 pairs of chromosomes. Each chromosome contains many genes, which are segments of DNA that code for proteins.

Here are three specific examples of genes and their functions within the human genome:

1. BRCA1 and BRCA2: The BRCA1 and BRCA2 genes are involved in the repair of damaged DNA, which helps to prevent the development of certain types of cancer. Mutations in these genes can increase a person's risk of developing breast and ovarian cancer.
2. CFTR: The CFTR gene codes for a protein that regulates the movement of salt and water in and out of cells. Mutations in this gene can cause cystic fibrosis, a genetic disorder that affects the lungs, pancreas, and other organs.
3. HBB: The HBB gene codes for the beta-globin subunit of hemoglobin, which is the protein in red blood cells that carries oxygen throughout the body. Mutations in this gene can cause sickle cell anemia, a genetic disorder in which the red blood cells are misshapen and can cause a variety of health problems.

3. Be Clear: In order to get the **best response from ChatGPT**, it's important to use **clear and straightforward language**. This means **avoiding technical terminology or phrases** that may be **unfamiliar** to the reader. A good prompt should be easily understood by ChatGPT so that it can provide a relevant answer. For instance, when dealing with artificial intelligence in the workplace, a better question would be **"What are the pros and cons of utilizing AI in the workplace?".**

By making sure that the prompt is **straightforward**, you can be confident that ChatGPT will be able to **answer it accurately**. Avoid using **ambiguous or vague language** in your prompts **at all costs**.

This can lead to confusing or irrelevant responses from ChatGPT. Instead, use clear, focussed and concise language for your query.

An example of a <u>vague prompt</u> could be "**Tell me about history**"

This prompt is **too extensive and vague**. History includes a **vast range of topics and periods**, making it difficult to know where to begin.

A more focused and specific prompt could be: "**Tell me about the events leading up to the Second World War**"

> The Second World War was a global conflict that lasted from 1939 to 1945. The events leading up to the war were complex and multifaceted, with many political, economic, and social factors playing a role. Here are some key events and developments that contributed to the outbreak of war:
>
> 1. Treaty of Versailles: The Treaty of Versailles, which was signed in 1919, ended World War I and imposed harsh penalties on Germany, including reparations payments and territorial losses. Many Germans were unhappy with the treaty and felt that it was unfair, which contributed to the rise of nationalism and militarism in Germany.

Ambiguous prompt: "**What is the best way to study?**"

This prompt shown above is ambiguous because it **does not specify what subject or type of study** the user is asking about. It could refer to studying for an exam, studying a new language, or studying a new skill.

Improved prompt: **"What are some effective study techniques for learning a new language?"**

This prompt **specifies the subject and the type of study**, making it easier for the user to understand what kind of response to expect.

It also **narrows down the scope** of the response, making it **more manageable for the AI** to provide useful information.

Learning a new language can be a challenging and rewarding experience. Here are some effective study techniques for improving language skills:

1. Immersion: Immersing oneself in a language is one of the most effective ways to learn. This can be done by traveling to a country where the language is spoken, watching movies or TV shows in the language, or speaking with native speakers. This helps learners to get a better sense of the language's grammar, pronunciation, and vocabulary.
2. Practice, practice, practice: Consistent practice is key to learning a new language. This includes practicing listening, speaking, reading, and writing skills. Setting aside time each day to practice these skills can help learners to progress more quickly.
3. Flashcards: Flashcards are a simple but effective tool for memorizing vocabulary words. They can be used to practice vocabulary in a variety of ways, such as by matching words with pictures or by translating words from one language to another.
4. Language learning apps: There are many language learning apps available that can help learners to practice their skills. These apps often include games, exercises, and quizzes that are designed to help learners improve their grammar, vocabulary, and pronunciation.

1. **Avoid Yes/No Questions:** Yes/No questions can **limit the scope of the response** generated by ChatGPT. Instead, try asking **open-ended questions** that encourage ChatGPT to provide **more detailed and informative** responses.

2. **Use Open-ended Questions:** An open-ended prompt **enables interpretation and creativity** in the response. It encourages ChatGPT to explore different ideas and perspectives. An **overly prescriptive or rigid prompt can limit ChatGPT's creativity** leading to a **less engaging** response.

> Regular exercise has numerous positive impacts on overall health and well-being, including:
>
> 1. Improved physical fitness: Regular exercise helps improve physical fitness by strengthening the cardiovascular and respiratory systems, building muscle and bone mass, and improving flexibility and balance.
> 2. Reduced risk of chronic diseases: Exercise has been shown to reduce the risk of chronic diseases such as heart disease, stroke, type 2 diabetes, and certain cancers.
> 3. Improved mental health: Exercise has been shown to reduce symptoms of depression and anxiety, improve mood and self-esteem, and increase cognitive function.
> 4. Better sleep: Exercise can improve sleep quality and duration, which is important for overall health and well-being.
> 5. Weight management: Exercise can help with weight loss and weight management by burning calories and increasing metabolism.
> 6. Reduced risk of falls: Regular exercise can improve balance, coordination, and strength, which can reduce the risk of falls in older adults.
> 7. Increased longevity: Studies have shown that regular exercise is associated with a longer lifespan and a reduced risk of premature death.

3. **Provide Context**: Providing context in your prompt can assist ChatGPT in **understanding the nature of your query** and generate a more relevant response. For example, if you are looking for information on a **specific topic**, provide some **background information** to help ChatGPT understand the **context of your query**.

   <u>Without context</u>: **"What is the best restaurant in town?"**

   This prompt is **too vague** and **doesn't provide any context** about what kind of restaurant the user is looking for.

With context: **"I'm in the mood for Indian food. What is the best Indian restaurant in Newtown, Sydney?"**

This prompt **provides context** by specifying the **type of cuisine** the user is **interested** in, which makes it **easier for the AI** to provide a relevant and helpful response.

Providing context in the prompt also **helps to avoid confusion** and ensures that the user gets the information they need.

> There are many great Indian restaurants in Newtown, Sydney, but some of the top-rated ones include:
>
> 1. Indian Home Diner: Known for their delicious curries and generous portion sizes, Indian Home Diner is a popular spot for locals and visitors alike.
> 2. Maya Da Dhaba: This family-run restaurant is known for its authentic Indian cuisine, friendly service, and welcoming atmosphere.
> 3. Faheem Fast Food: This casual eatery is known for its delicious biryani and flavorful curries, as well as its affordable prices.
> 4. The Spice Room: With its elegant decor and extensive menu, The Spice Room is a great choice for a special night out. Their dishes are made with high-quality ingredients and are bursting with flavor.

ChatGPT has **immense potential** for improving teaching and learning.

It can be used to create **personalized, engaging, and accessible educational experiences** that can help students **learn more effectively and efficiently**.

By following best practices for creating an effective prompt, educators can ensure that they are getting the most out of ChatGPT's capabilities.

Limitations of ChatGPT

As an **AI language model**, **ChatGPT** is a **versatile tool** that can perform a wide range of **useful tasks** such as **language translation**, **debating**, **research question answering**, and **code generation**. Its **remarkable abilities** have made it a **popular choice** for different types of **content creation**.

However, **ChatGPT** has its **limitations** and users must be aware of these issues that they might encounter when using ChatGPT.

Mid-way interruption when generating a response

At times, while attempting to write a longer response or answer, ChatGPT may encounter a mid-way interruption. In such cases, there are three available options:

1. **Continue** - by inputting a follow-up prompt **“continue” “go on” or “carry on”,** ChatGPT can resume from where it left off. This method is recommended to save time and effort in regenerating longer-type responses.
2. **Regenerate response** - by clicking the button above the chatbox, ChatGPT will rewrite the previous response from the beginning. However, it is possible to encounter the same error again so be **mentally prepared** to face such issues.
3. **New chat** - if the previous methods are unsuccessful, pressing the button on the top left of the page will initiate a new chat. It is important to note that this method does **not support follow-up questions**, and you will need to **start from the beginning**.

Lack of common sense and emotional intelligence

One of ChatGPT's limitations is its lack of common sense and background knowledge compared to humans.

Despite its ability to generate human-like responses and access vast amounts of information, it may occasionally provide nonsensical or inaccurate responses to certain questions or situations.

Additionally, ChatGPT does not possess true emotional intelligence, making it difficult for it to detect subtle emotional cues or respond appropriately to complex emotional situations.

Struggle with understanding context and generating long-form structured content

ChatGPT may also struggle with understanding context, particularly sarcasm and humour, and generating long-form structured content. Its performance is best when given a single task or objective to focus on and may provide biased or inaccurate responses based on the biases or prejudices present in the data on which it was trained.

Accuracy problems and grammatical issues

Accuracy problems or grammatical issues are another limitation of ChatGPT. It may not always provide entirely accurate responses in terms of context or relevance, especially when processing complex or specialized information.

Fine-tuning and computational resources

To use ChatGPT for specific use cases, fine-tuning may be necessary. This process involves training the model on a particular set of data to optimize its performance for a specific task or objective. However, fine-tuning can be time-consuming and resource-intensive.

Furthermore, ChatGPT is a highly complex and sophisticated AI language model that requires substantial computational resources to operate efficiently. Running it on low-end hardware or systems with limited computational power can result in slower processing times, reduced accuracy, and other performance issues.

Importance of verification and addressing biases

It is crucial to verify ChatGPT's answers whenever possible, as it can provide incorrect or even hilariously wrong answers, even though it may be confident in them. This underscores the importance of being critical of AI language models' output and approaching them with a critical eye while recognizing their limitations.

Finally, it is essential to acknowledge the potential for biases and discriminatory results in ChatGPT and other AI tools. Insufficient training data or biases in the data used for training can have a detrimental impact on the model's output. Therefore, it is important to recognize and address such biases to ensure fairness and reduce bias in technology.

Fifty Frequently Asked Questions About ChatGPT

In this section, you will find **answers** to **frequently asked questions** about ChatGPT, its **functionalities, capabilities, and best practices.**

Whether you're new to this platform or seeking in-depth knowledge, this section aims to address your queries comprehensively.

1. **What is ChatGPT, and what does it do?**

ChatGPT is a state-of-the-art language model developed by OpenAI. It employs the GPT (Generative Pre-trained

Transformer) architecture to generate human-like text in response to prompts. Specifically designed for interactive conversations, ChatGPT aims to provide contextually relevant and coherent responses.

2. **How does ChatGPT generate text?**

ChatGPT generates text through a process called autoregressive text generation. It predicts each word in a sequence based on the preceding words, leveraging patterns learnt from vast amounts of text in its training data. It employs a deep neural network to make these predictions.

3. **Is ChatGPT powered by artificial intelligence?**

Indeed, ChatGPT is powered by artificial intelligence. It falls under the category of natural language processing (NLP) models, utilising machine learning techniques to comprehend and produce human-like text.

4. **Can ChatGPT understand and respond to human conversations?**

Yes, ChatGPT is designed to engage in human-like conversations. It can maintain context within a dialogue, respond to prompts and questions, and create back-and-forth interactions.

5. **What are the primary applications of ChatGPT?**

ChatGPT finds applications in various domains, including answering questions, providing explanations, offering creative writing assistance, customer support interactions, content generation, and more. Its versatility allows it to cater to a wide range of text-based tasks.

6. **Can I use ChatGPT for creative writing?**

Absolutely, ChatGPT is a valuable tool for creative writing endeavours. It can assist in generating narratives, poems, scripts, and other forms of artistic expression. However, the quality of creative output might vary, and human review is advisable.

7. **Is ChatGPT available in languages other than English?**

Yes, OpenAI has expanded ChatGPT's language support beyond English. While it may be accessible in other languages, the level of proficiency and availability can vary depending on the language.

8. **How accurate are ChatGPT's responses?**

ChatGPT's responses are generated based on patterns in its training data. While it aims for accuracy, it can occasionally produce incorrect or nonsensical answers, especially when faced with ambiguous queries or topics it hasn't often encountered.

9. **What is the difference between ChatGPT and GPT-3?**

ChatGPT is a variant of the GPT-3 architecture, tailored to perform exceptionally well in conversational scenarios. While GPT-3 can also generate text, ChatGPT is optimised to provide contextually coherent responses in dynamic conversations.

10. **Can ChatGPT provide professional advice, like medical or legal information?**

No, ChatGPT's responses should not be considered as a substitute for professional advice. It doesn't possess the expertise of qualified professionals in fields like medicine or law.

11. **How can I control the tone or style of ChatGPT's responses?**

You can influence ChatGPT's tone and style by adjusting parameters such as "temperature" and "max tokens." Temperature affects the randomness of responses, while max tokens limit response length.

12. **Is ChatGPT's output always coherent and sensible?** While

While ChatGPT endeavours to generate coherent and sensible output, it might produce responses that seem sensible but are factually incorrect or nonsensical due to its reliance on training data patterns.

13. **What is fine-tuning, and can I customise ChatGPT's behaviour?**

Fine-tuning is the process of refining a pre-trained model like ChatGPT for specific tasks or behaviours. While OpenAI allows some customisation, it might be limited compared to full-scale fine-tuning.

14. **Can I use ChatGPT to translate languages?**

While ChatGPT can provide basic translation assistance, it's not a dedicated translation tool and might not match the accuracy of specialised translation services.

15. **How can businesses benefit from using ChatGPT?**

Businesses can leverage ChatGPT for various purposes, including customer support interactions, content generation, interactive user experiences, brainstorming sessions, and ideation processes.

16. **Is ChatGPT available for free, or is there a cost?**

OpenAI offers both free access and paid subscription plans for ChatGPT. Free usage might have limitations, while subscription plans provide enhanced features and usage.

17. **How does OpenAI ensure the ethical usage of ChatGPT?**

OpenAI has implemented safety mechanisms to mitigate the generation of inappropriate or harmful content. However, it might still display instances of false positives or negatives.

18. **Can I integrate ChatGPT into my website or application?**

Yes, OpenAI provides an API that enables developers to seamlessly integrate ChatGPT into their websites, applications, and other platforms to enhance user interactions.

19. **Is ChatGPT capable of generating code or programming scripts?**

While ChatGPT can generate code snippets, it might not consistently provide accurate or optimal coding solutions.

20. **Does ChatGPT have limitations in understanding context?**

ChatGPT understands the context within the current conversation, but its memory is limited. It might struggle to recall information from earlier parts of lengthy conversations.

21. **Can I have multi-turn conversations with ChatGPT?**

Yes, ChatGPT supports multi-turn conversations, allowing you to maintain context and refer to previous messages within the same conversation.

22. **How does ChatGPT handle offensive or inappropriate content?**

OpenAI has implemented a content filter to reduce the likelihood of ChatGPT generating offensive or inappropriate content. However, it might have instances of false positives or negatives.

23. **Can ChatGPT generate content for marketing or social media?**

ChatGPT can assist in generating marketing copy, social media posts, and other text-based content. However, it's advisable to review and edit the output for accuracy and alignment with brand messaging.

24. **What kind of feedback is OpenAI looking for from users?**

OpenAI welcomes user feedback on problematic model outputs, especially those that could be harmful or unintended. Feedback regarding false positives/negatives from the content filter is also valuable.

25. **Is ChatGPT's performance continuously improving?**

Yes, OpenAI strives to improve ChatGPT's performance over time based on user feedback and ongoing research. This leads to regular updates and refinements to the model.

26. **Can I use ChatGPT for tutoring or educational purposes?**

ChatGPT can provide explanations and answer questions, making it potentially useful for educational purposes. However, it's not a substitute for personalised instruction from educators.

27. **Is ChatGPT suitable for brainstorming or generating ideas?**

ChatGPT is a valuable tool for brainstorming sessions. It can assist in generating creative ideas, concepts, and solutions across various domains.

28. **Can I ask ChatGPT to summarise long passages of text?**

Yes, ChatGPT can assist in summarising text, although the quality and conciseness of the summary might vary based on the input text's complexity.

29. **Does ChatGPT generate original content, or does it copy from its training data?**

ChatGPT generates original text based on patterns learnt from its training data. It doesn't copy specific sentences verbatim from its training set.

30. **How does ChatGPT compare to other AI language models on the market?**

ChatGPT is among the leading AI language models and offers capabilities for generating text and engaging in conversations. Its performance might vary compared to other models in different contexts.

31. **Is there a character or word limit for input when using ChatGPT?**

Yes, there are limitations on input length, often referred to as "max tokens." If the input exceeds this limit, its response might be truncated or incomplete.

32. **Can ChatGPT understand technical or specialised subjects?**

ChatGPT has some capacity to understand technical content, but its expertise is limited to the breadth of information present in its training data.

33. **Is there a way to make ChatGPT's responses more concise?**

Yes, you can influence the length and conciseness of ChatGPT's responses by adjusting parameters like temperature and max tokens.

34. **Can I have a real-time conversation with ChatGPT?**

Yes, you can engage in real-time conversations with ChatGPT by sending messages sequentially and incorporating previous responses to maintain context.

35. **Is ChatGPT capable of recognising user emotions or sentiments?**

ChatGPT doesn't inherently recognise emotions but can generate text based on emotional cues provided in the conversation.

36. **What industries can benefit the most from using ChatGPT?**

Industries such as customer support, content creation, marketing, education, research, and creative writing can all benefit from ChatGPT's capabilities.

37. **Does ChatGPT provide citations or sources for the information it generates?**

ChatGPT doesn't provide citations or explicit sources for its responses. It's important to independently verify information for accuracy.

38. **Can I access historical chat logs when using ChatGPT?**

OpenAI's GPT models don't retain memory of past interactions, so you cannot access historical chat logs within the same session.

39. **Is ChatGPT suitable for storytelling or creating narratives?**

Yes, ChatGPT is adept at generating narratives and stories, making it useful for creative writing and storytelling purposes.

40. **How does ChatGPT handle ambiguous or unclear queries?**

ChatGPT might struggle with ambiguous or unclear queries, potentially leading to responses that don't align with the intended meaning.

41. **Is ChatGPT's API available for developers to build applications?**

Yes, OpenAI offers an API that developers can use to integrate ChatGPT into their websites, applications, and other platforms to enhance user interactions.

42. **Can I use ChatGPT to draft emails or other written correspondence?**

Yes, ChatGPT can assist in drafting emails or other written content. However, it's recommended to review and edit the output for accuracy and tone.

43. **How is user privacy and data security ensured when using ChatGPT?**

OpenAI retains user data for 30 days but has measures in place to protect user privacy. Review OpenAI's privacy policy for detailed information.

44. **Is there a limit to the number of requests I can make to ChatGPT?**

Usage limits depend on the pricing plan. Free users and paid subscribers have different levels of access and usage.

45. **Does ChatGPT learn and improve from the conversations it has?**

While ChatGPT doesn't learn in the traditional sense, OpenAI utilises user feedback to enhance the model over time, leading to updates and refinements.

46. **What types of conversations are better suited for ChatGPT?**

ChatGPT is suitable for a wide range of conversations, including answering questions, brainstorming, storytelling, explanations, and more.

47. **Can I give ChatGPT a persona or character to emulate?** While

ChatGPT doesn't inherently emulate personas, you can guide the model's responses by providing specific context or instructions.

48. **Is ChatGPT effective for content localisation or translation?**

While ChatGPT can provide basic translations, its expertise might not match specialised translation tools for complex or nuanced content.

49. **What are the technical requirements for integrating ChatGPT into my platform?**

OpenAI's API documentation provides technical details and guidelines for integrating ChatGPT into various platforms and applications.

50. **Where can I access ChatGPT and its documentation?**

You can access ChatGPT and its documentation through OpenAI's official website. The documentation offers information on usage, guidelines, and API access.

You can find the help section for ChatGPT on OpenAI's website which gets updated regularly. Here is the shortened URL for your convenience along with QR Code.

https://tinyurl.com/ChatGPThelpSupport

CHAPTER 2

USE CHATGPT TO DEVELOP LESSON PLANS FOR ANY TOPIC

2. Use ChatGPT to Develop Lesson Plans for Any Topic

In today's fast-paced education landscape, **lesson planning** is an essential component of **effective teaching**. Teachers need to create **engaging and effective lessons** that cater to the diverse needs and interests of their students. ChatGPT, an **advanced natural language processing model**, can be a game-changer in this process.

In this chapter, we will **explore** how ChatGPT can be **utilised for lesson planning**, including **ways to generate ideas for lesson plans**, creating **customized lesson plans** based on student needs and interests, and **strategies for incorporating ChatGPT-generated content** into lesson plans.

ChatGPT can be **leveraged to optimize lesson planning**, however, it must be used **thoughtfully**. Lesson plans should be **crafted with a specific intent**, such as outlining the objectives and results, encouraging conversations about **inclusivity and individualized instruction**, and confirming **alignment with the curriculum** and other educators.

The **first step** in using ChatGPT for lesson planning is to **generate ideas for your lesson plans**. To do this, you can **provide ChatGPT with a topic** or theme, and it will generate relevant text that can be used as a **starting point** for your lesson plan. For example, if you want to create a lesson plan on the Industrial Revolution, you could input **"Industrial Revolution"** into ChatGPT, and it might generate text such as:

JS Industrial Revolution

The Industrial Revolution was a period of rapid industrialization and technological advancement that began in the late 18th century and continued through the 19th century. The Industrial Revolution began in Britain and then spread to other parts of Europe, North America, and eventually the world.

The Industrial Revolution was characterized by several key developments, including the invention of new machinery and tools, the development of new manufacturing techniques, and the growth of the factory system. These changes led to significant increases in productivity and efficiency, which in turn drove economic growth and increased wealth.

This text **"Industrial Revolution"** can be used as a starting point for your lesson plan, and you can build on it by adding more **specific information, activities, and assessments**.

Basic Level Lesson Plan

Before you start **using ChatGPT to generate answers or text**, it's important to note that the response may be generated **in parts and not all at once**. If you receive a **partial answer**, simply **write "continue" in the prompt** to request the next part of the answer.

Depending on the **complexity and criteria** of your question, you may need to **use "continue" multiple times until the full response is generated**. This is a normal part of using ChatGPT.

Here is an example of how to create a **basic lesson plan.**

ChatGPT Prompt Template:

> Create **[no. of weeks]** weeks lesson plan with subtopics for teaching about **[topic]** to **[teaching level – eg. primary, high school, college, degree, postgraduate, doctoral]** students.

Customised ChatGPT Prompt Created from the Template:

> **Create a 12-week lesson plan with subtopics for teaching about "Industrial Revolution" to postgraduate students.**

ChatGPT video URL and QR code:

https://tinyurl.com/Basic-LessonPlan

ChatGPT Output:

Week 1: Introduction to the Industrial Revolution

- Defining the Industrial Revolution
- Understanding the social, economic, and political contexts that gave rise to the Industrial Revolution

Week 2: Key Inventions of the Industrial Revolution

- The steam engine
- The spinning jenny
- The power loom
- The telegraph
- The railroad

Week 3: Industrialization and Urbanization

- How industrialization transformed cities
- Urbanization and the growth of the middle class
- The impact of the Industrial Revolution on migration patterns

Week 4: Working Conditions in the Industrial Revolution

- The rise of factory work
- Poor working conditions
- Child labour
- The growth of labour unions

Week 5: The Impact of the Industrial Revolution on Agriculture

- Changes in farming practices
- The growth of agriculture and the food industry
- The impact of the Industrial Revolution on rural communities

Week 6: Transportation and Communication

- The impact of the Industrial Revolution on transportation and communication
- The development of the railroad
- The invention of the telegraph

Week 7: The Industrial Revolution and Globalization

- The spread of industrialization to other parts of the world
- The impact of the Industrial Revolution on international trade

- The role of imperialism and colonialism in the spread of industrialization

Week 8: The Industrial Revolution and the Environment

- The impact of industrialization on the environment
- The growth of pollution
- The emergence of environmentalism

Week 9: The Industrial Revolution and Science

- The role of science and technology in the Industrial Revolution
- Scientific developments during the Industrial Revolution
- The impact of the Industrial Revolution on scientific progress

Week 10: Women in the Industrial Revolution

- The role of women in the Industrial Revolution
- Women in the workforce
- Women's rights and suffrage movements

Week 11: The Industrial Revolution and Art

- The impact of the Industrial Revolution on art
- The rise of industrial design

- The emergence of new art movements

Week 12: The Legacy of the Industrial Revolution

- The lasting impact of the Industrial Revolution on society, politics, and the economy
- Debates surrounding the Industrial Revolution and its legacy
- The relevance of the Industrial Revolution in contemporary society

Intermediate Level Lesson Plan

You can also use more **specific prompts** with **detailed requirements** for the lesson plan. The lesson plan may include requirements such as **topics, subtopics, activities and learning outcomes.**

Here is an example of how to create an **intermediate lesson plan** with **various requirements.**

ChatGPT Prompt Template:

Create a **[no. of weeks]** week lesson plan with **[no. of subtopics]** subtopics for teaching **[topic]** to **[teaching level]** students. Include **[no. of activities]** activities and **[no of learning outcomes]** learning outcomes for each week.

Customised ChatGPT Prompt Created from the Template:

Create a 12-week lesson plan with 5 subtopics for each week for teaching about "Java Programming for beginners" to Diploma students. Include 3 activities and 3 learning outcomes for each week.

ChatGPT Video Output URL and QR Code:

https://tinyurl.com/IntermediateLessonPlan

ChatGPT Output:

Week 1: Introduction to Java Programming

- Introduction to Java Programming language
- Setting up the development environment
- Basic Syntax of Java Programming

- Data Types and Variables
- Control Statements

Activities:

1. Write a program to print "Hello World" on the console
2. Create a program that takes user input and performs basic arithmetic operations
3. Create a program that uses control statements to determine whether a number is even or odd

Learning Outcomes:

1. Understand the basic syntax of Java programming
2. Understand the importance of setting up the development environment
3. Be able to create simple programs using control statements and data types

Week 2: Object-Oriented Programming in Java

- Introduction to Object-Oriented Programming (OOP)
- Classes and Objects in Java
- Encapsulation in Java
- Inheritance in Java
- Polymorphism in Java

Activities:

1. Create a class to represent a student and use encapsulation to protect the student's information
2. Create a subclass of the student class to represent a graduate student
3. Implement polymorphism by creating an interface and using it to create multiple classes that implement it

Learning Outcomes:

1. Understand the principles of Object-Oriented Programming
2. Be able to create classes and objects in Java
3. Understand the concept of inheritance and polymorphism in Java

Week 3: Arrays and Strings in Java

- Arrays in Java
- Multi-dimensional arrays in Java
- Strings in Java
- String methods in Java
- StringBuilder class in Java

Activities:

1. Write a program to sort an array of integers using the bubble sort algorithm

2. Create a program to find the sum of two matrices using multi-dimensional arrays

3. Implement the StringBuilder class to manipulate a string

Learning Outcomes:

1. Understand the use of arrays and strings in Java

2. Use arrays to solve programming problems

3. Understand the use of String and StringBuilder classes in Java

Week 4: Exception Handling in Java

- Introduction to Exception Handling
- Types of Exceptions in Java
- Handling Exceptions in Java
- The try-catch-finally block
- Custom Exception Handling

Activities:

1. Create a program that throws an exception and handle it using the try-catch block

2. Implement a custom exception class to handle a specific exception

3. Create a program that reads data from a file and handle the exceptions that may occur

Learning Outcomes:

1. Understand the concept of exception handling in Java
2. Be able to handle exceptions using the try-catch block
3. Understand the use of custom exceptions in Java

Week 5: File Input and Output in Java

- Reading and Writing to files in Java
- FileInputStream and FileOutputStream classes
- BufferedReader and BufferedWriter classes
- Serialization and Deserialization in Java
- ObjectInputStream and ObjectOutputStream classes

Activities:

1. Create a program that writes data to a file
2. Implement serialization and deserialization in a program
3. Create a program that reads data from a file using BufferedReader and BufferedWriter classes

Learning Outcomes:

1. Understand the concept of file input and output in Java
2. Be able to write to and read from files in Java
3. Understand the use of serialization

Week 6: Graphical User Interface (GUI) in Java

- Introduction to GUI Programming
- JFrame and JPanel classes
- Layout Managers in Java
- Event Handling in Java
- ActionListener and MouseListener interfaces

Activities:

1. Create a simple GUI application that displays a text field and a button
2. Implement a layout manager to manage the components in the GUI
3. Handle events using the ActionListener and MouseListener interfaces

Learning Outcomes

1. Understand how to display a text field and a button
2. Be able to use layout manager to manage the components in the GUI
3. Be able to use the ActionListener and MouseListener interfaces

Week 7: Introduction to JavaFX

- Introduction to JavaFX
- Scene and Stage in JavaFX

- Layouts in JavaFX
- Controls in JavaFX
- CSS in JavaFX

Activities:

1. Create a simple JavaFX application that displays a button and a label
2. Implement a layout manager to manage the components in the JavaFX application
3. Customize the appearance of the components using CSS

Learning Outcomes:

1. Understand the basics of JavaFX
2. Be able to create a JavaFX application with basic controls
3. Understand how to customize the appearance of components using CSS

Week 8: JavaFX Event Handling

- Event Handling in JavaFX
- ActionEvent class in JavaFX
- MouseEvent class in JavaFX
- KeyEvent class in JavaFX
- Animation in JavaFX

Activities:

1. Handle events using the ActionEvent class in JavaFX
2. Handle events using the MouseEvent class in JavaFX
3. Implement animation in a JavaFX application

Learning Outcomes:

1. Understand how to handle events in JavaFX
2. Be able to handle different types of events using the appropriate class
3. Understand how to implement animation in a JavaFX application

Week 9: JavaFX UI Controls

- JavaFX UI Controls
- Text Input Controls in JavaFX
- ChoiceBox and ComboBox in JavaFX
- ListView and TreeView in JavaFX
- TableView in JavaFX

Activities:

1. Create a JavaFX application that uses Text Input Controls
2. Create a JavaFX application that uses ChoiceBox and ComboBox
3. Create a JavaFX application that uses ListView and TableView

Learning Outcomes:

4. Understand the different UI Controls available in JavaFX
5. Be able to use Text Input Controls, ChoiceBox and ComboBox in JavaFX applications
6. Be able to use ListView and TableView in JavaFX applications

Week 10: JavaFX Layouts

- Layouts in JavaFX
- HBox and VBox in JavaFX
- BorderPane in JavaFX
- GridPane in JavaFX
- StackPane in JavaFX

Activities:

1. Create a JavaFX application that uses HBox and VBox
2. Create a JavaFX application that uses BorderPane
3. Create a JavaFX application that uses GridPane and StackPane

Learning Outcomes:

1. Understand the different layout managers available in JavaFX
2. Be able to use HBox, VBox and BorderPane in JavaFX applications

3. Be able to use GridPane and StackPane in JavaFX applications

Week 11: Java Collections

- Introduction to Java Collections
- List Interface in Java Collections
- Set Interface in Java Collections
- Map Interface in Java Collections
- Queue Interface in Java Collections

Activities:

1. Create a program that uses ArrayList to store data
2. Create a Java program that uses HashSet to store data
3. Create a Java program that uses HashMap to store data

Learning Outcomes:

1. Understand the concept of Java Collections
2. Be able to use List, Set, Map and Queue interfaces in Java Collections
3. Understand the differences between the different interfaces in Java Collections

Week 12: Java Generics

- Introduction to Java Generics
- Generic Classes in Java
- Generic Methods in Java
- Bounded Type Parameters in Java Generics
- Wildcard Types in Java Generics

Activities:

1. Create a Java program that uses a Generic Class
2. Create a Java program that uses a Generic Method
3. Implement Bounded Type Parameters and Wildcard Types in Java Generics

Learning Outcomes:

1. Understand the concept of Java Generics
2. Be able to use Generic Classes and Generic Methods

Advanced Level Lesson Plan

You can create a **more detailed lesson plan** with **detailed specific and complex requirements**. You will need to use **more permutations and combinations of criteria** in the prompt to generate an **advanced level lesson plan**.

Here is an example of how to create an **advanced lesson plan** with more **specific** and **complex requirements.**

ChatGPT Prompt Template:

> Create **[no. of weeks]** weeks lesson plan about **[topic]** for **[teaching level – eg. primary, high school, college, degree, postgraduate, doctoral]** students. Include **2** relevant **[topic]** research activities, **[no. of learning outcomes]** learning outcomes, and **[no. of websites]** websites for each week.

Customised ChatGPT Prompt Created from the Template:

> **Create a 14-week lesson plan about "Creating sustainable housing for future living in Australia" for Doctoral students. Include 2 relevant sustainability research activities, 3 learning outcomes and 5 sustainability websites for each week.**

ChatGPT Video Output URL and QR Code:

https://tinyurl.com/AdvancedLessonPlan

ChatGPT Output:

Week 1: Introduction to Sustainable Housing

Learning outcomes:

- Define sustainable housing and its importance for future living in Australia
- Understand the principles and practices of sustainable housing
- Identify the challenges and opportunities for sustainable housing in Australia

Research activities:

1. Students will research and present a case study of a sustainable housing project in Australia or abroad.
2. Students will conduct a sustainability audit of a residential building and propose recommendations for improving its sustainability performance.

Sustainability websites:

1. Green Building Council of Australia: https://new.gbca.org.au/
2. Sustainable Living Tasmania: https://www.sustainablelivingtasmania.org.au/

3. Alternative Technology Association: https://www.ata.org.au/

4. Australian Passive House Association: https://passivehouseaustralia.org/

5. Your Home: https://www.yourhome.gov.au/

Week 2: Sustainable Building Materials

Learning outcomes:

- Understand the importance of sustainable building materials in sustainable housing
- Identify sustainable building materials and their properties
- Analyse the life cycle of building materials and their impact on the environment

Research activities:

1. Students will research and present a case study of a building project that uses sustainable building materials.
2. Students will conduct a life cycle assessment of a building material and propose alternatives that have a lower environmental impact.

Sustainability websites:

1. Green Building Council of Australia: https://new.gbca.org.au/
2. Forest Stewardship Council Australia: https://au.fsc.org/en-au
3. Good Environmental Choice Australia: https://www.geca.org.au/

4. Global GreenTag: https://www.globalgreentag.com/
5. The Cradle to Cradle Products Innovation Institute: https://www.c2ccertified.org/

Week 3: Renewable Energy in Sustainable Housing

Learning outcomes:

- Understand the importance of renewable energy in sustainable housing
- Identify different renewable energy technologies and their applications
- Analyse the economic and environmental benefits of renewable energy in sustainable housing

Research activities:

1. Students will research and present a case study of a sustainable housing project that uses renewable energy technologies.
2. Students will design a renewable energy system for a residential building and analyse its performance and economic viability.

Sustainability websites:

1. Clean Energy Council: https://www.cleanenergycouncil.org.au/
2. Australian Solar Council: https://www.solar.org.au/
3. Renew Economy: https://reneweconomy.com.au/
4. Energy Efficiency Council: https://www.eec.org.au/

5. Zero Carbon Australia: https://www.zca2020.org/

Week 4: Energy Efficiency in Sustainable Housing

Learning outcomes:

- Understand the importance of energy efficiency in sustainable housing
- Identify different strategies and technologies for improving energy efficiency in buildings
- Analyse the economic and environmental benefits of energy efficiency in sustainable housing

Research activities:

1. Students will research and present a case study of a sustainable housing project that achieved high energy efficiency performance.
2. Students will conduct an energy audit of a residential building and propose recommendations for improving its energy efficiency.

Sustainability websites:

1. Green Building Council of Australia: https://new.gbca.org.au/
2. National Home Energy Rating Scheme: https://www.nathers.gov.au/
3. Your Home: https://www.yourhome.gov.au/
4. Energy Rating: https://www.energyrating.gov.au/
5. Energy Star: https://www.energystar.gov/

Week 5: Water Efficiency in Sustainable Housing

Learning outcomes:

- Understand the importance of water efficiency in sustainable housing
- Identify different strategies and technologies for improving water efficiency in buildings
- Analyse the economic and environmental benefits of water efficiency in sustainable

Research activities:

1. Students will research and present a case study of a sustainable housing project that achieved high water efficiency performance.
2. Students will conduct a water audit of a residential building and propose recommendations for improving its water efficiency.

Sustainability websites:

1. Smart Watermark: https://www.smartwatermark.org/
2. Water Efficiency Labelling and Standards Scheme: https://www.waterrating.gov.au/
3. Australian Water Association: https://www.awa.asn.au/
4. Alliance for Water Efficiency: https://www.allianceforwaterefficiency.org/
5. WaterSense: https://www.epa.gov/watersense/

Week 6: Sustainable Urban Planning

Learning outcomes:

- Understand the principles and practices of sustainable urban planning
- Identify the challenges and opportunities for sustainable urban development in Australia
- Analyse the economic, social, and environmental benefits of sustainable urban planning

Research activities:

1. Students will research and present a case study of a sustainable urban development project in Australia or abroad.
2. Students will analyse the urban planning in their local area and propose recommendations for improving their sustainability performance.

Sustainability websites:

1. Australian Sustainable Built Environment Council: https://www.asbec.asn.au/
2. The Fifth Estate: https://www.thefifthestate.com.au/
3. Bioregional Australia: https://www.bioregional.com.au/
4. Institute for Sustainable Futures: https://www.uts.edu.au/research-and-teaching/our-research/institute-sustainable-futures
5. UN-Habitat: https://unhabitat.org/

Week 7: Sustainable Transportation in Urban Areas

Learning outcomes:

- Understand the importance of sustainable transportation in sustainable urban development
- Identify different sustainable transportation options and their applications
- Analyse the economic, social, and environmental benefits of sustainable transportation in urban areas

Research activities:

1. Students will research and present a case study of a sustainable transportation project in an urban area.
2. Students will propose a sustainable transportation plan for a local urban area and analyse its performance and feasibility.

Sustainability websites:

1. Transport for NSW: https://www.transport.nsw.gov.au/
2. City of Sydney: https://www.cityofsydney.nsw.gov.au/
3. Institute for Transportation and Development Policy: https://www.itdp.org/
4. WalkScore: https://www.walkscore.com/
5. BikeSafe: https://www.bikesafe.com.au/

Week 8: Sustainable Landscaping and Green Spaces in Urban Areas

Learning outcomes:

- Understand the importance of sustainable landscaping and green spaces in sustainable urban development
- Identify different sustainable landscaping and green space design strategies and technologies
- Analyse the economic, social, and environmental benefits of sustainable landscaping and green spaces in urban areas

Research activities:

1. Students will research and present a case study of a sustainable landscaping and green space project in an urban area.
2. Students will propose a sustainable landscaping and green space plan for a local urban area and analyse its performance and feasibility.

Sustainability websites:

1. Green Building Council of Australia: https://new.gbca.org.au/
2. Australian Institute of Landscape Architects: https://www.aila.org.au/
3. City of Melbourne: https://www.melbourne.vic.gov.au/
4. Parks Victoria: https://www.parks.vic.gov.au/
5. Green Cities: https://greencities.com.au/

Week 9: Sustainable Waste Management in Buildings and Urban Areas

Learning outcomes:

- Understand the importance of sustainable waste management in sustainable housing and urban development
- Identify different strategies and technologies for reducing, reusing, and recycling waste in buildings and urban areas
- Analyse the economic, social, and environmental benefits of sustainable waste management in buildings and urban areas

Research activities:

1. Students will research and present a case study of a sustainable waste management project in a building or urban area.
2. Students will conduct a waste audit of a building or urban area and propose recommendations for improving its waste reduction, reuse, and recycling performance.

Sustainability websites:

1. Planet Ark: https://planetark.org/
2. Waste Management and Resource Recovery Association of Australia: https://www.wmrr.asn.au/
3. Cleanaway: https://www.cleanaway.com.au/
4. Keep Australia Beautiful: https://kab.org.au/
5. Sustainability Victoria: https://www.sustainability.vic.gov.au/

Week 10: Sustainable Materials and Construction Practices

Learning outcomes:

- Understand the importance of sustainable materials and construction practices in sustainable housing and urban development
- Identify different sustainable materials and construction practices and their applications
- Analyse the economic, social, and environmental benefits of sustainable materials and construction practices

Research activities:

1. Students will research and present a case study of a sustainable building project that uses innovative sustainable materials and construction practices.
2. Students will propose a sustainable building design using sustainable materials and construction practices and analyse its performance and feasibility.

Sustainability websites:

1. Green Star: https://new.gbca.org.au/green-star/
2. Architecture and Design: https://www.architectureanddesign.com.au/
3. Building Designers Association of Australia: https://bdaa.com.au/
4. Forest Stewardship Council Australia: https://au.fsc.org/en-au
5. Embodied Carbon Network: https://www.embodiedcarbon.com/

Week 11: Sustainable Energy Use in Buildings

Learning outcomes:

- Understand the importance of sustainable energy use in sustainable housing and urban development
- Identify different strategies and technologies for reducing energy consumption in buildings
- Analyse the economic, social, and environmental benefits of sustainable energy use in buildings

Research activities:

1. Students will research and present a case study of a sustainable building project that achieved high energy efficiency performance.
2. Students will conduct an energy audit of a building and propose recommendations for improving its energy efficiency performance.

Sustainability websites:

1. Green Building Council of Australia: https://new.gbca.org.au/
2. National Australian Built Environment Rating System (NABERS): https://www.nabers.gov.au/
3. YourHome: https://www.yourhome.gov.au/
4. Australian Energy Foundation: https://www.aef.com.au/
5. Renew: https://renew.org.au/

Week 12: Sustainable Technologies for Smart and Connected Buildings

Learning outcomes:

- Understand the principles and applications of smart and connected buildings in sustainable housing and urban development
- Identify different sustainable technologies for smart and connected buildings and their applications
- Analyse the economic, social, and environmental benefits of sustainable technologies for smart and connected buildings

Research activities:

1. Students will research and present a case study of a sustainable building project that uses smart and connected technologies.
2. Students will propose a sustainable building design using smart and connected technologies and analyse its performance and feasibility.

Sustainability websites:

1. Smart Cities Council Australia and New Zealand: https://anz.smartcitiescouncil.com/
2. Australian Smart Communities Association: https://ascaustralasia.com/
3. Green Building Council of Australia - Future Homes: https://new.gbca.org.au/future-homes/
4. Internet of Things Alliance Australia: https://www.iot.org.au/

5. Property Council of Australia:
   https://www.propertycouncil.com.au/

Week 13: Sustainable Urban Design and Planning

Learning outcomes:

- Understand the principles and applications of sustainable urban design and planning
- Identify different strategies and technologies for creating sustainable urban areas
- Analyse the economic, social, and environmental benefits of sustainable urban design and planning

Research activities:

1. Students will research and present a case study of a sustainable urban design and planning project.
2. Students will propose a sustainable urban design and planning project and analyse its performance and feasibility

Sustainability websites:

1. Australian Sustainable Built Environment Council:
   https://www.asbec.asn.au/
2. Urban Development Institute of Australia:
   https://www.udia.com.au/
3. Smart Urban Futures:
   https://www.smarturbanfutures.com.au/
4. City of Melbourne - Sustainability:
   https://www.melbourne.vic.gov.au/about-melbourne/sustainability/Pages/sustainability.aspx

5. Urban Design Forum: https://www.urbandesignforum.org.au/

Week 14: Sustainable Living and Community Engagement

Learning outcomes:

- Understand the importance of sustainable living and community engagement in sustainable housing and urban development
- Identify different strategies and initiatives for promoting sustainable living and community engagement
- Analyse the economic, social, and environmental benefits of sustainable living and community engagement

Research activities:

1. Students will research and present a case study of a sustainable living and community engagement project.
2. Students will propose a sustainable living and community engagement initiative and analyse its performance and feasibility.

Sustainability websites:

1. Australian Conservation Foundation: https://www.acf.org.au/
2. Beyond Zero Emissions: https://bze.org.au/
3. Greenpeace Australia Pacific: https://www.greenpeace.org/australia/
4. 350.org Australia: https://350.org.au/
5. Sustainable Living Tasmania: https://www.slt.org.au/

Note: The above lesson plan is only a suggested outline and can be adapted to fit the specific needs and requirements of the doctoral students and the course. The research activities and sustainability websites provided are also just examples and not an exhaustive list of resources available on sustainable housing and urban development.

Lesson Plans from Your Resources

It is also possible and **easy** to create **lesson plans** based on your **own custom or personal resources** that you may be using for teaching and learning. All you need to do is paste your **"personal content or resource text"** into the ChatGPT and magically and effortlessly ChatGPT will generate the **lesson plan based on the content** or resources you have **provided**.

Here is an example of creating a **lesson plan** from your **own resources** on "**networking" topic**.

ChatGPT Prompt Template:

Create **[no. of weeks]** weeks lesson plan with subtopics for teaching about **[Paste here your own content or resources in text format]** to **[teaching level – eg. primary, high school, college, degree, postgraduate, doctoral]** students.

Customised ChatGPT Prompt Created from the Template:

Create a 10-week lesson plan with subtopics for teaching about [*Networking is the exchange of information and ideas among people with a common profession or special interest, usually in an informal social setting. Networking often begins with a single point of common ground. Professionals use networking to expand their circles of acquaintances, find out about job opportunities in their fields, and increase their awareness of news and trends in their fields or the greater world. Key Takeaways Networking is used by professionals to widen their circles of acquaintances, find out about job opportunities, and increase their awareness of news and trends in their fields. Business owners may network to develop relationships with people and companies they may do business with in the future. Professional networking platforms provide an online location for people to engage with other professionals, join groups, post blogs, and share information. The coronavirus pandemic drove many professionals to network solely online rather than in person. Many colleges and universities provide opportunities for alumni to network with one another. How Networking Works People generally join networking groups based on a single common point of interest that all members share. The most obvious is a professional affiliation, such as stockbrokers. Still, some people find effective networking opportunities in a college alumni group, a church or synagogue* *social group, or a private club. For professionals, the best networking opportunities may occur at trade shows, seminars, and conferences, designed to attract a large crowd of like-minded individuals. Networking helps a professional keep up with current events in the field and develops relationships that may boost future business or employment prospects. Needless to say, it also provides opportunities to help other people find jobs, make connections, and catch up on the news. Small business owners network to develop relationships with people and companies they may do business with in the future. These connections help them establish rapport and trust among people in their own communities. Successful business networking involves regularly following up with contacts to exchange valuable information that may not be readily available outside the network. Business owners and entrepreneurs often join their local chamber of commerce to promote their business interests and help others in their community do the same. There are many additional benefits to joining a chamber of commerce, such as receiving deals and discounts from other chamber members, having one's business listed in the chamber directory, and the ability to influence policies related to the area's business and economic activity. Online Networking Professional networking platforms such as LinkedIn provide an online location for people to engage with other professionals, join groups, post blogs, and share information. And, of course, they provide a place to post a resume that can be seen by prospective employers, to search for jobs, or to identify job candidates. These days, a business-to-business (B2B) customer pipeline can be developed almost entirely through the use of a social networking site. Online networking forums allow professionals to demonstrate their knowledge and connect with like-minded people. LinkedIn is the largest professional network, but there are many others.1 Some cater to particular subsets of people, such as Black Business Women Online. Others have a different focus, such as Meetup, which encourages its members to meet in person off-site or virtually through online video conferences. The term computer networking refers to linking multiple devices to share information and software resources directly. Special Considerations Given the growing number of networking opportunities available to people looking to start or advance their careers, it's important to take some time to explore your options before committing to a specific networking group. While it's tempting for a new business owner or someone looking for a dream job to join as many networks as possible, a better strategy is to target your time and efforts toward those groups that best fit your needs and interests. Many networking organisations will host a special meet and greet events that allow potential new members to attend a meeting before becoming a member. Once you join a networking group, it's important to become a contributing member. Rather than just using the association to further their own goals, people who use networking effectively look to offer something of value to other group members. Networking can help you identify opportunities for collaboration, strategic joint ventures, partnerships, and new areas to expand your business. How Can I Network Efficiently? It's important to take some time to explore your options before committing to a specific networking group. While it's tempting for a new business owner or someone looking for a dream job to join as many networks as possible, a better strategy is to target your time and efforts toward those groups that best fit your needs and interests. Many networking organisations will host a special meet and greet events that allow potential new members to attend a meeting before becoming members. Once you join a networking group, it's important to become a contributing member. Rather than just using the association to further their own goals, people who use networking effectively look to offer something of value to other group members. Why Is Networking Useful? Professionals use networking to expand their circles of acquaintances, find out about job opportunities in their fields, and increase their awareness of news and trends in their fields or the greater world. It helps a professional keep up with current events in the field and develops relationships that may boost future business or employment prospects. Why Should Businesses Network? Small business owners network to develop relationships with people and companies they may do business with in the future. These connections help them establish rapport and trust among people in their own communities. Successful business networking involves regularly following up with contacts to exchange valuable information that may not be readily available outside the network. Business owners and entrepreneurs often join their local chamber of commerce to promote their business interests and help others in their community do the same. Networking can help you identify opportunities for collaboration, strategic joint ventures, partnerships, and new areas to expand your business. What Is Online Networking? Professional networking platforms such as LinkedIn provide an online location for people to engage with other professionals, join groups, post blogs, and share information. And, of course, they provide a place to post a resume that can be seen by prospective employers, to search for jobs, or to identify job candidates. These days, a business-to-business (B2B) customer pipeline can be developed almost entirely through the use of a social networking site. Online networking forums allow professionals to demonstrate their knowledge and connect with like-minded people. Sponsored Access to World-Class Learning From Top Universities Are you interested in developing skills related to banking, investment management, or other fields related to finance? Browse hundreds of online certificate programs the world's leading universities offer in partnership with Emeritus. From core fundamentals to the latest research studies, you'll find a range of courses taught by industry experts. Learn more about developing future-ready skills and get started.*] **to college** students.

ChatGPT Video Output URL and QR Code:

https://tinyurl.com/ResourceLessonPlan

ChatGPT Output:

Here is a 10 week lesson plan for "What is Networking":

Week 1: Introduction to Networking

- Definition of networking and its importance
- Benefits of networking for professionals and business owners
- Types of networking groups and platforms

Week 2: Building Your Network

- Strategies for building a professional network
- How to identify and join relevant networking groups
- Tips for making connections and growing your network

Week 3: Effective Networking Techniques

- Best practices for networking in person and online
- How to make a good first impression
- Importance of follow-up and relationship building

Week 4: Leveraging Social Media for Networking

- Overview of social media platforms for networking
- Tips for creating a professional online presence
- How to use social media to expand your network

Week 5: Networking Events and Opportunities

- Overview of networking events and opportunities
- How to prepare for networking events
- Tips for making the most out of networking opportunities

Week 6: Elevator Pitch and Personal Branding

- Importance of creating a personal brand
- How to craft an effective elevator pitch
- Strategies for communicating your value proposition

Week 7: Networking for Business Owners

- Benefits of networking for small business owners
- How to identify potential business partners and clients
- Tips for building trust and credibility with your network

Week 8: Networking for Career Advancement

- How networking can help you advance your career

- How to identify and approach potential mentors
- Tips for leveraging your network to find job opportunities

Week 9: Overcoming Networking Challenges

- Common networking challenges and how to overcome them
- How to deal with networking anxiety and shyness
- Tips for navigating difficult networking situations

Week 10: Networking Follow-Up and Maintenance

- Importance of follow-up and maintenance in networking
- How to maintain relationships and stay in touch with your network
- Strategies for keeping your network engaged and active.

Customised Lesson Plans Based on Student Needs and Interests

One of the **most powerful features** of ChatGPT is its ability to generate **personalized content** based on user input. This means that it can create lesson plans that are **customised** to your student's **needs and interests**.

For example, if you have a student who is **interested in space exploration**, you could input **"space exploration"** into ChatGPT, and it might **generate text** such as:

> *"Space exploration is the investigation of outer space using various technologies and methods. It has led to many important discoveries and advances in science and technology, such as the development of the International Space Station, the discovery of new planets, and the study of the effects of space on human physiology."*

Using this text as a **starting point**, you can create a **lesson plan that incorporates your student's interest in space exploration**.

For example, you might have your student research a **specific aspect** of space exploration, such as the **history of the International Space Station**, and present their **findings** to the class.

Here is an example of how to do it using a **few prompts** in a conversation style so that it can **refined** and **targeted** well.

User Prompt:

> <u>Starting Prompt:</u> **"Space exploration"**

ChatGPT Video Output URL and QR Code:

https://tinyurl.com/ConversationPrompt

ChatGPT Output:

Space exploration is the study and exploration of outer space beyond the Earth's atmosphere. It encompasses a wide range of activities, including the use of manned and unmanned spacecraft, telescopes, and other technologies to study and explore the universe. The primary goals of space exploration include understanding the origin and evolution of the universe, exploring the possibility of life beyond Earth, and developing new technologies that can benefit humanity.

Followup Prompt:

Create a lesson plan for a postgraduate student named "Victor Hugo" who needs to learn about "the history of the International Space Station" and present his findings to the class.

ChatGPT Video Output URL and QR Code:

https://tinyurl.com/Custom-LessonPlan

ChatGPT Output:

Sure! Here's a sample lesson plan for a postgraduate student named Victor Hugo, who needs to learn about the history of the International Space Station and present his findings to the class.

Lesson Plan: History of the International Space Station

Objectives:

- Understand the history and development of the International Space Station (ISS)
- Explain the purpose and goals of the ISS
- Prepare a presentation on the history of the ISS and its significance

Materials:

- Computer with Internet access
- Books, articles, and other resources on the ISS
- Presentation software (such as PowerPoint or Google Slides)

Procedure:

1. Introduction (10 minutes)

   - Introduce the topic of the ISS and its significance in space exploration and research.
   - Discuss the objectives of the lesson plan and what Victor Hugo will be expected to learn and present.

2. Research and Study (60 minutes)

   - Provide Victor Hugo with a list of resources, such as books, articles, and websites, that he can use to research the history of the ISS.
   - Instruct Victor to spend the next hour studying and taking notes on the history and development of the ISS, including its major milestones and achievements.

3. Presentation Preparation (60 minutes)

   - Instruct Victor to create a presentation on the history of the ISS using the notes he took during his research.
   - Encourage him to use visuals such as images, graphs, and charts to enhance his presentation.
   - Provide feedback and assistance as needed.

4. Presentation Delivery (10 minutes per student)

   - Have each student, including Victor, present their findings on the history of the ISS to the class.
   - Encourage questions and discussion among the students.

5. Conclusion (10 minutes)

   - Summarize the key takeaways from the lesson, including the history, purpose, and goals of the ISS.

- Discuss the significance of the ISS in space exploration and research and its potential for future discoveries and advancements.

Assessment:

- Victor Hugo's presentation will be evaluated based on the accuracy and completeness of his research, the clarity and organisation of his presentation, and his ability to engage the audience and answer questions.

If you want this **customised lesson plan** to be **adapted** to another **student called Peter Pan** who is in **year 10**, ChapGPT could be used for that.

You will need to use a **similar prompt** as shown to achieve this.

User Prompt:

> **Regenerate the lesson plan for Year 10 student named "Peter Pan.**

ChatGPT Video Output URL and QR Code:

https://tinyurl.com/RegenerateLessonPlan

ChatGPT Output:

Sure, here's a lesson plan for a Year 10 student named Peter Pan on the history of the International Space Station.

Lesson Plan: History of the International Space Station for Year 10 Student Peter Pan

Objectives:

- Understand the history and development of the International Space Station (ISS)
- Explain the purpose and goals of the ISS
- Prepare a presentation on the history of the ISS and its significance

Materials:

- Computer with Internet access
- Books, articles, and other resources on the ISS
- Presentation software (such as PowerPoint or Google Slides)

Procedure:

1. Introduction (10 minutes)
    - Introduce the topic of the ISS and its significance in space exploration and research.
    - Discuss the objectives of the lesson plan and what Peter Pan will be expected to learn and present.
2. Research and Study (60 minutes)

- Provide Peter with a list of resources, such as books, articles, and websites, that he can use to research the history of the ISS.
- Instruct Peter to spend the next hour studying and taking notes on the history and development of the ISS, including its major milestones and achievements.

3. Presentation Preparation (60 minutes)

- Instruct Peter to create a presentation on the history of the ISS using the notes he took during his research.
- Encourage him to use visuals such as images, graphs, and charts to enhance his presentation.
- Provide feedback and assistance as needed.

4. Presentation Delivery (5-10 minutes per student)

- Have each student, including Peter, present their findings on the history of the ISS to the class.
- Encourage questions and discussion among the students.

5. Conclusion (10 minutes)

- Summarize the key takeaways from the lesson, including the history, purpose, and goals of the ISS.
- Discuss the significance of the ISS in space exploration and research and its potential for future discoveries and advancements.

Assessment:

- Peter's presentation will be evaluated based on the accuracy and completeness of his research, the clarity and organisation of his presentation, and his ability to engage the audience and answer questions.

Overall, ChatGPT is a **valuable tool for lesson planning** that can help teachers **create engaging and effective lessons** that are **tailored to their student's needs and interests**.

By using ChatGPT, teachers can **save time and effort** in the lesson planning process while still maintaining a high level of **quality** and **relevance** in their teaching.

It is important to remember that **ChatGPT should not replace the teacher's expertise** and **experience**.

While ChatGPT can provide valuable insights and ideas for lesson planning, it is still up to the teacher to design and deliver effective lessons that meet the needs of their students. Teachers should verify the information presented by ChatGPT and make required updates to make it accurate, effective and appropriate for the learners.

Fifteen Lesson Plan Prompts

Here are some **example prompts** that can be **customised** for generating **lesson plans**:

1. Develop a detailed plan for teaching **[topic]** to **[teaching level]** students, covering key subtopics and skills for **[no. of weeks]** weeks.
2. Design a comprehensive curriculum that explores **[topic]** with **[teaching level]** students, outlining a series of lessons and activities that build upon one another over **[no. of weeks]** weeks.
3. Craft an engaging and effective lesson plan for **[teaching level]** students, focused on deepening their understanding of **[topic]** and its related concepts throughout **[no. of weeks]** weeks.
4. Create a structured course of study that introduces **[teaching level]** students to **[topic]**, with a particular emphasis on developing their critical thinking and problem-solving skills over **[no. of weeks]** weeks.
5. Plan a series of lessons and projects that allow **[teaching level]** students to explore the intricacies of **[topic]** in depth, building their knowledge and understanding over **[no. of weeks]** weeks.

6. Develop a **[no. of weeks]**-week lesson plan for **[teaching level]** students that explores **[topic]** through **[no. of subtopics]** subtopics. Design engaging activities and measurable learning outcomes for each week to ensure students' success.

7. Create a lesson plan for a comprehensive curriculum that delves into **[topic]** with **[teaching level]** students over **[no. of weeks]** weeks. Include **[no of subtopics]** subtopics, **[no of activities]** activities, and **[no of learning outcomes]** learning outcomes for each week to support student learning and growth.

8. Design a structured **[no. of weeks]**-week lesson plan that introduces **[teaching level]** students to **[topic]** through **[no of subtopics]** subtopics. Develop **[no of activities]** activities and **[no of learning outcomes]** learning outcomes for each week that foster deep understanding and engagement.

9. Craft a detailed **[no. of weeks]**-week course of study that teaches **[teaching level]** students about **[topic]** through **[no of subtopics]** subtopics. Incorporate engaging activities and measurable learning outcomes for each week to ensure students are achieving their goals.

10. Plan a dynamic **[no. of weeks]**-week lesson plan that explores **[topic]** with **[teaching level]** students through **[no of subtopics]** subtopics. Design **[no of activities]** activities and **[no of learning outcomes]**

learning outcomes for each week that foster critical thinking and skill development.

11. Develop a comprehensive course outline that spans **[no. of weeks]** weeks, and covers **[no. of subtopics]** subtopics on **[topic]** for **[teaching level]** students. Design engaging activities and measurable learning outcomes for each week to ensure a deep understanding of the material.

12. Create a detailed lesson plan that introduces **[teaching level]** students to **[topic]** through **[no. of subtopics]** subtopics over **[no. of weeks]** weeks. Include **[no. of activities]** activities and **[no. of learning outcomes]** learning outcomes for each week to promote an immersive and effective learning experience.

13. Craft a structured curriculum that explores **[topic]** with **[teaching level]** students over **[no. of weeks]** weeks through **[no. of subtopics]** subtopics. Develop **[no. of activities]** activities and **[no. of learning outcomes]** learning outcomes for each week to foster critical thinking and skill development.

14. Plan a dynamic and engaging **[no. of weeks]** week course that covers **[no. of subtopics]** subtopics on **[topic]** for **[teaching level]** students. Outline **[no. of activities]** activities and **[no. of learning outcomes]**

learning outcomes for each week to ensure measurable student progress.

15. Design a comprehensive **[no. of weeks]** week lesson plan that delves into **[topic]** with **[teaching level]** students through **[no. of subtopics]** subtopics. Incorporate **[no. of activities]** activities and **[no. of learning outcomes]** learning outcomes for each week to ensure that students build a strong foundation of knowledge and skills.

While ChatGPT can provide valuable insights and ideas for lesson planning, it is still up to the teacher to design and deliver effective lessons that meet the needs of their students. Teachers should verify the information presented by ChatGPT and make required updates to make it accurate, effective and appropriate for the learners.

CHAPTER 3

CREATE ASSESSMENT ACTIVITIES BASED ON YOUTUBE VIDEOS AND OTHER CONTENT

3. Create Assessment Activities Based on YouTube Videos and Other Content

With ChatGPT you can **quickly create various types** of **assessment**s using ChatGPT to **suit different types of learners** and improve the learning outcomes.

You can use three different types of resources for creating assessments:

- **Transcript of educational videos** from **YouTube** or any other source.

- **Your own text**-based **resources**
- ChatGPT's **trained knowledge** is composed of **300 billion words**

> Please note that ChatGPT currently supports inputs of approximately 3,000 words, but it is expected to increase to around 25,000 words.

In this section, you will learn how to create **five** different types of **assessments** based on the **transcript** of the video on the topic **"Phases of Mitosis"**.

You can **use your own learning resources** as long as it is in **text format**.

Forty-Five Diverse Domains for Assessments

It's worth mentioning that ChatGPT already **knows many topics** and can **generate assessments on topics** directly **without even the need** to supply **your own text.**

Here are some of the areas that may be of interest to you.

1. **Agriculture:** agronomy, animal husbandry, horticulture, etc.
2. **Anthropology:** archaeology, cultural anthropology, physical anthropology, etc.
3. **Architecture:** architectural history, building technology, design principles, etc.
4. **Art and design:** art history, drawing, graphic design, painting, etc.
5. **Biology:** cell biology, ecology, evolutionary biology, genetics, etc.
6. **Business:** accounting, finance, management, marketing, etc.
7. **Communication:** interpersonal communication, mass communication, public speaking, etc.
8. **Computer science:** algorithms, data structures, programming, etc.
9. **Criminology:** criminal justice, criminological theory, penology, etc.
10. **Culinary arts:** cooking methods, culinary techniques, food safety, etc.
11. **Economics:** international trade, macroeconomics, microeconomics, etc.
12. **Education:** assessment and evaluation, curriculum development, educational psychology, etc.
13. **Engineering:** civil engineering, electrical engineering, mechanical engineering, etc.
14. **Environmental science:** climate change, conservation biology, ecology, etc.
15. **Fashion:** fashion design, fashion history, textiles, etc.

16. **Film and media:** film analysis, film history, media theory, etc.
17. **Foreign languages:** French, German, Mandarin, Spanish, etc.
18. **Gender and sexuality studies:** gender identity, feminist theory, queer theory, etc.
19. **Geography:** cartography, human geography, physical geography, etc.
20. **Health and medicine:** anatomy, epidemiology, pharmacology, physiology, etc.
21. **Health sciences:** exercise science, nutrition, public health, etc.
22. **History:** American history, European history, world history, etc.
23. **Information technology:** computer networking, database systems, software development, etc.
24. **Journalism:** media ethics, news writing, reporting, etc.
25. **Language arts:** grammar, reading comprehension, vocabulary, writing skills, etc.
26. **Law:** civil law, contract law, criminal law, international law, etc.
27. **Linguistics:** language acquisition, morphology, phonetics, pragmatics, etc.
28. **Literature:** drama, literary analysis, poetry, etc.
29. **Mathematics:** algebra, calculus, geometry, statistics, etc.
30. **Medicine:** anatomy, pathology, pharmacology, physiology, etc.
31. **Military science:** leadership, military history, strategy, tactics, etc.

32. **Music:** music history, music performance, music theory, etc.
33. **Philosophy:** aesthetics, ethics, logic, metaphysics, etc.
34. **Physics:** electromagnetism, mechanics, quantum mechanics, thermodynamics, etc.
35. **Political science:** comparative politics, international relations, political theory, etc.
36. **Psychology:** abnormal psychology, clinical psychology, developmental psychology, etc.
37. **Public administration:** governance, public finance, public policy, etc.
38. **Religion:** comparative religion, religious studies, theology, etc.
39. **Science and technology:** artificial intelligence, nanotechnology, robotics, etc.
40. **Social sciences:** anthropology, economics, political science, sociology, etc.
41. **Social studies:** economics, geography, government, history, etc.
42. **Social work:** human behaviour, social welfare policy, social work practice, etc.
43. **Sociology:** deviance and social control, social change, social stratification, etc.
44. **Sports:** rules, sports history, sports science, strategies, etc.
45. **Test preparation:** ACT, GMAT, GRE, SAT, TOEFL, etc.

True-False Assessment Type

ChatGPT Prompt Template:

Create a **[no. of questions]** questions **[assessment type]** assessment for **[teaching level]** students from the following content **[paste the video transcript or your text here]**.

ChatGPT Prompt Created from the Template:

Create a 10-question true-false type assessment for high school students from the following content "*Welcome to today's educational tutorial, where we'll take an in-depth journey into one of the fundamental processes in cell biology: the phases of mitosis. Mitosis is the process by which a single eukaryotic cell meticulously divides into two identical daughter cells. Its significance extends to the maintenance of tissue integrity, the replacement of damaged cells, and the promotion of growth in multicellular organisms. In this comprehensive video, we will dissect the various stages of mitosis, simplifying the complexities to make them accessible to all. So, let's embark on this cellular adventure!*

To start, let's clarify what mitosis is all about. In essence, mitosis is a highly orchestrated cellular dance aimed at ensuring that each resulting daughter cell receives an identical set of genetic material.

This process is vital for a wide range of biological functions, including growth, development, and tissue repair.

Before we delve into the phases of mitosis, it's crucial to understand the context of the cell cycle. The cell cycle comprises two main phases: the interphase and the mitotic phase. Interphase serves as the preparation phase for mitosis, during which the cell undergoes growth, replicates its DNA, and makes essential preparations for the impending division.

Mitosis, which is part of the mitotic phase, can be broken down into distinct stages, often remembered by the acronym PMAT: Prophase, Metaphase, Anaphase, and Telophase. Each of these phases contributes uniquely to the precision of cell division.

Let's begin our exploration with Prophase. During Prophase, remarkable transformations occur within the cell. Chromatin, the complex of DNA and associated proteins, condenses into visible, compact structures known as chromosomes. Each chromosome consists of two sister chromatids connected by a centromere. Simultaneously, the nuclear envelope starts breaking down, providing spindle fibres access to the chromosomes. This is a critical early step in preparing for cell division.

Progressing to Metaphase, we encounter a pivotal moment in mitosis. During this phase, the chromosomes align meticulously at the cell's equatorial plane, known as the metaphase plate. This alignment is meticulously orchestrated by spindle fibres extending from opposite poles of the cell. Ensuring precise chromosome alignment is essential to guarantee that genetic material is distributed accurately to the upcoming daughter cells.

The action intensifies during Anaphase, where chromatids part ways. The centromere, previously holding sister chromatids together, divides, releasing the tension on the spindle fibres. As these spindle fibres shorten, they begin the process of chromatid separation, pulling the sister chromatids towards opposite poles of the cell. It's worth noting that this separation ensures that each daughter cell inherits a complete and identical set of chromosomes.

Following Anaphase, we reach Telophase, the culmination of the mitotic process. Here, the cell effectively unwinds what it began in Prophase. The chromatin starts to expand, reverting to its more diffuse form. Simultaneously, nuclear envelopes begin to reform around each set of chromosomes, creating two distinct nuclei. This marks the beginning of the end of the cell's division journey.

But the journey doesn't conclude with Telophase; it transitions into cytokinesis. Cytokinesis, often considered the last step in cell division, focuses on dividing the cellular contents and organelles between the two emerging daughter cells. In animal cells, a cleavage furrow forms and pinches the cell in two, while in plant cells, a cell plate develops to facilitate division. Cytokinesis ensures that each daughter cell is fully equipped for autonomous functioning.

In summary, mitosis is an intricate, choreographed performance within a cell that ensures the precise distribution of genetic material. Its significance extends far beyond the confines of cellular biology, playing a pivotal role in the growth, repair, and maintenance of multicellular organisms.

Thank you for accompanying us on this exploration of the phases of mitosis. If you found this video informative, we invite you to like, share, and subscribe for more enlightening content. We encourage you to continue your journey into the fascinating realms of cell biology and genetics. Don't hesitate to reach out with any questions or comments; we're here to support your learning!

Our journey ends here, but your exploration continues. Keep your curiosity alive as you delve deeper into the captivating world of biology. Until next time, stay curious and keep learning!"

ChatGPT Video Output URL and QR Code:

https://tinyurl.com/TrueFalseAssess

ChatGPT response for true-false assessment created from YouTube video transcript.

Question 1: True or False? Mitosis is the process of cell division that results in the formation of four genetically different daughter cells.

Answer: False. Mitosis results in the formation of two genetically identical daughter cells.

Question 2: True or False? Interphase is a part of mitosis, where the cell undergoes preparations for division.

Answer: False. Interphase is a separate phase of the cell cycle that precedes mitosis.

Question 3: True or False? During Prophase, chromatin condenses into visible chromosomes, and the nuclear envelope breaks down.

Answer: True.

Question 4: True or False? In Metaphase, chromosomes align randomly within the cell, without any specific order.

Answer: False. Chromosomes align at the metaphase plate in an organised and precise manner.

Question 5: True or False? Anaphase is the phase in which sister chromatids are pulled apart and move toward opposite poles of the cell.

Answer: True.

Question 6: True or False? During Telophase, the chromatin condenses into chromosomes, and the nuclear envelope reforms.

Answer: False. In Telophase, the chromatin expands back into its diffuse form, and nuclear envelopes re-form around the separated sets of chromosomes.

Question 7: True or False? Cytokinesis in plant cells involves the formation of a cleavage furrow.

Answer: False. Plant cells undergo cytokinesis through the formation of a cell plate.

Question 8: True or False? The primary goal of mitosis is to create genetically diverse daughter cells.

Answer: False. The primary goal of mitosis is to create genetically identical daughter cells.

Question 9: True or False? Mitosis plays a crucial role in growth, development, and tissue repair in multicellular organisms.

Answer: True.

Question 10: True or False? The cell cycle consists of two main phases: the interphase and the mitotic phase.

Answer: True.

Multiple Choice Assessment Type

ChatGPT Prompt Created from the Template:

Create a 10 questions multiple-choice type assessment for Bachelor of Science students from the following content *"Paste YouTube video Phases of Mitosis transcript"*

NOTE: To save space and avoid duplication, I have refrained from pasting/including the entire transcript of the video again in the prompt above.

ChatGPT Video Output URL and QR Code:

https://tinyurl.com/MCQVideoAssess

ChatGPT response for multiple-choice assessment created from YouTube video transcript:

Question 1: What is the primary purpose of mitosis?

A) To produce gametes (sperm and egg cells)

B) To maintain tissue integrity and replace damaged cells

C) To create genetic diversity

D) To perform photosynthesis

Answer: B) To maintain tissue integrity and replace damaged cells

Question 2: Which phase of the cell cycle precedes mitosis?

A) Prophase

B) Interphase

C) Anaphase

D) Telophase

Answer: B) Interphase

Question 3: What is the correct sequence of the phases of mitosis?

A) Telophase, Metaphase, Anaphase, Prophase

B) Prophase, Metaphase, Anaphase, Telophase

C) Anaphase, Metaphase, Prophase, Telophase

D) Metaphase, Prophase, Telophase, Anaphase

Answer: B) Prophase, Metaphase, Anaphase, Telophase

Question 4: During which phase of mitosis do sister chromatids separate and move towards opposite poles of the cell?

A) Prophase

B) Metaphase

C) Anaphase

D) Telophase

Answer: C) Anaphase

Question 5: What is the role of spindle fibres in mitosis?

A) To hold the nucleus together

B) To maintain cell shape

C) To separate chromatids during Anaphase

D) To synthesize DNA

Answer: C) To separate chromatids during Anaphase

Question 6: What happens to the nuclear envelope during Prophase?

A) It reforms around the chromosomes

B) It remains unchanged

C) It begins to break down

D) It turns into mitochondria

Answer: C) It begins to break down

Question 7: Which phase of mitosis is characterized by the alignment of chromosomes at the metaphase plate?

A) Prophase

B) Metaphase

C) Anaphase

D) Telophase

Answer: B) Metaphase

Question 8: What is the outcome of cytokinesis in animal cells?

A) Formation of a cell plate

B) Formation of a cleavage furrow

C) Formation of a nuclear envelope

D) Formation of two distinct nuclei

Answer: B) Formation of a cleavage furrow

Question 9: Why is mitosis important for multicellular organisms?

A) To create genetic diversity

B) To ensure the survival of the cell

C) To maintain tissue integrity and promote growth

D) To perform cellular respiration

Answer: C) To maintain tissue integrity and promote growth

Question 10: What is the purpose of the cell cycle's interphase?

A) To prepare for cytokinesis

B) To replicate DNA and prepare for mitosis

C) To separate chromatids

D) To ensure chromosome alignment

Answer: B) To replicate DNA and prepare for mitosis

Fill-in-the-Blanks Assessment Type

ChatGPT Prompt Created from the Template:

Create a fill-in-the-blanks type assessment for high school from the following content "*Paste YouTube video Phases of Mitosis transcript"*

NOTE: To save space and avoid duplication, I have refrained from pasting/including the entire transcript of the video again in the prompt above.

ChatGPT Video Output URL and QR Code:

https://tinyurl.com/FillBlanksAssess

ChatGPT response for role-play assessment created from YouTube video transcript:

10-question fill-in-the-blanks assessment based on the provided content about the phases of mitosis:

Question 1: Mitosis is a process by which a single eukaryotic cell divides into two ______________ daughter cells.

Question 2: Mitosis is essential for growth, development, tissue repair, and the maintenance of tissue ______________.

Question 3: The cell cycle consists of two main phases: ______________ and the mitotic phase.

Question 4: The acronym PMAT stands for ______________, ______________, ______________, and ______________.

Question 5: During Prophase, chromatin condenses into visible structures called ______________.

Question 6: Chromosomes consist of two sisters ______________ connected by a centromere.

Question 7: In Metaphase, chromosomes align at the cell's ______________ plate.

Question 8: Anaphase is the phase in which chromatids are ______________.

Question 9: Telophase marks the beginning of the end of the cell's ______________ journey.

Question 10: Cytokinesis is the step that focuses on dividing cellular contents between the two emerging ______________ cells.

Answers:

1. identical
2. integrity
3. interphase
4. Prophase, Metaphase, Anaphase, Telophase
5. chromosomes
6. chromatids
7. metaphase
8. separated
9. division
10. daughter

Role-Play Assessment Type

ChatGPT Prompt Created from the Template:

Create a role-play type assessment for high school from the following content "*Paste YouTube video Phases of Mitosis transcript***"**

NOTE: To save space and avoid duplication, I have refrained from pasting/including the entire transcript of the video again in the prompt above.

ChatGPT Video Output URL and QR Code:

https://tinyurl.com/Role-PlayAssess

ChatGPT response for role-play assessment created from YouTube video transcript:

Role-play assessment: "Mitosis Explorers Challenge"

Objective: In this role-play assessment, you will take on the role of a budding biologist participating in the "Mitosis Explorers Challenge." Your task is to demonstrate your understanding of the phases of mitosis by engaging in a role-play scenario. Imagine you are presenting the key concepts of mitosis to a fellow student.

Instructions:

1. Find a partner or fellow student to participate in this role-play with you.
2. Decide who will play the role of the presenter (you) and who will play the role of the eager student.
3. The presenter will use the provided content about mitosis to explain the phases of mitosis to the students, using their own words and examples.
4. The student should actively engage by asking questions, seeking clarification, and showing enthusiasm for learning.
5. Feel free to use props or visual aids if available to enhance your presentation.
6. The role-play should cover the key points from the provided content, including the phases of mitosis, their significance, and the role of cytokinesis.

7. After the role-play, switch roles, allowing the student to become the presenter and the presenter to become the eager learner.
8. Each role-play should last approximately 10-15 minutes.

Assessment Criteria:

- Accuracy: Ensure that the information presented is factually accurate and covers the key points of mitosis.
- Clarity: Communicate the concepts clearly and effectively.
- Engagement: Both the presenter and the student should actively participate in the role-play, demonstrating enthusiasm for learning.
- Understanding: Show a deep understanding of the phases of mitosis, their significance, and the relationship between mitosis and the cell cycle.
- Creativity: Feel free to use creative ways to explain the concepts and make the role-play engaging.

Role-play Scenario Example:

Presenter (You): "Welcome to today's session of the Mitosis Explorers Challenge! I'm here to guide you through the fascinating world of mitosis. Imagine you're a cell biologist, and I'm your mentor. We're going to explore the phases of mitosis, which is like a well-choreographed dance inside a cell. Are you ready?"

Student: "Absolutely! I'm excited to learn."

Presenter: "Great! So, let's start with the basics. Mitosis is the process by which a single cell divides into two identical daughter cells. It's like a cell's way of creating clones of itself. Mitosis is crucial for growth, tissue repair, and maintaining our body's integrity."

(Student and presenter continue to discuss the cell cycle, interphase, and the significance of mitosis.)

Presenter: "Now, let's dive into the actual phases of mitosis. There are four main phases: Prophase, Metaphase, Anaphase, and Telophase. Think of them as the acts of our cellular play."

(Student asks questions and engages in the discussion.)

(Presenter and student continue to discuss each phase, using examples and creative explanations.)

After the role-play, switch roles, and the student becomes the presenter, following the same format.

Assessment:

- Assess each participant based on the criteria mentioned above.
- Provide feedback and suggestions for improvement.
- Encourage discussions and questions during the role-play to ensure a thorough understanding of the topic.
- Emphasize the importance of accurate information and clear communication.

This role-play assessment allows students to actively engage with the material, reinforce their understanding, and promote effective communication of scientific concepts.

Case Study Assessment Type

ChatGPT Prompt Created from the Template:

Create a case study type assessment for Bachelor of Science students from the following content *"Paste YouTube video Phases of Mitosis transcript"*

NOTE: To save space and avoid duplication, I have refrained from pasting/including the entire transcript of the video again in the prompt above.

ChatGPT Video Output URL and QR Code:

https://tinyurl.com/GPTCaseStudyRubric

ChatGPT response for case study assessment created from YouTube video transcript.

Case Study Assessment: Exploring Mitosis in Cell Biology

Introduction:

Welcome to this case study assessment, designed to test your understanding of the phases of mitosis and their significance in cell biology. In this case study, you will be presented with scenarios and questions related to the content discussed in the video on the phases of mitosis. You are a Bachelor of Science student specializing in biology, and this assessment aims to evaluate your knowledge and critical thinking skills in this area.

Case Study: The Cellular Adventure

Imagine you are a biologist working in a research lab. Your team has discovered a new species of multicellular organisms and wants to understand the mitotic process in these creatures. You are tasked with analyzing their cell division, specifically focusing on the phases of mitosis.

Case Scenario 1: The Discovery

Your research team has collected samples of the new species and has performed microscopic analysis of their cells. You observe cells undergoing mitosis, and your goal is to identify which phase of mitosis these cells are currently in. You are provided with microscope images of these cells.

Question 1: Examine the provided microscope image and determine which phase of mitosis is depicted. Explain the key features and characteristics that led to your identification.

[Insert Microscope Image - Image should depict one of the phases of mitosis]

Case Scenario 2: The Importance of Mitosis

As you continue your research, you realize the importance of understanding mitosis in these organisms. You need to explain to your colleagues why studying mitosis is crucial for understanding the life cycle and growth of this new species.

Question 2: Write a brief explanation, not exceeding 150 words, highlighting the significance of mitosis in multicellular organisms, particularly in terms of growth and development. Use the knowledge you gained from the video to support your explanation.

Case Scenario 3: The Mystery Cell

While analyzing the samples, you come across a peculiar cell that seems to be stuck in one of the mitotic phases. This cell is not progressing as it should, and you need to investigate the possible reasons for this abnormality.

Question 3: Identify and explain at least two factors or events that could lead to a cell being stuck in a specific phase of mitosis, preventing it from advancing to the next stage. How might this abnormality impact the overall process of cell division?

Case Scenario 4: The Educational Initiative

Impressed by your work, your research team decided to create an educational video on mitosis for students pursuing a Bachelor of Science degree in biology. You are tasked with providing guidance on how to effectively explain the phases of mitosis to ensure a clear and comprehensive understanding.

Question 4: Outline at least three key strategies or visual aids that should be included in the educational video to help students grasp the complexities of the phases of mitosis. Provide a brief explanation of why each strategy or visual aid is essential for clarity and comprehension.

Conclusion:

Congratulations! You have completed this case study assessment on the phases of mitosis in cell biology. Your ability to identify mitotic phases, explain their significance, analyse abnormalities, and propose effective teaching strategies has been assessed. Your knowledge and critical thinking skills in this area will serve you well as you continue your Bachelor of Science journey in biology.

By continually refining and tweaking your question prompts, you can enhance the quality of the outputs you receive. This will allow you to tailor the

assessment activities to better align with the educational objectives and the learning needs of your students. Whether you're interested in multiple-choice questions, short answer exercises, or project-based assessments, taking the time to fine-tune your prompts can lead to more accurate and insightful outputs.

Creating A Grading Rubric for Assessments

Using ChatGPT can **come in handy** when we need to create a **grading rubric for an assessment**. As we all know, a **grading rubric** is a **structured** and **organised tool** that **outlines the specific expectations and criteria** for an **assignment or assessment**.

The grading rubric provides a **clear and detailed** description of what is expected of the student and **how their work will be evaluated** based on **specific performance levels**.

Grading can be a **time-consuming** process, especially for large classes. A rubric streamlines the **grading process** by providing a predetermined set of criteria to evaluate.

Grading rubrics typically include **several categories or criteria** on which the **student will be evaluated**, each with corresponding levels of achievement.

The use of grading rubrics **promotes fairness, consistency, and transparency** in marking student's work, making the evaluation process **clearer** and more **objective** for both students and teachers.

Here is an example prompt to create a **grading rubric** for an assessment:

ChatGPT Prompt Template:

> Create a grading rubric for **[assessment type]** type assessment for **[teaching level or qualification]** students. The topic is **[topic]**.

ChatGPT Prompt Created from the Template:

> **Create a grading rubric for essay-type assessments for high school students. The topic is "Sending a man to the moon".**

ChatGPT Video Output URL and QR Code:

https://tinyurl.com/GPTGradingRubric

ChatGPT Output:

Criteria	Excellent (5)	Good (4)	Fair (3)	Poor (2)	Needs Improvement (1)
Introduction	Captures the reader's attention, provides clear and concise thesis statement	Provides a clear thesis statement, but lacks a hook	Provides a thesis statement, but lacks clarity or hook	Provides a vague or unclear thesis statement	No clear thesis statement
Content	Demonstrates thorough research and understanding of the topic; provides detailed and well-supported arguments with relevant examples and evidence	Demonstrates good understanding of the topic; provides relevant examples and evidence, but lacks detail or depth	Demonstrates some understanding of the topic, but lacks relevant examples and evidence	Demonstrates little understanding of the topic; provides irrelevant or inaccurate information	Does not address the topic
Organisation	Logical and effective organisation of ideas; uses clear transitions between paragraphs	Organises ideas logically, but may lack clear transitions between paragraphs	Organises ideas, but may lack a clear structure or flow; may have some awkward transitions	Lacks organisation or structure; ideas are disjointed and difficult to follow	No organisation or structure

Criteria	Excellent (5)	Good (4)	Fair (3)	Poor (2)	Needs Improvement (1)
Language Use	Uses sophisticated and varied vocabulary; sentence structure is varied and effective; few errors in grammar and mechanics	Uses appropriate vocabulary; sentence structure is generally effective; may have some errors in grammar and mechanics	Uses simple vocabulary and sentence structure; errors in grammar and mechanics are frequent and may interfere with understanding	Uses basic vocabulary and sentence structure; errors in grammar and mechanics are frequent and interfere with understanding	Language use is unclear or inappropriate
Conclusion	Restates thesis and provides a compelling conclusion; leaves a lasting impression on the reader	Restates thesis, but may lack a compelling conclusion; may not leave a lasting impression on the reader	Restates thesis, but lacks a clear conclusion; may not summarize key points	Does not restate the thesis or provide a clear conclusion	No conclusion
Overall Score	20-25	16-19	12-15	8-11	0-7

Here are some additional **grading rubric prompts** created from the **rubric prompt template.**

These **simple example prompts** can **serve as a starting point** for creating your **rubric prompts for your cohorts** and **subjects**.

1. Create a grading **rubric** for a **persuasive essay assessment** for **high school** students. The topic is **"Social media and its impact on mental health"**.
2. Design a grading **rubric** for a **lab report assessment** for **undergraduate biology** students. The topic is **"The effects of pH on enzyme activity."**
3. Develop a grading **rubric** for a **group project** assessment for **graduate-level business** students. The topic is **"Strategic planning and market analysis for a new product launch**."
4. Create a grading **rubric** for a **research paper** assessment for **doctoral-level** education students. The topic is **"The effectiveness of technology in enhancing student learning outcomes."**
5. Design a grading **rubric** for a **presentation** assessment for **elementary school** students. The topic is **"Famous inventors and their inventions."**

Here are some **specific, complex and detailed** grading **rubric prompt** examples **created** from the **rubric prompt template** to **provide more ideas for your own rubric prompts.**

1. Develop a **comprehensive** grading **rubric** for a **research paper** assessment for **undergraduate** students. The research paper should explore the topic of **environmental policy**.

2. Create a detailed **grading rubric** for a **group presentation** assessment for **high school** students. The presentation should focus on an aspect of **American history**, and the rubric should evaluate both **individual and group performance.**

3. Design an effective **grading rubric** for a **midterm exam** assessment for **graduate students**. The exam should cover the topic of **neuroscience**, and the rubric should assess the depth of **understanding and critical thinking skills** demonstrated by the students.

4. Create a **clear and concise grading rubric** for a **final project** assessment for **elementary students**. The project should focus on **animal habitats**, and the rubric should evaluate both the **scientific accuracy and creative presentation** of the project.

5. Develop a **rigorous grading rubric** for a **reflective essay** assessment for **professional development courses**. The essay should explore the topic of **diversity and inclusion in the workplace**, and the rubric should assess both the **depth of analysis and the effectiveness of communication** demonstrated by the writer.

Creating Assessment Case Studies or Scenarios with Rubric Evaluation

Here is an example prompt to create a **case study or scenario-type** assessment with a **grading rubric**.

ChatGPT Prompt Template:

> Create a role-play assessment for **[teaching level or qualification]** students about **[topic]**. Create a case study-based assessment for **[teaching level or qualification]** students who need to learn about **[topic]**. Include **[no of assessment types]** types assessments with a rubric

ChatGPT Prompt Created from the Template:

> **Create a case study based assessment for medical school students who need to learn about "How to do CPR on infants". Include 2 types of assessments with a rubric.**

ChatGPT Video Output URL and QR Code:

https://tinyurl.com/Video-CaseStudy

ChatGPT response for creating case study type assessments with the rubric:

Assessment 1: Written Case Study Assessment

Case Study: Infant Cardiac Arrest

You are a medical student who is observing an emergency department team during a cardiac arrest of a 4-month-old infant. The infant was brought in by ambulance after the parents found him unresponsive and not breathing. You observe the team as they perform CPR on the infant and work to resuscitate him.

Assignment:

Write a case study analysis of the infant's cardiac arrest, including the following:

1. Identification of potential causes of the infant's cardiac arrest.
2. Discussion of the importance of early recognition and initiation of CPR in the management of cardiac arrest in infants.
3. Evaluation of the team's performance during the resuscitation, including an assessment of their communication and teamwork.
4. Analysis of any ethical considerations that may arise during the management of a pediatric cardiac arrest.

Rubric for Assessment 1

Criteria	Exceptional (5)	Good (4)	Basic (3)	Poor (2)	Very Poor (1)
Identification of Potential Causes	Accurately identifies all potential causes of the infant's cardiac arrest, with detailed explanation and relevant supporting evidence.	Identifies most potential causes of the infant's cardiac arrest, with good explanation and some supporting evidence.	Identifies some potential causes of the infant's cardiac arrest, with limited explanation and minimal supporting evidence.	Identifies a few potential causes of the infant's cardiac arrest, with poor explanation and no supporting evidence.	Does not identify any potential causes of the infant's cardiac arrest.
Importance of Early Recognition and CPR	Provides a detailed and comprehensive discussion of the importance of early recognition and initiation of CPR in the management of cardiac arrest in infants.	Provides a good discussion of the importance of early recognition and initiation of CPR in the management of cardiac arrest in infants.	Provides a limited discussion of the importance of early recognition and initiation of CPR in the management of cardiac arrest in infants.	Provides a poor discussion of the importance of early recognition and initiation of CPR in the management of cardiac arrest in infants.	Does not provide any discussion of the importance of early recognition and initiation of CPR in the management of cardiac arrest in infants.

Criteria	Exceptional (5)	Good (4)	Basic (3)	Poor (2)	Very Poor (1)
Evaluation of Team Performance	Provides a comprehensive evaluation of the team's performance during the resuscitation, with a detailed assessment of their communication and teamwork.	Provides a good evaluation of the team's performance during the resuscitation, with a good assessment of their communication and teamwork.	Provides a limited evaluation of the team's performance during the resuscitation, with a limited assessment of their communication and teamwork.	Provides a poor evaluation of the team's performance during the resuscitation, with a poor assessment of their communication and teamwork.	Does not provide any evaluation of the team's performance during the resuscitation.
Analysis of Ethical Considerations	Provides a comprehensive analysis of any ethical considerations that may arise during the management of a pediatric cardiac arrest, with detailed explanation and relevant supporting evidence.	Provides a good analysis of any ethical considerations that may arise during the management of a pediatric cardiac arrest, with a good explanation and some supporting evidence.	Provides a limited analysis of any ethical considerations that may arise during the management of a pediatric cardiac arrest, with limited explanation and minimal supporting evidence.	Provides a poor analysis of any ethical considerations that may arise during the management of a pediatric cardiac arrest, with poor explanation and no supporting evidence.	Does not provide any analysis of ethical considerations that may arise during the management of a pediatric cardiac arrest.

ChatGPT Output:

Assessment 2: Practical Case Study Assessment

Case Study: Infant Cardiac Arrest

You are a medical student who is participating in a practical simulation of a pediatric cardiac arrest scenario in a clinical skills lab. The scenario involves a 6-month-old infant who is found unresponsive and not breathing. Your task is to perform CPR on the infant, following the correct procedures and protocols.

Assignment:

1. Perform CPR on the infant manikin, following the correct procedures and protocols for infant CPR.
2. Evaluate your own performance and identify areas of strength and weakness.

Write a reflection on your experience, discussing your thoughts and feelings during the simulation, as well as any insights gained or lessons learned.

Rubric for Assessment 2

Criteria	Exceptional (5)	Good (4)	Basic (3)	Poor (2)	Very Poor (1)
CPR Performance	Performs all steps of infant CPR correctly, with proper timing and technique.	Performs most steps of infant CPR correctly, with some minor errors in timing or technique.	Performs some steps of infant CPR correctly, with noticeable errors in timing or technique.	Performs a few steps of infant CPR correctly, with significant errors in timing or technique.	Does not perform any steps of infant CPR correctly.
Self-Evaluation	Provides a comprehensive evaluation of own performance, identifying strengths and weaknesses with specific examples and detailed explanations.	Provides a good evaluation of own performance, identifying most strengths and weaknesses with some examples and explanations.	Provides a limited evaluation of own performance, identifying some strengths and weaknesses with limited examples and explanations.	Provides a poor evaluation of own performance, identifying few strengths and weaknesses with minimal examples and explanations.	Does not provide any evaluation of its own performance.

Criteria	Exceptional (5)	Good (4)	Basic (3)	Poor (2)	Very Poor (1)
Reflection	Provides a comprehensive reflection on the experience, discussing thoughts and feelings during the simulation and insights gained or lessons learned, with specific examples and detailed explanations.	Provides a good reflection on the experience, discussing most thoughts and feelings during the simulation and insights gained or lessons learned, with some examples and explanations.	Provides a limited reflection on the experience, discussing some thoughts and feelings during the simulation and insights gained or lessons learned, with limited examples and explanations.	Provides a poor reflection on the experience, discussing a few thoughts and feelings during the simulation and insights gained or lessons learned, with minimal examples and explanations.	Does not provide any reflection on the experience.

Note: In the practical case study assessment, the evaluation of CPR performance will be observed by an instructor or evaluator and scored according to the rubric. The self-evaluation and reflection portions will be completed by the student and submitted along with the observed performance evaluation.

Twenty-Five Assessment Activity Prompts

Here are some **example prompts** that can be customised for creating **various types of assessment** activities:

1. Create a quiz with 10 multiple-choice questions on **[topic of your choice]**.
2. Create a quiz with 15 true and false type questions on **[topic of your choice]**.
3. Create a quiz with 20 fill-in-the-blank-type questions on **[topic of your choice]**.
4. Create a quiz with 20 short answer questions on **[topic of your choice]**.
5. Create a quiz with 10 multiple choice questions based on the following content **[paste the content here]**.
6. Create a quiz with 15 true and false type questions on the following content **[paste the content here]**.
7. Create a quiz with 20 fill-in-the-blank-type questions on the following content **[paste the content here]**.
8. Create a quiz with 20 short answer questions on the following content **[paste the content here]**.
9. Design a test with 10 multiple-choice items on **[topic you select]**.

10. Design a test with 15 yes or no questions on **[topic you select]**.
11. Design a test with 20 complete the sentence questions on **[topic you select]**.
12. Design a test with 20 brief response items on **[topic you select]**.
13. Design a test with 10 multiple-choice items using the following material **[insert the material here]**.
14. Design a test with 15 yes or no questions using the following material **[insert the material here]**.
15. Design a test with 20 complete the sentence questions using the following material **[insert the material here]**.
16. Design a test with 20 brief response items using the following material **[insert the material here]**.
17. Construct an assessment with 20 gap-filling tasks using the following material **[insert the material here]**.
18. Construct an assessment with 20 concise answer tasks using the following material **[insert the material here]**.
19. Formulate a quiz with 10 option-based questions on **[your chosen subject]**.
20. Formulate a quiz with 15 affirmation or negation queries on **[your chosen subject]**.
21. Formulate a quiz with 20 sentence completion tasks on **[your chosen subject]**.

22. Formulate a quiz with 20 succinct reply challenges on **[your chosen subject]**.
23. Draft an exam with 20 sentence finishing tasks on **[your preferred topic]**.
24. Draft an exam with 20 short-answer segments on **[your preferred topic]**.
25. Draft an exam with 10 selection-based queries using the following content **[provide the content here]**.

ChatGPT can adapt to the level of the student, providing questions or problems that are appropriately challenging. This adaptability allows for a more personalised assessment experience, which can be more engaging and relevant for the student.

CHAPTER 4

USE CHATGPT TO GRADE ASSESSMENTS AND PROVIDE FEEDBACK

4. Use ChatGPT to Grade Assessments and Provide Feedback

ChatGPT can provide **student feedback** on their work such as **essays, reports and any other type of writing**. You can provide **criteria or marking rubrics to ChatGPT** and it can provide feedback based on those **criteria**.

However, please be **warned that at times ChatGPT grading and feedback may be inaccurate** and therefore **teachers need to review** and adjust the ChatGPT produced **grade and feedback**.

Grading and Feedback for Essay Assessments

ChatGPT can provide student **feedback** on **essay type assessments.**

Here is an example that can **help you understand** how to **use** the following **prompt for grading assessment** and give feedback.

ChatGPT Prompt Template:

> Act as a teacher and provide **[no. of words]** words long feedback and a total grade out of **[marks]** marks based on the **[criteria 1]**, **[criteria 2]**, **[criteria 3]**, **[criteria 4]**, and **[criteria 5]** for this **[essay]** **"Paste student assessment text – essay, report, presentation, etc."**

Customised ChatGPT Prompt Created from the Template:

> **Act as a teacher and provide 100 word long feedback and a total grade out of 50 marks based on the quality of definitions and**

concepts, explanation of concepts, examples and references, critical analysis and inclusion of high-quality resources

for this essay *"Ancient human refers to the cultural and social developments of human societies that emerged in the prehistoric era, before the advent of writing systems. These s were characterized by their unique beliefs, customs, and practices that shaped the way of life for the people of that time. Some of the most well-known ancient s include the Mesopotamian, Egyptian, Indus Valley, Chinese, and Mayan s.*

The Mesopotamian, located in the region that is now Iraq, was one of the earliest s to develop. It emerged in the fourth millennium BCE and lasted until the sixth century BCE. Mesopotamia was the site of the first cities and urban centres, as well as the development of agriculture and the invention of the wheel. The Mesopotamians were also responsible for the invention of writing, which allowed for the recording of important events and the development of literature. Their religion was polytheistic and their gods and goddesses were believed to have a significant influence on daily life.

The Egyptian, located in the northeastern region of Africa, was one of the most advanced and enduring s in ancient history. It emerged around 3150 BCE and lasted until the fourth century CE. The Egyptians are known for their impressive architecture, including the pyramids and temples, as well as their sophisticated hieroglyphic writing system. They were skilled in mathematics and astronomy, and their religion was also polytheistic, with many gods and goddesses that were worshipped in temples throughout the region.

The Indus Valley, located in present-day Pakistan and India, emerged around 2600 BCE and lasted until 1900 BCE. It is one of the earliest s in the world and was characterized by its advanced urban planning and sanitation systems. The people of the Indus Valley were skilled in metallurgy, including the production of bronze and copper, and they had a writing system that had yet to be deciphered. The was also notable for its trade networks, which extended as far as Mesopotamia and Egypt.

The Chinese, located in East Asia, emerged around 2100 BCE and lasted until the twentieth century CE. It is known for its rich cultural heritage, including the development of Confucianism and Taoism, as well as its significant contributions to art, literature, and philosophy. The Chinese were skilled in agriculture, metallurgy, and the production of silk, which was a highly valued commodity in the ancient world. Their writing system, which includes characters that represent ideas rather than sounds, is one of the oldest in the world.

The Mayan, located in Mesoamerica, emerged around 2000 BCE and lasted until the fifteenth century CE. The Mayans were skilled astronomers and mathematicians, and they developed a complex calendar system that is still used by some indigenous communities today. They were also skilled in agriculture, with a diet that included corn, beans, and squash. The Mayan religion was polytheistic, with gods and goddesses that represented natural phenomena and important aspects of daily life.

Despite their differences, these ancient s all shared several commonalities. They were characterized by their social hierarchies, with rulers and elites at the top and commoners at the bottom. They also shared a reliance on agriculture and the natural environment for their survival, and they were skilled in various trades and crafts, including metallurgy, pottery, and weaving. Religion played a significant role in all of these s, with gods and goddesses that were believed to have a powerful influence on daily life.

1. *In conclusion, ancient human was a period of great innovation and cultural development. The Mesopotamian, Egyptian, Indus Valley, Chinese, and Mayan s all contributed to our understanding of the ancient world and its legacies Johnson, M. (2019). The Development of Ancient s. Routledge.*

2. *Fagan, B. M. (2004). Ancient s. National Geographic Society.*

3. *Trigger, B. G. (2003). Understanding Early s: A Comparative Study. Cambridge University Press."*

ChatGPT Video Output URL and QR Code:

https://tinyurl.com/Grade-Feedback

ChatGPT Output:

Feedback:

Overall, your essay provides a concise overview of five of the most well-known ancient human s. You have effectively defined the concept of ancient human and provided specific examples of s, along with their notable achievements, such as the invention of writing, architecture, and advances in mathematics and astronomy. Additionally, you have highlighted some of the similarities and differences between these s.

You have cited high-quality references to support your points and have included a range of information on each. However, there are some areas where you could improve. For instance, you could have provided a more in-depth critical analysis of the impact of these s on the modern world. Additionally, you could have explored how these interacted with each other and the impact of this interaction on their respective societies.

Grade: 42/50

You have demonstrated a good understanding of the concepts and provided relevant examples and references. However, there is room for improvement in the critical analysis and use of additional resources.

Ten Grading and Feedback Prompts for Essay

Here are a few **helpful prompts** to assist you in **generating** your **own essay grading prompt**.

1. Assume the role of a **[teacher]** and provide feedback of **[150 words]** along with a total grade out of **[100 marks]** based on **[clarity of ideas]**, **[coherence of argument]**, **[evidence and supporting references]**, **[critical analysis]**, and **[overall presentation]** of the essay titled "Paste student text here".
2. As an **[evaluator]**, write **[200 word feedback]** and provide a total grade out of **[75 marks]** based on the **[use of appropriate terminology]**, **[understanding of key concepts]**, **[analysis of key points]**, **[use of**

relevant examples], and **[overall structure]** of the essay titled "Paste student text here".

3. Assume the role of a **[teacher]** and provide **[250-word feedback]** along with a total grade out of **[60 marks]** based on the **[quality of introduction and conclusion]**, **[integration of sources]**, **[critical evaluation]**, **[originality of ideas]**, and **[overall coherence]** of the essay titled "Paste student text here".

4. In the **[role of a teacher]**, provide **[300 word feedback]** and a total grade out of **[80 marks]** based on the **[accuracy of information]**, **[depth of analysis]**, **[use of appropriate evidence and references]**, **[effective organisation]**, and **[overall writing style]** of this essay "Paste student text here".

5. As a **[teacher]**, evaluate the essay by providing **[350-word feedback]** and a total grade out of **[90 marks]** based on the **[understanding of the subject matter]**, **[integration of key concepts]**, **[supporting evidence and references]**, **[critical analysis]**, and **[overall presentation and writing style]** for "Paste student text here".

6. Act as a **[teacher]** and provide feedback of **[150 words]** and a grade out of **[100 marks]** based on the **[structure]**, **[coherence]**, **[use of evidence]**,

[creativity], and **[language proficiency]** of this essay "Paste student text here".

7. In the **[capacity of a teacher]**, evaluate the following essay "Paste student text here" and assign a grade out of **[50 marks]**, based on the **[level of detail]**, **[organisation]**, **[argumentation]**, **[grammar]**, and **[originality]**. Provide feedback in **[100 words]**.
8. As an **[instructor]**, grade this "Paste student text here" essay out of **[80 marks]**, considering the **[research depth]**, **[writing style]**, **[coherence]**, **[flow]**, and **[incorporation of diverse viewpoints]**. Provide feedback in **[150 words]**.
9. Assume the role of a **[teacher]** and evaluate this essay "Paste student text here" based on the **[accuracy of the information]**, **[persuasive arguments]**, **[use of examples]**, **[logical flow]**, and **[adherence to instructions]**. Assign a grade out of **[60 marks]** and provide feedback in **[120 words]**.
10. Assume the role of a **[educator]** and evaluate this essay "Paste student text here" based on its **[clarity]**, **[relevance]**, **[coherence]**, **[creativity]**, and **[language proficiency]**. Provide feedback in **[100 words]** and assign a grade out of **[70 marks]**.

Grading And Feedback for Multiple-Choice Assessments

ChatGPT can provide student feedback on **multiple-choice** type assessments.

Here is an example that can help you understand how to generate assessment **grading and feedback** for **multiple-choice** type assessments.

ChatGPT Prompt Template:

> **Act as a teacher and provide [no. of words] words long feedback and total a grade out of [marks] marks for multiple-choice assessment including these responses *"Paste student multiple choice response"***

Customised ChatGPT Prompt Created from the Template:

> **Act as a teacher and provide 50 word long feedback and a total grade out of 10 marks for multiple-choice assessment for this student's response** "Which planet in our Solar System is closest to the Sun?"
>
> A) Jupiter

B) Mars

C) Venus

D) Mercury

Answer: D) Mercury

Which planet in our Solar System has the most rings?

A) Uranus

B) Saturn

C) Neptune

D) Jupiter

Answer: B) Saturn

What is the largest planet in our Solar System?

A) Earth

B) Mars

C) Jupiter

D) Saturn

Answer: C) Jupiter

What is the name of the planet known for its beautiful rings?

A) Jupiter

B) Saturn

C) Uranus

D) Neptune

Answer: B) Saturn

Which planet in our Solar System has the highest density?

A) Mercury

B) Earth

C) Venus

D) Mars

Answer: B) Earth

Which planet has the shortest year?

A) Mercury

B) Mars

C) Jupiter

D) Neptune

Answer: A) Mercury

What is the name of the largest volcano in our Solar System, located on Mars?

A) Olympus Mons

B) Mount Everest

C) Mount Kilimanjaro

D) Mount Rainier

Answer: A) Olympus Mons

Which planet in our Solar System has the most known moons?

A) Earth

B) Jupiter

C) Saturn

D) Uranus

Answer: B) Jupiter

What is the name of the spacecraft that was the first to visit all four of the outer planets in our Solar System?

A) Voyager 1

B) Mars Pathfinder

C) Apollo 11

D) Hubble Space Telescope

Answer: A) Voyager 1

What is the name of the dwarf planet located in the Kuiper Belt?

A) Eris

B) Pluto

C) Makemake

D) Haumea

Answer: B) Pluto”

ChatGPT Video Output URL and QR Code:

https://tinyurl.com/MCQGrade

ChatGPT Output:

Feedback:

Great job, you have scored 10/10 on this multiple-choice assessment! Your answers were all correct and demonstrated a strong understanding of the basics of our Solar System. Your response to each question was concise and to the point, which is a great approach for this type of assessment. Keep up the good work!

Utilising AI for assessments can significantly reduce the workload for educators, especially in larger classes or online settings where immediate human feedback may be time-consuming. This scalability allows for more frequent assessments without increasing the administrative burden on educators. These benefits are balanced by challenges, such as ensuring the AI's understanding and evaluation are accurate and fair. However, the technology holds promise for enhancing educational assessment practices.

Ten Grading and Feedback Prompts for Multiple-Choice Assessments

Here are a few **helpful prompts** to assist you in **generating** your **own multiple-choice grading prompt**.

1. Serve as an **[English instructor]** and offer **[75 words]** of feedback, grading up to **[50 marks]** for this **[multiple-choice evaluation]** "Insert student's multiple-choice answer here".
2. Function as a **[geography educator]** and deliver **[50 words]** of commentary, with a score out of **[100 marks]** for this **[multiple-choice evaluation]** "Insert student's multiple-choice answer here".
3. Take on the role of a **[chemistry professor]** and give general remarks, assigning a grade out of **[15 marks]** for this **[multiple-choice evaluation]** "Insert student's multiple-choice answer here".
4. Act as an **[economics lecturer]** and provide concise feedback, marking up to **[40 marks]** for this **[multiple-choice evaluation]** "Insert student's multiple-choice answer here".
5. Act in the capacity of a **[social science tutor]** and offer succinct comments, grading out of **[100 marks]** for this **[multiple-choice evaluation]** "Insert student's multiple-choice answer here".
6. Act as an **[English teacher]** and provide **[75 words]** long feedback and total grade out of **[50 marks]** for this **[multiple-choice assessment]** "Paste student's multiple-choice response".
7. Act as a **[geography teacher]** and provide **[50 words]** long feedback and total grade out of **[100 marks]** for

this **[multiple-choice assessment]** "Paste student's multiple-choice response".

8. Act as a **[chemistry teacher]** and provide general feedback and total grade out of **[15 marks]** for this **[multiple-choice assessment]** "Paste student's multiple-choice response".
9. Act as an **[economics teacher]** and provide short feedback and total grade out of **[40 marks]** for this **[multiple-choice assessment]** "Paste student's multiple-choice response".
10. Act as a **[social science teacher]** and provide short feedback and total grade out of **[100 marks]** for this **[multiple-choice assessment]** "Paste student's multiple-choice response".

Grading And Feedback for True-False Assessments

ChatGPT can also provide student feedback **for true-false type** assessments.

Here is an example that can help you **provide assessment grading and feedback** for true-false type assessments.

ChatGPT Prompt Template:

> Act as a teacher and provide **[no. of words]** words long feedback and total grade out of **[marks]** marks for this fill-in-the-blanks assessment **"Paste student's true-false response"**.

Customised ChatGPT Prompt Created from the Template:

> Act as a teacher and provide 50 word long feedback and a total grade out of 10 marks for this true-false assessment "
>
> 1. Mitochondria are *found in plant cells, but not in animal cells. [False]*
> 2. Mitochondria *are responsible for producing energy in the form of ATP. [True]*
> 3. Mitochondria *have their own DNA separate from the cell's nucleus. [True]*
> 4. Mitochondria *are typically shaped like spheres or cubes. [False]*
> 5. Mitochondria *play a role in regulating cell death through a process called apoptosis. [True]*

6. Mitochondria *can only produce ATP through aerobic respiration. [False]*
7. Mitochondria *are found in every type of eukaryotic cell. [True]*
8. Mitochondria *are involved in the synthesis of proteins. [False]*
9. Mitochondria *are surrounded by a double membrane. [True]*
10. Mitochondria *are the only organelles that contain their own DNA. [False]”*

ChatGPT Video Output URL and QR Code:

https://tinyurl.com/TrueFalseGrade

ChatGPT Output:

Feedback:

Great job on this assessment! You demonstrated a good understanding of the role and structure of mitochondria. Your score is 10 out of 10. Keep up the good work and continue to review the material to reinforce your understanding.

One of the most significant advantages of using ChatGPT for generating feedback is the speed at which it can be provided. Traditional feedback methods often require manual effort from teachers or instructors, which can result in delays. Immediate feedback allows students to make quick adjustments and reinforces learning more effectively. ChatGPT can offer a level of consistency that is hard to achieve manually. Additionally, ChatGPT can generate personalised feedback based on each student's specific errors or areas for improvement.

Ten Grading and Feedback Prompts for True-False Assessments

Here are some **helpful prompts** to assist you in **generating** your **own true-false grading prompt**.

1. Act as a **[English teacher]** and provide **[75 words]** long feedback and a total grade out of **[50 marks]** for this true-false assessment "Paste student's true-false response".
2. Act as a **[geography teacher]** and provide **[50 words]** long feedback and a total grade out of **[100 marks]** for this true-false assessment "Paste student's true-false response".
3. Act as a **[chemistry teacher]** and provide **[general feedback]** and total grade out of **[15 marks]** for this true-false assessment "Paste student's true-false response".
4. Be a **[economics teacher]** and provide **[short feedback]** and a total grade out of **[40 marks]** for this true-false assessment "Paste student's true-false response".
5. Act as a **[social science teacher]** and provide **[short feedback]** and total grade out of **[100 marks]** for this true-false assessment "Paste student's true-false response".
6. Be a **[English instructor]** and offer **[75-word]** feedback along with a grade out of **[50 points]** for this true-false test "Insert student's true-false answers".

7. Act as a **[geography educator]** and give **[50-word]** feedback and a score out of **[100 points]** for this true-false quiz "Insert student's true-false answers".
8. Be a **[chemistry mentor]** and deliver **[generalized feedback]** with a score out of **[15 points]** for this true-false evaluation "Insert student's true-false answers".
9. As an **[economics lecturer]** and present **[concise feedback]** and a grade out of **[40 points]** for this true-false test "Insert student's true-false answers".
10. As a **[social studies instructor]** and offer **[brief feedback]** with a score out of **[100 points]** for this true-false examination "Insert student's true-false answers".

Grading and Feedback for Fill-in-the-Blanks Assessments

ChatGPT can provide student feedback for **fill-in-the-blank type assessments.**

Here is an example that can help you **understand how to use ChatGPT for grading and providing feedback** for fill-in-the-blanks type assessment.

ChatGPT Prompt Template:

> **Act as a teacher and provide [no. of words] words long feedback and total grade out of [marks] marks for this fill-in-the-blanks assessment *"Paste student's fill-in-the-blanks response"*.**

IMPORTANT: ChatGPT **does not take input** as **underline** text so you will need to instead use tag *underline_answer.* This means if you want to input the following student response: ***"The reciprocal of sine is cosecant"*** for grading then the ChatGPT input should be: ***"The reciprocal of sine is underline__cosecant"***.

Customised ChatGPT Prompt Created from the Template:

> **Act as a** teacher **and provide 50 word long feedback and a total grade out of 10 marks for this fill-in-the-blanks assessment "**
>
> 1. *The three primary trigonometric functions are sine, cosine, and underline__tangent.*
> 2. The *reciprocal of sine is* ***underline_cosecant.***
> 3. The *reciprocal of cosine is* ***underline__secant.***

4. The reciprocal of tangent is **underline__cotangent**.

5. The unit circle has a radius of **underline__1**.

6. The measure of an angle in radians is equal to the length of the **underline__arc** on the unit circle.

7. The underline_**cosine** of an angle is equal to the sine of its complementary angle.

8. The underline__**sine** of an angle is equal to the cosine of its complementary angle.

9. The Pythagorean identity is sin^2(theta) + cos^2(theta) = **underline__1**.

10. The function y = A sin(Bx + C) + D is an example of an **underline_sinusoidal function**.

"

ChatGPT Video Output URL and QR Code:

https://tinyurl.com/FillBlanksGrade

ChatGPT Output:

Feedback:

Good effort on the fill-in-the-blanks assessment! Here's your feedback and grade:

1. Correct!
2. Correct!
3. Correct!
4. Correct!
5. Correct!
6. Correct!
7. Correct!
8. Correct!
9. Correct!
10. Correct!

Your score is 10 out of 10! Excellent job demonstrating your knowledge of trigonometric functions and identities. Keep up the great work!

Ten Grading and Feedback Prompts for Fill-in-the-Blanks Assessments

Here are a few **helpful prompts** to assist you in **generating** your **own fill-in-the-blanks grading prompt**.

1. In the role of a teacher, give a **[no. of words]** words long evaluation and a cumulative score out of **[marks]** marks for the fill-in-the-blanks test with these answers **"Paste student fill-in-the-blanks response"**.
2. Taking on the teacher's perspective, deliver feedback spanning **[no. of words]** words and determine a grade out of **[marks]** marks for this fill-in-the-blanks evaluation **"Paste student's fill-in-the-blanks response"**.
3. Emulating a teacher's role, provide an assessment of **[no. of words]** words and allocate a score out of **[marks]** marks for this fill-in-the-blanks test **"Paste student's fill-in-the-blanks response"**.
4. As a language teacher, offer a critique that is **[no. of words]** words long and a total grade out of **[marks]** marks for this fill-in-the-blanks exam "Insert student's fill-in-the-blanks answers".

5. Act as a trainer and provide **[no. of words]**-word review and assign a grade out of **[marks]** marks for this fill-in-the-blanks assessment "Insert student's fill-in-the-blanks answers".
6. As a teacher, provide a quick student appraisal comprising **[no. of words]** words and determine a score out of **[marks]** marks for this fill-in-the-blanks quiz "Insert student's fill-in-the-blanks answers".
7. As someone in the teaching profession, provide a **[no. of words]**-word commentary and decide on a score out of **[marks]** marks for this fill-in-the-blanks challenge "Insert student's fill-in-the-blanks answers".
8. Act as a tutor and provide a critique spanning **[no. of words]** words and award a grade out of **[marks]** marks for this fill-in-the-blanks task "Insert student's fill-in-the-blanks answers".
9. As an English tutor, provide an evaluation that is **[no. of words]** words in length and allocate marks out of a total of **[marks]** for this fill-in-the-blanks assignment "Insert student's fill-in-the-blanks answers".
10. Act as a teacher, generate an evaluation that spans **[no. of words]** words and set a grade out of **[marks]** marks for this fill-in-the-blanks test "Insert student's fill-in-the-blanks answers".

CHAPTER 5

HOW TO USE CHATGPT TO BRAINSTORM TOPICS TO STUDY

5. How to Use ChatGPT to Brainstorm Topics to Study

Using ChatGPT to **brainstorm topic areas to study** is an effective way for students to generate **ideas and inspiration** for their studies.

One of the key benefits of using ChatGPT for brainstorming is that it saves **time and effort**. Students can simply input their topic or area of interest, and ChatGPT will provide them with a **range of relevant suggestions** for what to study.

This can be particularly helpful for students who are new to a topic or who **are struggling to come up with ideas** for their coursework.

Another benefit of using ChatGPT for brainstorming is the **diversity of perspectives** it provides. ChatGPT has been trained on a wide variety of sources, including **academic research, news articles, and other publications**. As a result, it can provide students with unique perspectives on a topic, including perspectives they may not have previously considered. This can help students gain a more **well-rounded understanding of their chosen topic**.

Using ChatGPT for brainstorming can also encourage **critical thinking**. By exploring different ideas and perspectives suggested by ChatGPT, students can learn how to evaluate and analyse information and develop their ideas and insights based on the suggestions provided.

This can help students develop important critical thinking skills that will be valuable in their **academic and professional lives**.

By leveraging the power of this language model, students can generate new ideas and insights that will help them excel in their studies and beyond.

How to Brainstorm Topics to Study

To use ChatGPT to brainstorm things to study about a topic, you can follow these steps:

1. Start by selecting a topic to study.
2. Ask ChatGPT to provide a brief overview of the topic to gain a basic understanding.
3. Use ChatGPT to generate a list of subtopics related to the main topic.
4. Narrow down the list of subtopics to those that seem most relevant or interesting.
5. Ask ChatGPT to provide more detailed information about each subtopic.
6. Use ChatGPT to generate potential research questions or hypotheses related to each subtopic.
7. Choose a few research questions to focus on and use ChatGPT to generate potential sources or materials to aid in further exploration of each question.

8. Use the sources and materials gathered from ChatGPT to conduct research and further deepen your understanding of the topic.

Sample ChatGPT Prompts:

- Can you give me a brief overview of the topic of climate change?
- What are some subtopics related to the effects of climate change on the oceans?
- Can you provide more detailed information about the impact of ocean acidification on marine life?
- What are some potential research questions related to the impact of ocean acidification on marine life?
- Can you give me a brief overview of the topic of deforestation?
- What are some subtopics related to the effects of deforestation on biodiversity?
- Can you provide more detailed information about the impact of deforestation on native species?
- What are some potential research questions related to the loss of habitat due to deforestation?

Use the ideas generated by ChatGPT as a starting point for your research. You can further explore each subtopic.

Step-by-Step Technique of Brainstorming

Here is another **step-by-step example** of how ChatGPT can be used to **brainstorm things to study** about a **topic**:

1. Define your topic of interest, for example, "Artificial Intelligence".
2. Use a prompt to ask ChatGPT to generate ideas related to the topic. Some example prompts could be:
   - Can you suggest some subtopics to study about Artificial Intelligence?

- What are some areas of focus when studying Artificial Intelligence?
- Can you provide me with some research topics related to Artificial Intelligence?

3. Review the ideas generated by ChatGPT and refine them according to your specific interests and goals. Some of the ideas generated by ChatGPT may be general or not directly relevant to your interests, so it's important to evaluate them critically and select the ones that are most useful for your purposes.

How to Use Multi-Prompt Conversation to Brainstorm

Here is an **example of a brainstorming conversation** between **ChatGPT and a student** that may help understand what a **typical brainstorming conversation** may look like.

User: Can you suggest some subtopics to study about Artificial Intelligence?

ChatGPT Video Output URL and QR Code:

https://tinyurl.com/GPTStudentChat

ChatGPT Output:

ChatGPT: Sure, here are some subtopics related to Artificial Intelligence:

- Machine learning algorithms
- Natural language processing
- Computer vision
- Robotics and automation
- Ethics and governance of AI Neural networks
- Expert systems

User: That's great, thank you. Can you suggest some research topics related to the ethics and governance of AI?

ChatGPT Video Output URL and QR Code:

https://tinyurl.com/GPTStudentPrompt01

ChatGPT Output:

ChatGPT: Of course, here are some research topics related to the ethics and governance of AI:

- The role of government in regulating AI development and deployment
- Ethical considerations for AI decision-making
- Bias and fairness in AI algorithms
- Privacy and security concerns with AI systems
- Transparency and accountability in AI development and use
- Social and economic implications of AI adoption

User: Can you suggest some research topics related to the social and economic implications of AI adoption?

ChatGPT Video Output URL and QR Code:

https://tinyurl.com/GPTStudentPrompt02

ChatGPT Output:

ChatGPT: Certainly! Here are some potential research topics related to the social and economic implications of AI adoption:

1. The impact of AI on employment: How will the widespread adoption of AI technologies affect the job market in different industries? What will be the short-term and long-term consequences for workers and businesses?

2. Ethics and accountability in AI: How can we ensure that AI systems are developed and deployed in an ethical and accountable manner? What are the potential risks of AI systems that are biased or discriminatory?

3. AI and inequality: How might the adoption of AI technologies exacerbate existing inequalities in society? What policies and interventions could be put in place to mitigate these risks?

4. The role of AI in healthcare: What are the potential benefits and risks of AI applications in healthcare, such as diagnostic tools and treatment recommendations? How can we ensure that AI is used safely and effectively in the healthcare sector?

5. AI and privacy: What are the implications of AI systems that collect and analyse vast amounts of personal data? How can we protect individuals' privacy rights while still leveraging the benefits of AI?

6. The economic implications of AI for different countries: How will the adoption of AI technologies affect the global economy, and

what will be the consequences for different countries and regions? How can we ensure that the benefits of AI are distributed fairly across the world?

7. AI and education: How might AI technologies transform education and learning? What are the potential benefits and risks of using AI in the classroom, and how can we ensure that it is used responsibly and effectively?

8. The impact of AI on decision-making: What are the potential consequences of relying on AI systems to make important decisions in fields such as finance, law, and politics? How can we ensure that AI systems are transparent and accountable in these contexts?

These are just a few examples of research topics related to the social and economic implications of AI adoption. Depending on your specific interests and expertise, there are many other avenues to explore in this field.

Five Brainstorming Prompts

Here are some ChatGPT prompts and examples for brainstorming:

Prompt 1: "Can you generate some questions that can help explore the topic of climate change?"

ChatGPT Video Output URL and QR Code:

https://tinyurl.com/ClimateChangeBrain

ChatGPT Output:

- What are some innovative solutions to combat climate change?
- What causes climate change?
- How does climate change affect different regions of the world?
- What are the potential consequences of climate change?

Prompt 2: "Can you suggest different angles to approach the topic of artificial intelligence?"

ChatGPT Video Output URL and QR Code:

https://tinyurl.com/AI-Brainstorming

ChatGPT Output:

- The history of artificial intelligence: How has AI evolved?
- Ethics and artificial intelligence: What are the ethical implications of developing AI?
- AI and healthcare: How is AI being used to improve healthcare?
- AI and the economy: What are the potential economic impacts of AI?
- AI and privacy: How does AI impact personal privacy?

Prompt 3: "Can you generate some keywords and phrases that can aid in research about renewable energy?"

ChatGPT Video Output URL and QR Code:

https://tinyurl.com/RenewableEnergyBrainstorm

ChatGPT Output:

- Solar energy
- Wind energy
- Geothermal energy
- Hydroelectric power
- Sustainable energy

Prompt 4: Provide suggestions for further reading or resources about World War II

ChatGPT Video Output URL and QR Code:

https://tinyurl.com/WWII-Brainstorm

ChatGPT Output:

Comprehensive Histories:

- "The Second World War" by Sir Winston S. Churchill (6 Volumes)
- "The Second World War" by Antony Beevor
- "The Storm of War: A New History of the Second World War" by Andrew Roberts

Memoirs and First-Hand Accounts:

- "With the Old Breed" by Eugene B. Sledge
- "Helmet for My Pillow" by Robert Leckie
- "Berlin Diary" by William L. Shirer
- "Maquis" by George Millar

Specific Battles or Fronts:

- "Stalingrad: The Fateful Siege: 1942-1943" by Antony Beevor
- "D-Day: June 6, 1944: The Climactic Battle of World War II" by Stephen E. Ambrose
- "The Battle of the Atlantic: How the Allies Won the War" by Jonathan Dimbleby

Prompt 5: Offer potential research questions or thesis statements.

ChatGPT Video Output URL and QR Code:

https://tinyurl.com/GPTResearch-Questions

ChatGPT Output:

Computer Science/Artificial Intelligence:

- Research Question: "How can explainable artificial intelligence techniques be integrated into complex deep learning models to enhance transparency and interpretability?"
- Thesis Statement: "Developing an AI-driven framework for real-time anomaly detection in cybersecurity using deep learning and interpretable feature attribution."

Environmental Science:

- Research Question: "What are the long-term effects of plastic pollution on marine ecosystems, and how can innovative biodegradable materials contribute to mitigating this issue?"
- Thesis Statement: "Assessing the impact of urban green spaces on air quality improvement and urban heat island reduction in rapidly growing cities."

Psychology:

- Research Question: "What are the psychological factors that influence individuals' adherence to exercise routines, and how can personalized interventions enhance long-term exercise compliance?"
- Thesis Statement: "Investigating the role of early childhood experiences in the development of resilience and coping strategies in adulthood."

Economics:

- Research Question: "How do different types of government interventions affect the income inequality gap, and what are the implications for social stability and economic growth?"
- Thesis Statement: "Analyzing the economic impact of automation and AI on the job market and exploring strategies for upskilling and reskilling the workforce."

Sociology:

- Research Question: "What are the social determinants contributing to the persistence of gender-based wage disparities, and how can organisational policies be redesigned to promote pay equity?"
- Thesis Statement: "Examining the influence of social media on shaping collective social movements and the challenges posed to traditional forms of activism."

Medical Science:

- Research Question: “How do genetic and environmental factors interact to predispose individuals to autoimmune disorders, and how can precision medicine approaches be employed for effective treatment?”
- Thesis Statement: “Investigating the potential of novel drug delivery systems to improve treatment efficacy and patient compliance in chronic diseases.”

Education:

- Research Question: "What are the key factors influencing the adoption of technology in classrooms, and how can educators leverage digital tools to enhance student engagement and learning outcomes?"
- Thesis Statement: "Exploring the impact of culturally responsive teaching strategies on narrowing the achievement gap among diverse student populations."

Thirty Brainstorming Prompts

Here are some **brainstorming prompts** that can be **further customised** for **brainstorming** on **multiple topics** using **ChatGPT**:

1. Can you identify **[music genres or artists]** that have influenced the **[culture or social landscape]** of a **[particular region or period]**?
2. Could you generate **[survey questions or metrics]** that can measure **[customer satisfaction or user experience]** for a **[product or service]**?
3. Could you compile a list of **[key historical events or figures]** that have shaped the **[politics or society]** of a **[specific region or nation]**?
4. Could you compile **[case studies or examples]** that illustrate the **[success or failure]** of **[particular initiatives or projects]**?
5. Could you generate a list of questions that explore the role of **[topic 1]** in accelerating **[topic 2]**?
6. Could you assemble a set of **[statistical data or metrics]** that can help evaluate the **[performance or effectiveness]** of **[specific program or policy]**?

7. Can you provide a list of **[experts or thought leaders]** who are influential in the field of **[specific subject or industry]**?
8. Could you recommend **[travel destinations or cultural experiences]** that offer insights into **[unique customs or traditions]**?
9. Could you list **[websites or online platforms]** that offer **[credible information or resources]** on **[specific subject or industry]**?
10. Can you pinpoint specific **[areas of study]** within **[major topic]** that are relevant to **[subtopic]**?
11. Can you put together a compilation of **[primary literature or source type]** that provides insights into **[specific aspect]** during **[historical event or period]**?
12. Could you suggest **[innovative methods or tools]** for **[data collection or analysis]** in **[research area or project]**?
13. Could you recommend **[podcasts or webinars]** that focus on **[emerging trends]** in **[specific industry or field]**?
14. Could you produce a list of **[search terms and phrases]** useful for studying the **[regulatory consequences]** of moving towards **[industry type]**?
15. Could you propose some **[focused topics]** that look into the **[barriers and issues]** of using **[artificial**

intelligence] in **[judicial systems]**? Can you recommend a few **[academic papers]** that explore the **[contributions of a specific group]** during **[historical event or period]**?

16. Can you curate a collection of **[artworks or literary pieces]** that reflect the **[cultural or social themes]** of a **[specific era or movement]**?
17. Can you suggest **[courses or training programs]** that can enhance skills in **[specific area or discipline]**?
18. Can you provide a curated list of **[primary source documents]** that offer insights into the **[diplomatic relations]** during **[World War II]**?
19. Could you identify **[networking opportunities or events]** that are beneficial for professionals in **[specific field or industry]**?
20. Could you recommend **[books or publications]** that offer a deep dive into the **[cultural aspects]** of **[specific community or region]**?
21. Could you recommend **[mobile apps or software]** that can improve **[productivity or well-being]** in a **[work or personal setting]**?
22. Can you suggest various **[perspectives]** from which to examine the **[ethical implications]** of **[artificial intelligence]**?

23. Can you list **[best practices or guidelines]** for achieving **[specific goals or outcomes]** in **[particular setting or industry]**?
24. Could you assemble a list of **[resources or materials]** that can aid in **[self-study or professional development]** in **[specific subject or skill]**?
25. Can you identify **[key debates or controversies]** within the field of **[academic discipline or industry]**?
26. Can you suggest **[volunteer opportunities or internships]** that provide experience in **[specific field or role]**?
27. Could you generate a set of **[keywords and phrases]** that can be used to research the **[policy implications]** of transitioning to **[topic]**?
28. Can you suggest **[investment opportunities or strategies]** for growing **[personal or business finances]**?
29. Can you compile a list of **[keywords and phrases]** that focus on the **[technological advancements]** in **[topic]**?
30. Could you generate a list of **[questions or topics]** for a panel discussion on the **[ethical or moral dilemmas]** in **[specific field or situation]**?

CHAPTER 6

USE CHATGPT TO IMPROVE LANGUAGE SKILLS

6. Use ChatGPT to Improve Language Skills

In an era dominated by **technological innovation**, leveraging the power of **artificial intelligence** to foster **language acquisition** presents an exciting frontier. **ChatGPT** holds immense potential to augment traditional language learning methods, offering learners a dynamic platform to **improve** their **linguistic skills**.

ChatGPT can be effectively employed to **enhance vocabulary**, **improve conversational abilities**, and foster a deeper understanding of **language nuances**.

Develop Writing Prompt

ChatGPT can be used to generate writing prompts for students that offer the following benefits:

1. **Wide range of topics**: ChatGPT has been trained on a vast amount of data, which makes it capable of generating prompts on a wide range of topics such as literature, history, science, and social studies.
2. **Personalisation**: ChatGPT can tailor prompts to individual students based on their interests and writing abilities. By analysing previous responses, ChatGPT can generate prompts that are challenging yet achievable for each student.
3. **Creative inspiration**: ChatGPT can generate unique and creative writing prompts that may inspire students to think outside the box and produce more innovative writing.
4. **Timesaving**: Teachers and educators can save time by using ChatGPT to generate writing prompts rather than spending time brainstorming ideas. This allows them to focus on other aspects of lesson planning and student engagement.
5. **Flexibility**: ChatGPT can generate prompts in a variety of formats, such as personal narratives, persuasive essays, and research papers. This allows educators to choose the

type of prompt that best fits their learning objectives and teaching style.

A teacher could ask ChatGPT to generate a **writing prompt** that requires students to use the present perfect tense, a **complex verb tense** that can be **difficult** for **language learners** to master.

The prompt looks as follows:

> **Write a narrative about a personal experience you have had that has changed your perspective on life. Use the present perfect tense to describe the actions you took and the impact they had on your life.**

This prompt would challenge students to use the present perfect tense to describe an experience that has ongoing relevance in their lives. By **focusing on this specific grammar structure**, students are encouraged to think deeply about how it functions in English and how they **can use it effectively** in their writing.

Similarly, teachers can also use ChatGPT to generate prompts that require students to use **specific vocabulary sets**. For instance, a prompt could ask students to write about a current event using a **set of words related** to politics or economics. By incorporating **challenging vocabulary words** into their writing, students can **expand their lexicons** and develop more **sophisticated** language skills.

Here are some examples of prompts generated by ChatGPT that can be used by students and educators.

Narrative Writing Prompts:

1. Write a story about a character who discovers a hidden talent they never knew they had.
2. Write about a time when you had to make a difficult decision and explain how you came to your choice.
3. Write a story about a character who goes on an adventure to an unknown place.
4. Write about a time when you experienced a significant cultural difference, and how it affected you.
5. Write a story about a character who faces a major setback but overcomes it through perseverance.

Persuasive Writing Prompts:

1. Write a persuasive essay arguing for or against the use of social media by teenagers.

2. Argue for or against the use of school uniforms.
3. Write a persuasive essay arguing for or against the use of technology in the classroom.
4. Argue for or against the idea of homework in schools.
5. Write a persuasive essay arguing for or against the idea of a four-day school week.

Expository Writing Prompts:

1. Write an informative essay about a historical event that has had a significant impact on the world.
2. Write an explanatory essay about the process of recycling and how it benefits the environment.
3. Write an essay explaining the benefits and drawbacks of social media.
4. Write an informative essay about the importance of exercise and a healthy lifestyle.
5. Write an essay explaining the impact of climate change on the environment.

Descriptive Writing Prompts:

1. Describe a person who has had a significant impact on your life and explain how they have influenced you.
2. Describe a favourite childhood memory and explain what makes it special to you.
3. Describe a food you love and explain why it is your favourite.
4. Describe a place that is special to you and explain why it is meaningful.
5. Describe your favourite holiday and explain what makes it special to you.

Creative Writing Prompts:

1. Write a poem about the changing seasons.
2. Write a short story that takes place in a dystopian society.
3. Write a fairy tale with a modern twist.
4. Write a script for a short film about a character who is trying to find their way home.

5. Write a letter to your future self, describing your goals and aspirations for the future.

Generate Conversation Prompts

Another strategy is to use **ChatGPT** to generate **conversation prompts**. These prompts can be used to facilitate conversations between **students**, or between a **student and a teacher**. For example, a teacher could **ask ChatGPT to generate a conversation prompt** that requires the use of a particular **vocabulary** or **grammar structure**.

One of the **advantages** of using ChatGPT to **generate conversation prompts** is that it can provide a **variety of prompts** that cater to different **learning levels** and **interests**. For instance, a teacher can ask ChatGPT to generate a prompt that is **straightforward** for **beginner learners** or a more **complex prompt** for **advanced learners**.

By providing prompts that are **tailored to students' language abilities and interests**, teachers can create a more **engaging** and **motivating** learning environment.

Another **benefit** of using ChatGPT to generate conversation prompts is that it can help students **build their confidence** in speaking and listening. By providing prompts that are **relevant and interesting** to students, ChatGPT encourages them to participate in conversations that are **meaningful** to them.

This can help students feel more comfortable speaking in English and can boost their **confidence** in their language skills.

Moreover, using ChatGPT to generate conversation prompts can help students develop their **critical thinking skills**.

By **engaging in conversations** that require them to think deeply about complex issues, students can practice **analysing** and **evaluating** different **perspectives**. This can help them develop their ability to **think critically** and express their **opinions** effectively.

> The beauty of writing prompts lies in their ability to stimulate creativity while still offering a guiding structure. They reduce the intimidation factor of starting from scratch, providing a framework that can be as restrictive or as liberating as the writer chooses. With the prompt as a starting point, writers can find it easier to unleash their creativity, turning that initial spark into a fully formed piece of writing.

Using ChatGPT **to generate conversation prompts** can also help students develop their **intercultural communication skills**. By discussing topics related to **culture, society,** and

politics, students **can learn about different perspectives** and **ways of thinking**.

This can help them develop a greater understanding of **cultural differences** and similarities and **can help** them **communicate more effectively** with people from **different backgrounds**.

Here are some conversational prompts generated by ChatGPT:

Personal Experience Conversation Prompts:

1. What is a memorable experience you have had that has shaped who you are today?
2. Can you describe a time when you had to overcome a difficult challenge? What did you learn from the experience?
3. What is a favourite childhood memory you have? Why is it important to you?
4. Have you ever experienced culture shock? If so, can you describe the experience and how it affected you?
5. Can you tell me about a personal accomplishment you are proud of and why?

Pop Culture Conversation Prompts:

1. Who is your favourite actor or actress? What is your favourite movie or TV show they have been in?
2. What is your favourite genre of music? Can you recommend a song or artist to me?
3. Do you have a favourite author? Can you describe why you enjoy their work?
4. Who is your favourite superhero or villain? What makes them interesting to you?
5. What is your favourite video game or board game? Can you explain why you enjoy playing it?

Current Events Conversation Prompts:

1. Can you describe a current event that has caught your attention recently? Why is it important to you?
2. What is your opinion on climate change and the environment? What can we do to make a positive impact?
3. How do you feel about the COVID-19 pandemic and the measures being taken to combat it?

4. Can you describe a political issue you are passionate about? Why is it important to you?
5. How do you feel about the use of social media and its impact on society?

Philosophical Conversation Prompts:

1. What does success mean to you? How do you define it?
2. What is your opinion on the concept of fate or destiny? Do you believe in it?
3. How do you feel about the concept of free will? Do we truly have control over our choices?
4. What is your opinion on the existence of a higher power or God? Do you believe in it?
5. What is your opinion on the meaning of life? What do you believe our purpose is?

Educational Conversation Prompts:

1. What is your favourite subject in school? Why do you enjoy it?
2. What is your opinion on homework? Do you believe it is beneficial or not?
3. Can you describe a teacher or mentor who has had a significant impact on your life? How have they influenced you?
4. How do you feel about standardised testing? Do you believe it is an accurate measure of a student's knowledge?
5. Can you describe a topic or subject you would like to learn more about? Why does it interest you?

Fifteen Conversational Prompts

Here are fifteen **conversational ChatGPT prompt templates** that can help you craft your own customised conversational prompts. These templates are designed to **stimulate engaging** and **thought-provoking** conversations.

They cover a wide range of topics, from **personal interests to current events.**

ChatGPT Conversational Prompt Templates:

1. What **[current event or issue]** do you have strong feelings about and why? What do you think can be done to make a positive impact in addressing this **[issue]**?
2. What **[form of media or entertainment]** do you enjoy the most, and why? Can you recommend a recent favourite? What role do you think **[this form of entertainment]** plays in society?
3. What **[historical event, figure, or era]** do you find intriguing, and why? How do you believe studying **[history]** can help us understand the present and shape the future?
4. What **[scientific concept or discovery]** do you find fascinating? Can you explain the science behind it? What role do you think **[science]** plays in society?
5. What is your **[belief system or philosophy]**, and how has it evolved? How do you find **[meaning]** or **[purpose]** in your life?
6. What is your favourite **[sport or physical activity]**, and what draws you to it? Have you ever attended a live **[sporting event]**? Can you describe the experience?

7. What is your favourite type of **[cuisine or food]**, and why? Have you ever tried a unique or exotic **[dish]**? Can you describe it?

8. Have you ever travelled to a foreign **[country or culture]**? Can you describe the experience? If not, where would you like to go and why?

9. What **[qualities or values]** do you look for in a **[friend/partner]**, and why? Can you describe a significant **[relationship]** in your life and how it has affected you?

10. Do you enjoy spending time in **[nature]**, and what activities do you enjoy doing outdoors? Can you describe a favourite natural **[landmark or location]** you have visited?

11. What is your **[dream job or career path]**, and how are you working towards it? If not, what other **[career paths or interests]** are you considering?

12. What is your favourite **[technology device or app]**, and how has it impacted your life? Do you have any concerns about the role of **[technology]** in society?

13. What is your **[personal style or fashion sense]**, and can you describe an **[outfit or accessory]** that represents it? What are your thoughts on the **[fashion industry]** and its impact on society?

14. Do you enjoy **[creating or appreciating]** art, and what **[medium or style]** do you prefer? Can you describe a favourite piece of **[artwork]** and explain why it is meaningful to you?
15. How do you manage your **[personal challenge or topic]**, and what are your thoughts on **[related subtopics]**? Do you have any **[specific goals or plans]** for addressing this **[challenge or topic]** in the future?

Five Key Reasons for Multilingual Translation

Multilingual translation using ChatGPT is an **innovative** and **highly effective** way for **students to improve** their foreign language skills. By leveraging the power of **natural language processing** and **advanced algorithms**, ChatGPT can help students learn new languages in a more **efficient**, **accurate**, and **personalized** way.

By **leveraging** the power of **natural language processing** and advanced **algorithms**, ChatGPT can help **students learn new languages** in a more **efficient, accurate, and personalized way**.

Here are **six key advantages of multilingual translation** using ChatGPT:

1. Increased Language Proficiency

ChatGPT can help students **practice their language skills** in both their **native language** and the **target language**, which can **boost their language proficiency**. **For instance**, a student learning Italian can use ChatGPT to **translate a sentence from English to Italian**, and then **translate it back to English** to check for accuracy. They could also use ChatGPT to **translate an Italian text to study it in depth**. Similarly, a student learning Arabic can use ChatGPT to **translate an Arabic song into English** to **better understand its meaning**.

2. Improved Accuracy

ChatGPT's advanced **algorithms** and **natural language processing capabilities** can help students **achieve more accurate translations**, which is **crucial** for **developing their language skills**.

For example, a student learning Japanese can use **ChatGPT to translate a sentence from Japanese to English** and then **analyse** the translation to identify any **errors in grammar or syntax**. They could also use **ChatGPT to translate an English text into Japanese** to **practice their language skills**.

3. Increased Efficiency

ChatGPT's quick and efficient translation abilities can **save students time** and help them **focus** on **other aspects** of their **language learning**. For instance, a student learning French can use ChatGPT to **translate a news article from French to English** and then spend time analysing the article to identify key **vocabulary and grammar structures**. Similarly, a student learning Mandarin can use **ChatGPT to translate a paragraph from Mandarin to English** and then **use the translation as a reference** while writing an essay.

4. Access to Multilingual Resources

ChatGPT's multilingual capabilities allow students to **access resources and materials** in different languages, **expanding** their **knowledge** and understanding of various **cultures and perspectives**. **For example**, a student learning Spanish can use ChatGPT to **translate a Spanish novel into English** to **broaden their reading list**. They could also use ChatGPT to **translate an English scientific article into Spanish** to **understand technical terms** in their **target language**.

5. Customised Learning

ChatGPT can be **customized** to meet the **individual needs and preferences** of students, making it a **valuable tool for personalised language learning**. **For instance**, a student learning Russian can use ChatGPT to **translate a sentence from Russian to English** and then practice speaking the English translation to **improve their pronunciation**. They could also use **ChatGPT to translate an English speech into Russian** and **practice** delivering it. Similarly, a student learning Portuguese can use **ChatGPT to translate a Portuguese text into English** and then **write a summary in English** to practice their writing skills.

6. Translating Phrases Simultaneously into Different Languages

ChatGPT can also **translate phrases simultaneously into multiple languages**. This can be a **novel way** for students to **improve** their **language skills**. This approach allows students to **practice translation**, **improve their vocabulary**, and **enhance** their understanding of **grammar and syntax** in multiple languages at the same time.

Using ChatGPT to **translate phrases into multiple languages can also help students develop a deeper appreciation and understanding of different cultures**.

By examining the **nuances and subtleties** of languages and cultures, students can **broaden their worldview** and gain a **greater appreciation for diversity**. One effective way to use ChatGPT for simultaneous translation is to provide students with a **list of vocabulary words or phrases in their native language**, and then ask them to translate those words into multiple target languages.

For example, a teacher might ask students to translate the following phrase into Spanish, French, German, and Chinese: **"My favourite colour is blue."** Another approach is to provide students with a **short passage or dialogue in one language** and then ask them to **translate it into multiple target languages using ChatGPT**.

This exercise can help students develop their **reading comprehension and translation skills more interactively and engagingly**. **For instance**, a teacher might ask students to translate a **dialogue between two people discussing their favourite foods** in Spanish, French, German, and Chinese.

Finally, teachers can use ChatGPT to create prompts that ask students to **translate phrases or passages from one language to multiple target languages**, and then **compare the results**.

> Translating idiomatic expressions or colloquialisms is particularly challenging for machine translation services like ChatGPT. These expressions often don't have direct equivalents in other languages, making it difficult for the algorithm to provide an accurate translation.

This approach allows students to see the **subtle differences in grammar, syntax, and vocabulary** between different languages and can be an **effective way to build their translation skills**.

The table includes a list of 99 unique languages that ChatGPT can translate across:

Afrikaans	Hausa	Palauan
Albanian	Hawaiian	Pashto
Amharic	Hebrew	Polish
Arabic	Hindi	Portuguese
Armenian	Hungarian	Punjabi
Assamese	Icelandic	Rapa Nui
Azerbaijani	Igbo	Romanian
Basque	Indonesian	Russian
Belarusian	Irish	Samoan
Bengali	Italian	Serbian
Bislama	Japanese	Sinhalese
Bulgarian	Kannada	Slovak
Burmese	Kazakh	Slovenian
Catalan	Khmer	Somali
Chamorro	Korean	Spanish
Chinese (Simplified)	Kyrgyz	Swahili
Chinese (Traditional)	Lao	Swedish
Croatian	Latin	Tahitian
Czech	Latvian	Tajik
Danish	Lithuanian	Tamil
Dari	Macedonian	Telugu
Dutch	Malagasy	Thai
English	Malay	Tigrinya
Esperanto	Malayalam	Tongan
Estonian	Maltese	Turkish

Farsi (Persian)	Maltese	Turkmen
Fijian	Maori	Ukrainian
Filipino (Tagalog)	Marathi	Urdu
Finnish	Marshallese	Uzbek
French	Nepali	Vietnamese
Georgian	Norwegian	Welsh
German	Odia (Oriya)	Yoruba
Greek	Oromo	Zulu
Gujarati		

Prompt Ideas and Examples for Multilingual Language Translation

Language teachers and instructors can create a **more engaging and interactive learning environment** for their students. By using ChatGPT, teachers can promote **cross-cultural communication** and understanding, thereby helping their students become more **global citizens**.

Example 1

Generate a prompt asking students to translate a short phrase or sentence into four different languages using ChatGPT. For example:

Prompt: "Translate the phrase 'I love you' into French, Spanish, German, and Chinese."

ChatGPT Video Output URL and QR Code:

https://tinyurl.com/Translate4Lang

ChatGPT Output:

I love you:

- French: Je t'aime
- Spanish: Te quiero / Te amo
- German: Ich liebe Dich
- Chinese: 我爱你 (wǒ ài nǐ)

Example 2

Give students a set of vocabulary words in their native language and ask them to use ChatGPT to translate them simultaneously into four different languages. For example:

Prompt: "Translate the following ten words from Portuguese into English, French, Spanish, and German using ChatGPT: amor, comida, felicidade, amigo, casa, beleza, saudade, sol, mar, lua."

ChatGPT Video Output URL and QR Code:

https://tinyurl.com/MultiWordTranslate

ChatGPT Output:

amor (love):

- English: love
- French: amour
- Spanish: amor
- German: Liebe

comida (food):

- English: food
- French: nourriture
- Spanish: comida
- German: Essen

felicidade (happiness):

- English: happiness
- French: bonheur
- Spanish: felicidad
- German: Glück

amigo (friend):

- English: friend
- French: ami(e)
- Spanish: amigo/amiga
- German: Freund(in)

casa (house/home):

- English: house/home
- French: maison
- Spanish: casa/hogar
- German: Haus

beleza (beauty):

- English: beauty
- French: beauté
- Spanish: belleza
- German: Schönheit

saudade (a feeling of longing or nostalgia):

- English: saudade (word without equivalent in other languages)
- French: saudade (mot sans équivalent dans d'autres langues)
- Spanish: saudade (palabra sin equivalente en otros idiomas)
- German: saudade (Wort ohne Entsprechung in anderen Sprachen)

sol (sun):

- English: sun
- French: soleil
- Spanish: sol
- German: Sonne

mar (sea):

- English: sea
- French: mer
- Spanish: mar
- German: Meer

lua (moon):

- English: moon

- French: lune
- Spanish: luna
- German: Mond

Example 3

Ask students to use ChatGPT to translate dialogue or conversation from one language into four different languages simultaneously. For example:

Prompt: "Translate this short dialogue from Spanish into English, French, German, and Chinese using ChatGPT: '¿Cómo te llamas?' 'Me llamo Ana. ¿Y tú?' 'Me llamo Carlos."

ChatGPT Video Output URL and QR Code:

https://tinyurl.com/MultiLangDialogue

ChatGPT Output:

Spanish: "¿Cómo te llamas?" "Me llamo Ana. ¿Y tú?" "Me llamo Carlos."

English: "What's your name?" "My name is Ana. And you?" "My name is Carlos."

French: "Comment t'appelles-tu?" "Je m'appelle Ana. Et toi?" "Je m'appelle Carlos."

German: "Wie heißt du?" "Ich heiße Ana. Und du?" "Ich heiße Carlos."

Chinese: "你叫什么名字？" "我叫安娜。你呢？" "我叫卡洛斯。"

Twenty-Five Multilingual Translation Prompts

Here are twenty-five prompts to spark some **ideas for translation** that can be **helpful for language learners and teachers**.

ChatGPT Prompt Template:

1. Translate the following **[Source Language]** sentence into **[Target Language]**: "**[Sentence to Translate]**"

2. Provide a **[Target Language]** translation for the phrase: "**[Phrase to Translate]**"
3. Convert this **[Source Language]** paragraph into **[Target Language]**: "**[Paragraph to Convert]**"
4. Can you translate this **[Source Language]** proverb into **[Target Language]**? "**[Proverb to Translate]**"
5. Please translate this **[Source Language]** recipe into **[Target Language]**: "**[Recipe to Translate]**"
6. Translate this **[Source Language]** poem into **[Target Language]** while preserving its rhyme and rhythm.
7. Provide a **[Target Language]** translation for the sentence: "**[Sentence to Translate]**"
8. Convert this **[Source Language]** dialogue into **[Target Language]**: "**[Dialogue to Convert]**"
9. Can you translate this **[Source Language]** quote into **[Target Language]**? "**[Quote to Translate]**"
10. Translate this **[Source Language]** haiku into **[Target Language]**: "**[Haiku to Translate]**"
11. Please translate this **[Source Language]** song lyrics into **[Target Language]**: "**[Lyrics to Translate]**"
12. Translate this **[Source Language]** news article into **[Target Language]** to make it accessible to a wider audience.

13. Convert this **[Source Language]** story into **[Target Language]** while retaining its cultural nuances.
14. Can you provide a **[Target Language]** translation for this famous **[Source Language]** phrase? "**[Phrase to Translate]**"
15. Translate this **[Source Language]** poem into **[Target Language]**, maintaining its poetic flow.
16. Translate this **[Source Language]** dialogue into **[Target Language]**: "**[Dialogue to Translate]**"
17. Please provide a **[Target Language]** translation for the phrase: "**[Phrase to Translate]**"
18. Convert this **[Source Language]** recipe into **[Target Language]**: "**[Recipe to Convert]**"
19. Translate this **[Source Language]** mythological tale into **[Target Language]**, capturing its mythos and charm.
20. Translate this **[Source Language]** folk song into **[Target Language]**, preserving its cultural significance.
21. Transform this **[Source Language]** culinary recipe into **[Target Language]**: "**[Recipe to Transform]**"
22. Convert this **[Source Language]** legendary narrative into **[Target Language]**, encapsulating its mythology and allure.

23. Convey the essence of this **[Source Language]** traditional melody into **[Target Language]**, safeguarding its cultural importance.
24. Translate this **[Source Language]** poem into **[Target Language],** retaining its poetic flow.
25. Convert this **[Source Language]** conversation into **[Target Language]: "[Dialogue to Convert]"**

CHAPTER 7

USING CHATGPT TO CREATE SUMMARY FOR BETTER COMPREHENSION AND RETENTION

7. Using ChatGPT to Create Summaries for Better Comprehension and Retention

ChatGPT can produce **concise** and **comprehensive summaries** of **complex concepts**, **historical events**, and **lengthy texts**, which can serve as a foundation for **in-depth discussions** and **analyses**. **ChatGPT generated summaries** can help students to **better understand** complex concepts and ideas.

For example, if students are reading a **challenging text**, they can use ChatGPT to generate a **summary** of the **key points**, which can then be used as a **reference point** for further **analysis** and **discussion**. This approach can be particularly helpful for students who are **struggling** with a specific concept or topic, as it allows them to **break down** the information into more **manageable parts**.

Five Reasons for Summarisation

Here are some **interesting benefits** of **summarisation** for both **students** and **educators**.

1. **Saving time and increasing productivity:** With the ability to generate summaries quickly and efficiently, ChatGPT can help students **save time and increase their productivity**. They can focus their attention on the most important **concepts and ideas** presented in educational content, rather than spending hours reading through **lengthy texts** or watching videos which may help to an extent but can be tiring for some students.

2. **Enhancing comprehension and retention:** ChatGPT summaries can improve **students' comprehension** and retention of **educational content**. By distilling complex information into concise and **easily understandable summaries**, students can more **effectively grasp** and remember **key concepts**.

3. **Encouraging critical thinking and analysis:** By providing a foundation of **essential information**, ChatGPT summaries can encourage students to engage in **critical thinking** and analysis. They can **identify key themes and issues**, evaluate the information presented, and **develop their own opinions** and ideas based on the content.

4. **Saving time and ensuring coverage of all of the necessary material:** ChatGPT's **summarisation capabilities** can also be a valuable resource for educators looking to prepare for lessons or discussions. By **generating concise summaries** of key **concepts or historical events**, teachers can **save time** and ensure that they are covering all of the necessary material. For example, a **history teacher** might use ChatGPT to generate a summary of the major events leading up to the **Industrial Revolution**, which could then be used as a **starting point for a more in-depth discussion** of the topic.

5. **Improving student's writing and analysis skills:** Another benefit of using ChatGPT for summarisation is that it can help to improve students' **writing and analysis skills**. By examining how ChatGPT generates summaries and **identifying the key points**, students can learn to better identify and **synthesize information**. This approach can be **particularly useful** for students who struggle with writing or who have difficulty organizing their thoughts.

With ChatGPT's **document summarisation prompts**, teachers can obtain a summary of a lengthy document that captures the **main points** and **key information**, saving them time and effort. It is important to note that while ChatGPT's summarization tool can assist in creating educational materials, it is still essential to **review the output** for **fact-checking and removing biases**. This ensures that the final output document meets the **desired expectations** and accurately conveys the intended message. Furthermore, educators can also utilise ChatGPT's **document rewriting feature** to **tailor the language and complexity level** of the summary to match different teaching levels.

ChatGPT's ability to produce concise and comprehensive summaries can be a powerful tool for both students and educators. Whether used as a reference point for deeper discussions or as a time-saving resource for lesson preparation, ChatGPT's summarization capabilities can help to facilitate learning and improve understanding of complex concepts and ideas

Here is an example of how to summarise a document.

ChatGPT Prompt Template:

Please summarise **[insert text content to be summarised]** for teaching **[teaching level]** students.

Customised ChatGPT Prompt Created from the Template:

Please summarise [*A lack of quality sleep affects nearly half of Australian adults. Like cricket or sausage sizzles, getting a good night's sleep has become a national obsession.*

Sleep is important for good health: poor sleep has been linked to heart disease, high blood pressure, diabetes, depression and more. Lack of sleep may also affect your mood, appetite, motivation, judgment and learning.

Here are 6 evidence-based ways to get a better night's sleep. Plus, the causes of poor sleep you should avoid. You're welcome.

6 tips for better sleep:

Have a warm bath

According to a systematic review by the University of Texas at Austin, bathing 1-2 hours before bedtime in water that's 40-42°C in temperature can significantly improve your sleep. It also speeds up, by an average of 10 minutes, how long it can take to fall asleep.

Exercise more (teenagers, in particular)

In a study of more than 400 teens, for every extra hour of moderate-to-vigorous daytime physical activity participants did, they fell asleep 18 minutes earlier than usual. They also slept 10 minutes longer, according to the journal Scientific Reports.

Sort out your snoring

Not always 'harmless', snoring — when accompanied by tiredness during the day — could be a sign of obstructive sleep apnoea. It can be treated, which will lead to a better night's shuteye (both for you and your partner if you have one). See your doctor if you suspect you have sleep apnea.

Get out of bed after 20 minutes

If you can't fall asleep within 20 to 30 minutes of going to bed, you should get up. Go to another dimly lit room and sit quietly. Try not to use a screen, eat, drink or do household chores, and go back to bed when you feel sleepy. This helps your mind link bed with sleep, rather than with frustration.

Stay out of bed

Yes, you read that right. According to the Sleep Health Foundation, it's important to train the brain to link your bed with sleep and intimacy only. So, if possible, avoid using your bedroom for 'living-room activities' such as studying, watching TV or making phone calls.

Seek natural bright light in the morning

If you're routinely having trouble falling asleep, going outside or near a window after sunrise will help your body clock switch off production of the 'sleepy' hormone, melatonin. This, in turn, will help reset your clock, so when it becomes darker at night, melatonin production will resume — making you feel tired.

Causes of poor sleep

Sleeping pills: In the long term, sleeping pills are unlikely to help with insomnia, reports NPS MedicineWise, and in some cases, might do more harm than good. Likewise, some people with chronic pain use prescription opioids to help them sleep but there is no evidence that this works long-term.

Sleep calculators: These calculators may not be the answer to work out how much sleep you need. Widely available on the internet, 'sleep calculators' give the user a precise time to go to sleep so they purportedly wake up refreshed. These calculators are not based on scientific evidence, according to the Sleep Health Foundation, and it's better to follow fuss-free good sleep habits.

Alcohol: It might make you feel sleepy, but alcohol can disrupt your sleep later — possibly leading to frequent waking, night sweats, headaches and restlessness. According to the Sleep Health Foundation, binge drinking can affect melatonin levels for up to a week.] **for teaching [undergraduate] students**

ChatGPT Video Output URL and QR Code:

https://tinyurl.com/TextSummaryUG

ChatGPT Output:

A lack of quality sleep affects a significant portion of Australian adults, underscoring the importance of good sleep for overall health. Poor sleep is linked to various health issues, including heart disease, high blood pressure, diabetes, depression, and more. Sleep also impacts mood, appetite, motivation, judgment, and learning.

Here are evidence-based strategies for better sleep:

1. **Have a Warm Bath:** Taking a warm bath 1-2 hours before bedtime (40-42°C) can significantly improve sleep quality and accelerate the time it takes to fall asleep.

2. **Exercise More:** Engaging in moderate-to-vigorous daytime physical activity, particularly for teenagers, can lead to falling asleep earlier and sleeping longer.

3. **Address Snoring:** Snoring, especially when accompanied by daytime tiredness, might indicate obstructive sleep apnea. Seeking medical help can improve sleep quality for both you and your partner.

4. **Get Out of Bed After 20 Minutes:** If unable to fall asleep within 20-30 minutes, get up, go to a dimly lit room, and return to bed when feeling sleepy to associate the bed with sleep rather than frustration.

5. **Stay Out of Bed:** Reserve the bed for sleep and intimacy only, avoiding activities like studying or watching TV in bed.

6. **Seek Natural Bright Light:** Exposing yourself to natural light after sunrise can help regulate the body's sleep-wake cycle by affecting melatonin production.

Causes of poor sleep to avoid:

1. **Sleeping Pills:** Long-term use of sleeping pills may not effectively treat insomnia and could have adverse effects.

2. **Sleep Calculators:** Online sleep calculators lack scientific evidence; it's better to establish good sleep habits.

3. **Alcohol:** While it may induce initial sleepiness, alcohol can disrupt sleep later and impact melatonin levels.

4. **Lack of Physical Activity:** Insufficient physical activity during the day can contribute to poor sleep quality.

5. **Stress and Anxiety:** High levels of stress and anxiety can lead to racing thoughts and restlessness, making it difficult to relax and fall asleep.

Note: This summary provides concise information for teaching undergraduate students about improving sleep quality and avoiding common causes of poor sleep.

Nine Major Types of Summarisation Prompt Templates

Here are **nine specific summarisation templates and examples** that you can **further customise** for your use:

ChatGPT Prompt Templates:

1. **Historical Event Template:** Generate a summary of the key events, figures, causes, and consequences of **[name of a particular historical event such as World War II or the French Revolution]**
2. **Literary Work Template:** Create a summary of the central themes, motifs, and plot points of a **[name of literary work, such as a novel, play, or poem]**
3. **Scientific Discoveries Template:** Generate a summary of the most important scientific discoveries and breakthroughs in **[name of a particular field such as genetics, medicine, or physics]**
4. **Social Movement Template:** Summarise the key events, figures, and outcomes of a particular social movement, such as the **[type of movement]** in the **[name of country, city, state or region]**

5. **Philosophical Ideas Template:** Create a summary of the major philosophical schools of thought, from ancient to contemporary times, and their key **[concepts and principles such as existentialism, utilitarianism, and postmodernism]**.

6. **Book Summary Template:** Summarise key points of **[Bo Title 1], [Book Title 2], [Book Title 3], [Book Title 4], [Book Title 4] and [Book Title 6]**.

7. **Business Case Study Template:** Generate a summary of challenges faced, strategies implemented, and outcomes achieved by **[name of a company or business endeavour]**

8. **Health and Wellness Tips Template:** Offer a summarised compilation of practical tips and advice for maintaining **[a specific aspect of health, such as mental well-being or physical fitness]**

9. **Social Issue Analysis Template:** Provide a summary of the causes, consequences, and potential solutions for **[name of a social issue, such as poverty or gender inequality]**

Ten Cause-and-Effect Type Summarisation Prompts

The following **example prompts** are great for **summarising historical events** or other situations where there are **clear cause-and-effect relationships.** The **bold keywords** in brackets can be customised for generating summarisation using ChatGPT.

ChatGPT Prompt Examples:

1. **[Summarise]** the events that led to the **[fall of** the **Roman Empire]** and its **[impact]** on **[world history]**.
2. **[Provide]** a **[summary]** of the key events leading up to the **[American Revolution]** and its **[outcome]**.
3. **[Summarise]** the events that led to the **[Non-violence movement]** in **[India]** and its **[impact]** on **[society]**.
4. **[Provide]** a **[summary]** of the key events leading up to the **[formation of the European Union]** and its **[impact]** on **[international relations]**.
5. **[Summarise]** the events leading up to the **[French Revolution]** and its **[impact]** on **[French society and culture]**.

6. **[Detail]** the key factors that contributed to the **[Renaissance]** and its **[effect]** on **[art and science]**.
7. **[Summarise]** the events that led to the **[Civil Rights Movement]** in the **[USA]** and its **[impact]** on **[racial equality]**.
8. **[Provide]** a **[summary]** of the key events leading up to the **[World War I]** and its **[consequences]** on **[global politics]**.
9. **[Describe]** the events leading up to the **[Russian Revolution]** and its **[repercussions]** on **[communism and global dynamics]**.
10. **[Highlight]** the key milestones in the **[Space Race]** and its **[significance]** in **[technological advancements]**.

Unlike human summarisers, who may introduce their own biases or overlook key points, ChatGPT aims to maintain a consistent approach to summarisation, focusing on the most salient points in the text.

Twelve Key Concepts and Principles Summarisation Prompts

The following **example prompts** are useful for summarising **academic or technical subjects**. Identify the main concepts or principles that underlie the subject, and then provide **brief explanations or examples** to illustrate each one.

ChatGPT Prompt Examples:

1. Identify the key principles of social psychology and provide examples of how they are applied in research. **[Summarise]** the **[key principles]** of **[microeconomics]** and provide examples of how they are applied in the **[business world]**.
2. **[Identify]** the **[main concepts]** of **[artificial intelligence]** and provide brief explanations of each one.
3. **[Summarise]** the **[key concepts]** of **[evolutionary biology]** and provide examples of how they are applied in **[research]**.

4. **[Identify]** the **[key principles]** of **[design thinking]** and provide examples of how they are used in **[problem-solving]**.
5. **[Summarise]** the **[key concepts]** of **[game theory]** and provide examples of how they are applied in **[economics and political science]**.
6. **[Identify]** the **[key principles]** of **[social psychology]** and provide examples of how they are applied in **[research]**.
7. **[Explain]** the **[fundamental principles]** of **[quantum physics]** and provide examples of how they are applied in **[modern technology]**.
8. **[Identify]** the **[core concepts]** of **[sustainable development]** and provide brief explanations of each one.
9. **[Summarise]** the **[key ideas]** of **[environmental science]** and provide examples of how they are applied in **[conservation efforts]**.
10. **[Highlight]** the **[central principles]** of **[biochemistry]** and provide examples of how they are used in **[medical research]**.
11. **[Describe]** the **[key tenets]** of **[cognitive psychology]** and provide examples of how they are applied in **[educational settings]**.

12. **[Identify]** the **[main pillars]** of **[ethical philosophy]** and provide examples of how they are applied in **[moral decision-making]**.

Twelve Main Ideas and Arguments Prompts

These example prompts are good for **summarising persuasive or argumentative texts**.

ChatGPT Prompt Examples:

1. **[Identify]** the **[main ideas]** or **[arguments]** presented in the text, and then provide **[brief explanations]** or **[evidence]** to support each one.
2. **[Summarise]** the **[main arguments]** for and against **[climate change]** as a human-caused phenomenon.
3. **[Summarise]** the **[main ideas]** in Jane Austen's Pride and Prejudice, providing some examples of how they are developed.

4. **[Summarise]** the **[main arguments]** in favour of and against **[free trade]**, providing evidence to support each position.
5. **[Identify]** and **[summarise]** the main ideas presented in Plato's Republic.
6. **[Summarise]** the **[main arguments]** for and against gun control in the United States, providing evidence to support each position.
7. **[Analyse]** the **[geographical factors]** influencing the **[distribution]** of **[wildlife species]** in a given region, then **[provide a rationale]** for your findings.
8. **[Examine]** the **[primary geographical features]** that shape **[climate patterns]** in a specific area, and **[elaborate on]** their effects.
9. **[Investigate]** the **[major geological processes]** responsible for the formation of **[mountain ranges]**, and offer **[illustrative examples]**.
10. **[Summarise]** the **[key concepts]** in the study of **[plate tectonics]**, about **[notable plate boundaries]**.
11. **[Identify]** and **[describe]** the **[significant natural hazards]** that can occur in coastal regions, and **[expound on]** their potential consequences.

12. **[Evaluate]** the **[environmental impacts]** of **[urbanisation]** in a particular geographic area, including **[both positive and negative aspects]**.

ChatGPT can provide a scalable solution that doesn't suffer from fatigue or reduced attention span.

Twelve Scientific Discoveries and Breakthroughs

These example prompts are ideal for **summarising scientific research or breakthroughs.**

ChatGPT Prompt Examples:

1. **[Investigate]** the **[groundbreaking discoveries]** in the field of **[quantum physics]**, elucidating their **[revolutionary implications]**.
2. **[Summarise]** the **[significant advancements]** in **[genomic research]**, with a focus on **[gene-editing techniques]** like CRISPR-Cas9.
3. **[Explore]** the **[milestones]** in **[space exploration]**, highlighting the **[technological innovations]** that made them possible.
4. **[Analyse]** the **[major findings]** in the realm of **[neuroscience]**, especially those pertaining to **[brain plasticity]**.
5. **[Examine]** the **[cutting-edge breakthroughs]** in **[artificial intelligence]**, emphasising their **[potential applications]** across industries.
6. **[Summarise]** the **[key revelations]** in the field of **[quantum computing]**, considering their **[game-changing implications]** for computation.
7. **[Delve into]** the **[landmark achievements]** in **[nanotechnology]**, underscoring their **[innovation potential]** in various sectors.

8. **[Investigate]** the **[seminal discoveries]** in the domain of **[medicine]**, with a particular focus on **[vaccination breakthroughs]**.
9. **[Explore]** the **[pioneering research]** in **[renewable energy sources]**, outlining the **[sustainability benefits]** they offer.
10. **[Analyse]** the **[breakthroughs]** in **[quantum cryptography]**, shedding light on their **[security implications]**.
11. **[Examine]** the **[noteworthy findings]** in the field of **[marine biology]**, highlighting their **[ecological significance]**.
12. **[Investigate]** the **[groundbreaking developments]** in **[renewable energy technology]**, emphasising their **[sustainability impact]**.

Sixty Miscellaneous Prompts for Summarisation

Here are some ChatGPT prompts that cover a range of topics across **history, science, literature, and social issues** and can be adapted for similar summarisation purposes.

ChatGPT Prompt Examples:

1. **[Summarise]** the **[causes and consequences]** of the **[First World War]**.
2. **[Create]** a **[summary]** of the **[major economic theories]** and their **[contributions]** to the **[field of economics]**.
3. **[Summarise]** the **[central themes and plot points]** of **[Shakespeare's 'Hamlet']**.
4. **[Summarise]** the **[key ideas and principles]** of the **[Enlightenment period]** in **[Europe]**.
5. **[Create]** a **[summary]** of the **[major advances]** in **[medical science]** over the **[last century]**.
6. **[Summarise]** the **[causes and effects]** of **[climate change]** on the **[environment and society]**.
7. **[Summarise]** the **[key concepts and principles]** of **[modern physics]**, including **[relativity and quantum mechanics]**.
8. **[Create]** a **[summary]** of the **[major philosophical schools of thought]**, from **[ancient to contemporary times]**.
9. **[Generate]** a **[summary]** of the **[technological advances]** and their **[impact]** on **[society].**
10. **[Provide]** a **[brief overview]** of the **[key principles and theories]** of **[psychology]**.
11. **[Summarise]** the **[causes and effects]** of the **[Industrial Revolution]** in **[Europe]**.
12. **[Provide]** a **[concise summary]** of the **[major themes and motifs]** in **[Shakespeare's play Macbeth]**.

13. **[Summarise]** the **[major contributions]** of the **[Enlightenment]** to the **[development of modern democracy]**.
14. **[Summarise]** the **[key ideas]** presented in **[Martin Luther King Jr.'s "I Have a Dream" speech]**.
15. **[Generate]** a **[summary]** of the **[causes and consequences]** of the **[Industrial Revolution]**.
16. **[Generate]** a **[summary]** of the **[plot and main themes]** of the novel **["To Kill a Mockingbird"]**.
17. **[Provide]** a **[summary]** of the **[major achievements and contributions]** of the **[ancient Greek]**.
18. **[Generate]** a **[summary]** of the **[key principles and teachings]** of **[Buddhism]**.
19. **[Summarise]** the **[most important scientific discoveries and breakthroughs]** in the **[field of genetics]**.
20. **[Generate]** a **[summary]** of the **[major economic theories and principles]** of **[capitalism]**.
21. **[Provide]** a **[summary]** of the **[main features and characteristics]** of the **[Romanticism literary movement]**.
22. **[Summarise]** the **[key ideas and arguments]** presented in a **[recent scientific research paper]** on **[climate change]**.
23. **[Summarise]** the **[main points]** of a **[TED talk]** on a topic related to **[technology and society]**.
24. **[Summarise]** the **[most notable events and individuals]** in a **[particular period of history]**, such as the **[Renaissance or the Civil Rights Movement]**.

25. **[Summarise]** the **[key takeaways and insights]** from a **[recent business or leadership book]**, such as **["The Lean Startup" or "Good to Great"]**.
26. **[Summarise]** the **[key elements and themes]** of a **[recent blockbuster movie]**, such as **["Black Panther" or "Avengers: Endgame"]**.
27. **[Provide]** a **[summary]** of the **[main principles and ideas]** of a **[particular political philosophy]**, such as **[libertarianism or Marxism]**.
28. **[Generate]** a **[summary]** of the **[main causes and effects]** of the **[global financial crisis of 2008]**.
29. **[Summarise]** the **[main events and outcomes]** of the **[French Revolution]**.
30. **[Create]** a **[summary]** of the **[key themes and motifs]** in a **[classic play]**, such as **["Oedipus Rex" or "Macbeth"]**.
31. **[Generate]** a **[summary]** of the **[most important theories and principles]** of **[social psychology]**.
32. **[Summarise]** the **[key ideas and arguments]** presented in a **[recent political speech or debate]**.
33. **[Provide]** a **[summary]** of the **[major technological advancements and innovations]** of the **[21st century]**.
34. **[Generate]** a **[summary]** of the **[key principles and practices]** of **[sustainable development]**.
35. **[Summarise]** the **[main events and significance]** of the **[feminist movement]** in the **[United States]**.
36. **[Create]** a **[summary]** of the **[major scientific discoveries and advancements]** in the **[field of**

astronomy]. **[Summarise]** the **[main events and outcomes]** of the **[Russian Revolution]**.

37. **[Provide]** a **[summary]** of the **[key principles and practices]** of **[organic farming]** and its **[impact on agriculture]**.
38. **[Generate]** a **[summary]** of the **[major milestones]** in **[space exploration]** and their **[significance]**.
39. **[Summarise]** the **[key themes and narratives]** of **[Jane Austen's 'Pride and Prejudice']**.
40. **[Detail]** the **[major contributions]** of the **[Scientific Revolution]** to the **[advancement of knowledge]**.
41. **[Summarise]** the **[main events and figures]** of the **[Renaissance period]** in **[Europe]**.
42. **[Provide]** a **[summary]** of the **[key principles and techniques]** of **[modern architecture]**.
43. **[Generate]** a **[summary]** of the **[major developments]** in **[renewable energy technologies]** in the last decade.
44. **[Summarise]** the **[key ideas and tenets]** of **[Confucianism]** and its **[impact on East Asian cultures]**.
45. **[Summarise]** the **[main themes and characters]** in **[George Orwell's '1984']**.
46. **[Provide]** a **[summary]** of the **[key principles and practices]** of **[yoga]** and its **[benefits for mental and physical health]**.
47. **[Generate]** a **[summary]** of the **[major innovations]** in **[virtual reality technology]** and their **[applications]**.
48. **[Detail]** the **[major contributions]** of the **[Postmodernism movement]** to **[art and literature]**.

49. **[Summarise]** the **[main events and outcomes]** of the **[Spanish Civil War]**.
50. **[Provide]** a **[summary]** of the **[key principles and techniques]** of **[digital marketing]**.
51. **[Generate]** a **[summary]** of the **[major developments]** in **[nanotechnology]** and their **[potential applications]**.
52. **[Summarise]** the **[key ideas and practices]** of **[Zen Buddhism]**.
53. **[Summarise]** the **[main themes and narratives]** of **[F. Scott Fitzgerald's 'The Great Gatsby']**.
54. **[Provide]** a **[summary]** of the **[key principles and practices]** of **[sustainable tourism]**.
55. **[Generate]** a **[summary]** of the **[major milestones]** in **[robotics]** and their **[impact on industries]**.
56. **[Detail]** the **[major contributions]** of the **[Impressionism movement]** to **[visual arts]**.
57. **[Provide]** a **[summary]** of the **[key principles and techniques]** of **[molecular gastronomy]** in **[culinary arts]**.
58. **[Generate]** a **[summary]** of the **[major developments]** in **[biotechnology]** over the past few decades.
59. **[Summarise]** the **[key ideas and tenets]** of **[Stoicism]** and its **[influence on Western thought]**.
60. **[Detail]** the **[major events and outcomes]** of the **[Mexican Revolution]**.

CHAPTER 8

PROOFREAD EDIT AND OBTAIN FEEDBACK USING CHATGPT

8. Proofread Edit and Obtain Feedback Using ChatGPT

ChatGPT's editing and feedback abilities can be used to provide **quick and effective reviews** of written work, enabling students to make necessary revisions such as **correcting grammatical errors**, incorporating transitional phrases, **better or refined vocabulary**, and **integrating examples and relevant facts** to support their claims within the written content.

This, as a result, can improve the overall quality of the **writing** and **facilitate students** in developing their **writing skills and taking it to the next level**.

Seven Prompts for Proofreading

Here are some **example prompts** that can be used to help with **proofreading, revising, editing, improving, refining, and getting feedback** on student's work:

ChatGPT Prompt Templates:

1. Revise **[Paste here the student's written content such as essay poem story].**
2. Edit **[Paste here the student's written content such as essay poem story].**
3. Improve **[Paste here student's written content such as essay poem story].**
4. Check **[Paste here student's written content such as essay poem story]** for errors.
5. Refine **[Paste here the student's written content such as essay poem story].**
6. Proofread **[Paste here the student's written content such as essay poem story].**
7. Correct formatting issues **[Paste here the student's written content such as essay poem story].**

Fifteen Prompts for Feedback

Here are some **example prompts** that can be **customised** for **obtaining feedback on students' work** from ChatGPT:

ChatGPT Prompt Templates:

1. Provide necessary editing recommendations on **[Paste here student's written content such as essay poem story]** at **[teaching level]**.
2. Provide feedback on **[type of error – eg. grammar and spelling errors]** on **[Paste here student-written content such as essay poem story]**.
3. Provide feedback on vocabulary and word choice, suggesting alternative words or phrasing where appropriate on **[Paste here student's written content]**.
4. Provide feedback on the structure of the piece, including suggestions for paragraph breaks or changes in organisation where needed on **[Paste here student's written content]**.
5. Provide feedback on the strength and clarity of the thesis statement or central argument on **[Paste here student's written content]**.

6. Provide feedback on the conclusion, including suggestions for how to summarise and reinforce the main points of the piece on **[Paste here student's written content]**.
7. Provide feedback on the introduction, suggesting ways to grab the reader's attention and clearly state the main topic about **[Paste here student's written content]**.
8. Provide feedback on the central theme, including suggestions for how to structure paragraphs and support the thesis with evidence or examples based on **[Paste here student's written content]**.
9. Provide feedback on language usage and style, offering suggestions for how to improve clarity and precision of **[Paste here student's written content]**.
10. Provide feedback on formatting and citations, ensuring that the piece is correctly formatted, and sources are cited properly in the following writing **[Paste here student's written content]**.
11. Provide feedback on the thesis, offering suggestions for how to make it stronger and more focused. Here is the thesis content **[Paste here the student's written content]**.
12. Provide feedback on the use of evidence or examples, ensuring that they are relevant and

effectively support your argument in the following writing **[Paste here student's written content]**.

13. Provide feedback on the structure of the piece, including suggestions for how to organise paragraphs and transitions to ensure a cohesive flow of ideas in the following writing **[Paste here student's written content]**.
14. Provide feedback on language usage and style, offering suggestions for how to improve clarity and precision in the following writing **[Paste here student's written content]**.
15. Provide feedback on overall coherence and impact, providing recommendations for how to create a strong and engaging piece of writing in the following writing **[Paste here student's written content]**.

CHAPTER 9

USE CHATGPT TO GENERATE ESSAY TOPICS AND OUTLINE

9. Use ChatGPT to Generate Essay Topics and Outline

In case you already have a **topic in mind**, ChatGPT can assist you in creating an **outline** for it. However, for those who haven't decided on a topic, ChatGPT can **help identify an appropriate** essay **topic**.

Here is a simple ChatGPT prompt for creating an **essay outline**.

Create an outline for an essay about Thomas Edison and his contributions to technology.

ChatGPT Video Output URL and QR Code:

https://tinyurl.com/GPTEssayOutline

ChatGPT Output:

I. Introduction

- Brief background information on Thomas Edison
- Importance of his contributions to technology

II. Early Life and Career of Thomas Edison

- Edison's childhood and education
- His early jobs and experiences with telegraphy
- The founding of Menlo Park, NJ laboratory

III. Inventions and Discoveries

- Phonograph and sound recording technology
- Incandescent light bulb and its impact on society
- Motion picture camera and the rise of the film industry
- Other notable contributions such as the alkaline storage battery and the fluoroscope

IV. Impact of Edison's Inventions on Society and Technology

- Changes to daily life and work
- Advancements in science and engineering
- Edison's influence on other inventors and entrepreneurs

V. Criticisms of Edison and Controversies

- The "War of Currents" and Edison's role in it
- Patent disputes and legal battles
- Criticisms of Edison's business practices and treatment of employees

VI. Legacy and Historical Significance

- Edison's lasting impact on technology and society
- Influence on future generations of inventors and entrepreneurs
- Edison's recognition and honours

VII. Conclusion

- Summary of Edison's contributions and impact on technology
- Reflection on Edison's legacy and relevance today

Ten Prompts for Essay Topic

Another way to generate a **catchy essay topic** could be using **similar ChatGPT prompts** as follows. You **can modify** the following prompts to **create your own** custom prompts.

ChatGPT Prompts Examples:

1. Could you provide me with five engaging essay topics related to the **[positive or negative effects]** of electric bikes on the environment? Also, could you give me some suggestions on how to approach each topic?
2. I'm seeking assistance in generating five captivating essay topics that revolve around **[electric bikes' environmental impacts]**. Can you also provide a brief outline for each topic?
3. Can you help me brainstorm five attention-grabbing essay topics on the **[impact of electric bikes on the environment]**? Additionally, can you provide some guidance on how to structure the essay for each topic?
4. I need your help to create five intriguing essay topics on **[electric bikes' impact on the environment]**. Can you also give me some tips on how to begin my research for each topic?

5. Would you be able to assist me in developing five compelling essay topics concerning **[electric bikes' effects on the environment]**? Additionally, could you provide me with some resources to get started on researching each topic?

6. Could you curate a list of five thought-provoking essay topics exploring the nuanced interplay between **[electric bike adoption]** and the **[socioeconomic dynamics]** of urban environments? Moreover, I'd appreciate insights on how to delve deep into each topic.

7. I'm looking for your expertise in crafting five multifaceted essay topics that delve into the **[ecological ramifications]** of the widespread use of electric bikes. Additionally, can you provide a comprehensive framework for structuring each essay?

8. Can you assist me in formulating five intellectually stimulating essay topics centred around the **[sustainability]** of electric bikes and their role in **[mitigating environmental challenges]**? It would be immensely valuable if you could guide me in initiating research for these topics.

9. I require your assistance to devise five intricate essay topics that scrutinize the **[technological advancements]** driving the popularity of electric bikes and their **[potential implications]** on

transportation systems. Furthermore, I'd appreciate your recommendations on scholarly resources for each topic.

10. Would you kindly help me generate five academically rigorous essay topics focusing on the **[ethical considerations]** surrounding electric bike usage and their **[broader societal consequences]**? Additionally, could you provide me with a curated list of primary and secondary sources for initiating research on these topics?

Twenty Prompts for Creating Essays

If the **essay topic has already been provided**, various ChatGPT **prompt variations** can be used **to generate a draft version** of the essay that can subsequently be **refined with personal input**. Here are **some prompt templates** that can be used to generate a **draft essay**.

ChatGPT Prompt Templates:

1. Discuss the main causes and effects of **[essay topic]**. Provide at least three supporting details for each cause and effect.

2. Analyse the different perspectives on **[essay topic]** and argue for the most compelling viewpoint. Support your argument with at least three pieces of evidence.

3. Compare and contrast **[topic A]** and **[topic B]**. Identify at least three similarities and three differences between the two and explain their significance.

4. Explain the history and evolution of **[essay topic]**. Describe at least three key events or milestones that shaped its development.

5. Evaluate the impact of **[essay topic]** on society. Identify at least three positive and negative consequences and provide evidence to support your analysis.

6. Make an argument for or against **[essay topic]**. Provide at least three reasons to support your position and refute any opposing arguments.

7. Describe the current state of **[essay topic]** and predict its future trajectory. Identify at least three challenges or opportunities that are likely to affect its development.

8. Explore the ethical implications of **[essay topic]**. Identify at least three ethical issues that arise from it and explain why they matter.

9. Examine the role of **[essay topic]** in a particular field or industry. Provide at least three examples of its application and analyse its significance.

10. Investigate the impact of **[essay topic]** on a specific group or population. Identify at least three ways in which it affects them and evaluate their experiences.

11. Examine the cultural significance of **[essay topic]**. Discuss how it has influenced art, literature, music, and other aspects of culture. Provide examples to illustrate its impact.

12. Investigate the role of **[essay topic]** in shaping historical events. Analyse how it has contributed to or influenced key moments in history, and discuss its lasting effects.

13. Explore the intersection of **[essay topic]** and technology. Discuss how advancements in technology have affected the way **[essay topic]** is understood, practised, or experienced.

14. Analyse the relationship between **essay [topic]** and socioeconomic factors. Explore how economic, political, and social conditions impact **[essay topic]**, and discuss potential solutions to related challenges.

15. Discuss the psychological effects of **[essay topic]**. Examine how **[essay topic]** influences human behaviour, emotions, and cognition, and consider both positive and negative effects.
16. Explain the concept of **[essay topic]** to a layperson. Break down complex concepts and terminology related to **[essay topic]** in a way that is accessible and understandable to a general audience.
17. Evaluate the effectiveness of current policies or strategies addressing **essay [topic]**. Assess the strengths and weaknesses of existing approaches and propose potential improvements.
18. Analyse the portrayal of **[essay topic]** in popular media. Discuss how **[essay topic]** is depicted in movies, TV shows, literature, or other forms of media, and consider its impact on public perception.
19. Investigate the connection between **[essay topic]** and global trends. Examine how **[essay topic]** is influenced by urbanization, globalization, or technological advancements.
20. Examine the historical context of **[essay topic]** in a specific period. Choose a particular era and discuss how **[essay topic]** was understood and experienced during that time, considering social, cultural, and political factors.

CHAPTER 10

PERFORM SENTIMENT ANALYSIS USING CHATGPT

10. Perform Sentiment Analysis Using ChatGPT

Sentiment analysis is a technique used to determine the **emotional tone** of a **piece of text**.

It involves **analysing the words** used in a text to determine whether it expresses a **positive, negative, or neutral** sentiment.

For **teachers**, sentiment analysis has **numerous benefits**, including gaining insight into **student emotions**, identifying areas of **improvement**, and improving **student engagement**.

As a teacher or trainer, sentiment analysis can help to **better understand** a student's **work, comments and discussions** in their writings. Some of the **ways it can be useful** for teachers are as follows:

- Analyse student feedback to determine the overall sentiment towards a particular lesson or course.
- Analyse social media posts to understand how students feel about a particular topic or issue.
- Analyse student writing to identify areas where they may be struggling or need additional support.
- Analyse student surveys to determine the overall sentiment towards a particular teaching method or strategy.
- Analyse chat logs to understand how students are engaging with online learning platforms.
- Analyse student performance data to identify trends in student sentiment over time.
- Analyse student comments to determine the overall sentiment towards a particular assignment or project.

Here is an example of a simple ChatGPT prompt template that can be customised to perform sentiment analysis.

ChatGPT Prompt Template:

> Perform sentiment analysis on **[Paste content]**

Customised ChatGPT Prompt Created from the Template:

Perform sentiment analysis on [*Climate change represents a challenge to the electricity sector. For example, Figure 1 shows how the fire season has advanced by nearly three months in one location over the last 70 years, potentially reducing the amount of time available for line maintenance and the reduction of fuel loads.***]**

ChatGPT Video Output URL and QR Code:

https://tinyurl.com/GPTSentimentAnalysis

ChatGPT Answer/Response:

The provided text seems to express a negative sentiment towards the impact of climate change on the electricity sector. Let's break down the sentiment:

1. **Climate Change Impact:** The text mentions that climate change represents a challenge to the electricity sector. This indicates that climate change is having a negative effect on the sector, which conveys a negative sentiment.

2. **Fire Season Advancement:** The text further describes how the fire season has advanced by nearly three months over the last 70 years. This advancement is likely attributed to the effects of

climate change, and it presents a potential problem. This suggests a negative sentiment as it highlights an undesirable consequence.

3. **Reduced Maintenance Time:** The advancement of the fire season could lead to a reduction in the amount of time available for line maintenance. This implies that the electricity sector may face difficulties in maintaining its infrastructure due to the changing conditions caused by climate change. This again expresses a negative sentiment.

4. **Fuel Load Reduction:** The text also mentions the reduction of fuel loads, which is likely a reference to efforts to mitigate fire risks. The fact that climate change is affecting this aspect negatively implies that the sector faces challenges in effectively reducing fuel loads. This adds to the negative sentiment.

Overall, the text conveys a negative sentiment by highlighting how climate change is posing challenges to the electricity sector, impacting maintenance schedules, and potentially hindering efforts to reduce fire risks.

Twenty Prompts for Sentiment Analysis

Here are some **ChatGPT prompts** to help you perform **sentiment analysis.**

1. Determine the sentiment conveyed in the following **[text/article/review]**.
2. What is the overall sentiment in this **[text/article/review]**? Is it positive, negative, or neutral?
3. On a scale of 1 to 10, how would you rate the sentiment expressed in the following **[text/article/review]**? (1 = very negative, 10 = very positive)
4. What emotions are being expressed in the following **[text/article/review]**?
5. Conduct a sentiment analysis of the following **[text/article/review]** and provide a summary of the emotions conveyed. Examine the sentiment expressed within the following [text/article/review].

6. What is the prevailing sentiment in this **[text/article/review]**? Would you categorize it as positive, negative, or neutral?
7. Rate the sentiment conveyed in the subsequent **[text/article/review]** on a scale of 1 to 10. (1 = extremely negative, 10 = extremely positive)
8. Decode the emotions being conveyed in the given **[text/article/review]**.
9. Explore the emotional tone of the following **[text/article/review]**.
10. Judge the mood and sentiment depicted in this **[text/article/review]**. Is it predominantly positive, negative, or neutral?
11. Assign a sentiment score from 1 to 10 for the emotions expressed in the ensuing **[text/article/review]**. (1 = highly pessimistic, 10 = extremely optimistic)
12. Uncover the underlying emotions within the provided **[text/article/review]**.
13. Evaluate the sentiment portrayed in the forthcoming **[text/article/review].**
14. Determine the emotional context of the given **[text/article/review].**
15. Analyse the sentiment portrayed in the subsequent **[text/article/review].**

16. Assess the general sentiment presented in this **[text/article/review].** Would you classify it as positive, negative, or neutral?
17. Using a scale of 1 to 10, indicate your perception of the sentiment conveyed in the ensuing **[text/article/review].** (1 = highly negative, 10 = highly positive)
18. Identify the emotions being articulated in the given **[text/article/review].**
19. Analyse the sentiment portrayed in the subsequent **[text/article/review].**
20. Assess the general sentiment presented in this **[text/article/review].** Would you classify it as positive, negative, or neutral?

ChtGPT's accuracy in sentiment analysis is only as good as the data on which it was trained. If the training data lacks diversity or is biased, the sentiment analysis may also be flawed.

CHAPTER 11

CREATE PROGRAM CODES USING CHATGPT

11. Create Program Codes Using ChatGPT

C **hatGPT** is a **versatile** language model that can provide **support** for a wide range of **programming languages**. Whether you need help **generating** new code, **editing** and **refining** existing code, or **converting** code between different languages, **ChatGPT** has the **expertise** to assist you. Some of the **programming languages** that **ChatGPT** can **assist** with include **Python**, **Java**, **C++**, **JavaScript**, **PHP**, **Ruby**, **HTML**, **CSS**, and **SQL**. With its **advanced** natural language processing **capabilities**, **ChatGPT** can help you **streamline** your

programming workflow and achieve your **coding objectives** with **greater efficiency** and **ease**.

Here are a **few examples** to get a feel for **ChatGPT** generated **programming codes**.

Java Program for Sorting ArrayList of String in Descending Order

Here is an example of a **simple Java program** that illustrates the programming capabilities of ChatGPT.

ChatGPT Prompt:

> **Provide Java code for Sorting ArrayList of String in Descending Order**

ChatGPT Video Output URL and QR Code:

https://tinyurl.com/SimpleJavaProg

ChatGPT Output:

JAVA CODE

```
import java.util.ArrayList;

import java.util.Collections;


public class SortArrayListDescending {

   public static void main(String[] args) {

      // Create an ArrayList of Strings

      ArrayList<String> list = new ArrayList<>();

      list.add("apple");

      list.add("banana");

      list.add("cherry");

      list.add("date");

      list.add("elderberry");


      // Sort the ArrayList in descending order using Collections.sort()
method

      Collections.sort(list, Collections.reverseOrder());


      // Print the sorted ArrayList

      System.out.println("Sorted ArrayList (descending order):");

      for (String str : list) {
```

```
            System.out.println(str);
        }
    }
}
```

OUTPUT OF THE PROGRAM

```
Sorted ArrayList (descending order):
elderberry
date
cherry
banana
apple
```

CODE EXPLANATION

In this example, we create an ArrayList of Strings and add some elements to it. We then use the Collections.sort() method to sort the ArrayList in descending order, using the Collections.reverseOrder() method to get a comparator that sorts the elements in reverse order. Finally, we iterate over the sorted ArrayList and print its elements.

Do not rely heavily on ChatGPT coding skills as it generates erroneous codes at times. Please check and verify that the codes are working appropriately.

Python Program to Find the Factorial of a Given Number

ChatGPT is capable of generating Python code.

It can be a **useful tool** for anyone who wants to save time and effort by generating code using plain English descriptions of the desired functionality.

Additionally, ChatGPT can help optimise the code by suggesting **improvements and identifying potential performance issues**.

ChatGPT's ability to generate Python code and provide valuable insights can be a **valuable asset for people** looking to streamline their **development processes** and create more **efficient applications.**

ChatGPT does not maintain a deep understanding of the overall project or task at hand. As such, the code snippets generated may need to be adapted to fit effectively into a larger codebase. For simple tasks like generating a "Hello, World!" program or basic arithmetic calculations, ChatGPT is generally quite reliable. However, for more complex tasks like developing full-fledged applications, the model's accuracy may be less reliable.

Here is an example of **simple Python code** created by using ChatGPT.

ChatGPT Prompt:

Write a Python program to find the factorial of a given number.

ChatGPT Video Output URL and QR Code:

https://tinyurl.com/SimplePythonProg

ChatGPT Output:

PYTHON CODE

```
num = int(input("Enter a number: "))
factorial = 1

if num < 0:
   print("Factorial cannot be found for negative numbers.")
elif num == 0:
   print("Factorial of 0 is 1.")
else:
   for i in range(1, num + 1):
      factorial *= i
   print("Factorial of", num, "is", factorial)
```

OUTPUT OF THE PROGRAM

```
Enter a number: 5
Factorial of 5 is 120
```

CODE EXPLANATION

In this program, we first take the input number from the user using the input() function and convert it into an integer using the int() function. We then initialize a variable factorial to 1, as the factorial of 0 and 1 is 1.

We then use an if-elif-else statement to check whether the input number is negative, zero, or positive. If it's negative, we print an error message, as the factorial of negative numbers is undefined. If it's zero, we print the factorial as 1. If it's positive, we use a for loop to iterate from 1 to the input number, and multiply the factorial variable with the loop variable at each iteration.

Finally, we print the value of the factorial as the output.

Ten Java Programming Prompts

Here are some **ChatGPT prompts** to help you generate **Java Programs.**

ChatGPT Prompt Templates:

1. Develop **[JAVA]** code that computes the sum of two provided numbers and shows the outcome.

2. Craft **[JAVA]** code that employs **[regular expressions]** to verify the validity of a user-inputted **[email address]**.

3. Design a **[JAVA method]** that accepts a **[number array]** as an argument and returns the maximum value.

4. Produce **[JAVA]** code that establishes a connection with a **[MySQL database]** and fetches all entries from a specific table.

5. Compose **[JAVA]** code that **[uploads an image file]** and stores it in a designated server directory.

6. Construct a **[JAVA]** code that creates a **[random password]** of a given length using both letters and numbers.

7. Formulate **[JAVA]** code that iterates through a **[string array]** and outputs each string in capital letters.

8. Implement **[JAVA]** code that calculates the **[factorial]** of a specified number through **[recursion]**.

9. Develop a **[JAVA GUI application]** that takes a name and age from the user and displays an age-appropriate greeting.

10. Create **[JAVA]** code that offers **[basic shopping cart features]** for an e-commerce site, such as item addition and removal.

ChatGPT can help quickly sketch out code snippets or algorithms, saving time during the initial phases of development.

HTML File with JavaScript Code for 12-Digit Calculator

Using ChatGPT, **developers** can **describe** the **desired functionality** and **layout** of their **web page** in **plain English**, and **ChatGPT** can **generate** the corresponding **HTML and JavaScript code**. This can **save time and effort** when creating **complex web pages** that involve **multiple functions**, **events**, and **libraries**. Moreover, **ChatGPT** can **help developers optimise** their **HTML and JavaScript code** by **suggesting improvements** or identifying **potential performance issues**. With its **natural language processing capabilities**, **ChatGPT** can **analyse and interpret** the input data to provide **valuable insights** into the most **efficient way** to structure and write the code. Additionally, **ChatGPT** can be **useful in debugging HTML and JavaScript code** by identifying **errors** and suggesting solutions. With its **natural language processing capabilities**, **ChatGPT** can **analyse and interpret code snippets** to **identify issues** and provide potential solutions. Here is an example of an **HTML file with JavaScript** created **using ChatGPT**.

ChatGPT Prompt:

> **Write a HTML file that includes JavaScript code for a 12-digit calculator**

ChatGPT Video Output URL and QR Code:

https://tinyurl.com/HTMLwJavaScript

ChatGPT Output:

HTML WITH JAVASCRIPT CODE

```
<!DOCTYPE html>

<html>

<head>

        <title>12-Digit Calculator</title>

        <script type="text/JavaScript">

                // Function to clear the calculator display
```

```
                    function clearDisplay() {
                              document.getElementById("calculator-
display").value = "";
                    }


                    // Function to evaluate the expression entered in
the calculator display
                    function calculate() {
                              var          expression          =
document.getElementById("calculator-display").value;
                              var result = eval(expression);
                              document.getElementById("calculator-
display").value = result;
                    }


                    // Function to add a number or operator to the
calculator display
                    function addToDisplay(input) {
                              document.getElementById("calculator-
display").value += input;
                    }
          </script>
</head>
<body>
```

```
    <h1>12-Digit Calculator</h1>
    <input         type="text"         id="calculator-display"
size="16"><br><br>
    <button onclick="addToDisplay('1')">1</button>
    <button onclick="addToDisplay('2')">2</button>
    <button onclick="addToDisplay('3')">3</button>
    <button onclick="addToDisplay('+')">+</button><br>
    <button onclick="addToDisplay('4')">4</button>
    <button onclick="addToDisplay('5')">5</button>
    <button onclick="addToDisplay('6')">6</button>
    <button onclick="addToDisplay('-')">-</button><br>
    <button onclick="addToDisplay('7')">7</button>
    <button onclick="addToDisplay('8')">8</button>
    <button onclick="addToDisplay('9')">9</button>
    <button onclick="addToDisplay('*')">*</button><br>
    <button onclick="addToDisplay('0')">0</button>
    <button onclick="addToDisplay('.')">.</button>
    <button onclick="calculate()">=</button>
    <button onclick="addToDisplay('/')">/</button><br><br>
    <button onclick="clearDisplay()">Clear</button>
</body>
</html>
```

CODE EXPLANATION

This HTML file creates a simple 12-digit calculator. It includes four functions: clearDisplay() to clear the calculator display, calculate() to evaluate the expression entered in the display, addToDisplay(input) to add a number or operator to the display, and an onload function to initialize the calculator when the page loads. The calculator display is an <input> element with an ID of calculator-display, and the calculator buttons are created using <button> elements with onclick attributes that call the appropriate functions.

Ten JavaScript Prompts

Here are some **useful JavaScript prompts** that can help you create your **own prompts** for JavaScript.

.

ChatGPT Prompt Templates:

1. Construct **[JavaScript]** code that determines the total of two given numbers and displays the result.
2. Develop a **[JavaScript]** function that reverses a **[string]** and returns the reversed version.

3. Engineer **[JavaScript]** code that uses **[WebRTC]** to enable **[video conferencing]** between two users.
4. Develop a **[JavaScript]** program that uses **[Canvas API]** to draw **[geometric shapes]** on a web page.
5. Compose **[JavaScript]** code that leverages **[WebSockets]** for **[real-time communication]** between a client and server.
6. Implement a **[JavaScript]** function that sorts an **[array of objects]** based on a specific **[property]**.
7. Create a **[JavaScript]** program that uses **[localStorage]** to save and retrieve **[user settings]**.
8. Write **[JavaScript]** code that uses **[Fetch API]** to make **[HTTP requests]** and handle **[JSON responses]**.
9. Construct a **[JavaScript]** function that calculates the **[Fibonacci sequence]** up to a given number.
10. Generate **[JavaScript]** code that uses **[Promises]** to handle **[asynchronous operations]**.

The ChatGPT generated code is not usually optimised for performance and may not follow best practices. The code should be reviewed for potential security vulnerabilities, as ChatGPT cannot ensure security best practices.

PHP Code to Detect and Prevent SQL Injection Attacks

ChatGPT can **generate PHP code** alongside other **programming languages**. Consequently, it can serve as a **valuable resource** for individuals tasked with **writing PHP code** for their applications.

Using **ChatGPT**, you can **describe** the desired **functionality** of your **PHP code** in clear **plain English**. The model then generates the corresponding **PHP code**, leading to significant time and effort savings, especially when dealing with intricate PHP code involving **multiple functions**, **classes**, and **libraries**.

Beyond just **generating PHP code**, **ChatGPT** also offers assistance in **optimizing** existing **PHP code** by providing suggestions for improvements and identifying potential **performance issues**. Additionally, it offers **valuable insights** into the most **efficient approach** for structuring **PHP code** to accomplish specific tasks.

Below is an example of **simple PHP code** created using **ChatGPT**.

ChatGPT Prompt:

Generate PHP code that detects and prevents SQL injection attacks

ChatGPT Video Output URL and QR Code:

https://tinyurl.com/SQLInjectPHP

ChatGPT Output:

Create **PHP CODE**

```
<?php

// Get input data from the user
```

```
$username = $ POST['username'];

$password = $ POST['password'];


// Establish database connection

$servername = "localhost";

$dbusername = "username";

$dbpassword = "password";

$dbname = "mydatabase";


$conn = new mysqli($servername, $dbusername, $dbpassword,
$dbname);


// Prepare SQL statement with placeholders

$stmt = $conn->prepare("SELECT * FROM users WHERE username =
? AND password = ?");


// Bind parameters to statement

$stmt->bind param("ss", $username, $password);


// Execute statement

$stmt->execute();


// Get results
```

```
$result = $stmt->get result();


// Check if user exists

if ($result->num rows > 0) {

    // User exists, do something

} else {

    // User does not exist, do something else

}


// Close statement and connection

$stmt->close();

$conn->close();

?>
```

CODE EXPLANATION

In this example, we use prepared statements to prepare an SQL query with placeholders for user input. We then bind the user input to the statement and execute it. This way, even if the user enters malicious input, the placeholders will prevent the SQL injection attack from being successful.

Ten PHP Prompts

Here are some **useful PHP prompts** that can help you create your **own prompts** for PHP coding.

ChatGPT Prompt Templates:

1. Create a **[PHP]** code to **[calculate]** the **[sum]** of two **[given numbers]** and **[display]** the **[result]**.
2. Write **[PHP]** code to **[validate]** an **[email address]** entered by a **[user]** using **[regular expressions]**.
3. Create a **[PHP function]** that takes an **[array of numbers]** as **[input]** and **[returns]** the **[highest value]**.
4. Generate **[PHP]** code to **[connect]** to a **[MySQL database]** and **[retrieve]** all **[records]** from a **[table]**.
5. Write **[PHP]** code to **[upload]** an **[image file]** and **[save]** it to a **[specific directory]** on the **[server]**.
6. Create a **[PHP script]** that **[generates]** a **[random password]** of a **[specified length]** using **[alphanumeric characters]**.
7. Generate **[PHP]** code to **[loop]** through an **[array of strings]** and **[display]** each **[string]** in **[uppercase]**.

8. Write **[PHP]** code to **[calculate]** the **[factorial]** of a **[given number]** using **[recursion]**.
9. Create a **[PHP form]** that **[accepts]** **[user input]** for a **[name]** and **[age]**, then **[displays]** a **[greeting]** based on the **[age]**.
10. Generate **[PHP]** code to **[implement]** a **[basic shopping cart functionality]** for an **[online store]**, including **[adding and removing items]**.

SQL Queries

ChatGPT can even **help** to **create SQL queries**. **ChatGPT** has been **trained** on a **diverse range** of **text data**, including **SQL query language**. Due to its **ability** to **understand and generate SQL queries**, it can be a **valuable resource** for **developers** who are **tasked with creating SQL queries** for their applications.

You can **describe** the **data** you wish to **retrieve** in **plain English**, and the **model** can **generate** the corresponding **SQL**

query. This can **save significant time and effort** when creating **complex SQL queries** that involve **multiple tables** and **complex joins**.

Furthermore, **ChatGPT** can also **help optimize** existing **SQL queries** by **suggesting improvements** to the **query structure** or identifying **potential performance issues**.

With its **ability to analyse and interpret data**, **ChatGPT** can provide **valuable insights** into the most **efficient way** to structure an **SQL query** to retrieve the required data.

Here is an example of a **simple SQL query** created using **ChatGPT**.

ChatGPT Prompt:

Create an SQL query to find all users who live in Sydney and have over 3,000 credits

ChatGPT Video Output URL and QR Code:

https://tinyurl.com/SimpleSQLQuery

ChatGPT Output:

Assuming that there is a table called **users** with columns **name**, **city**, and **credits**, the SQL query to find all users who live in Sydney and have over 3000 credits would be:

```
SELECT name

FROM users

WHERE city = 'Sydney' AND credits > 3000;
```

This query will select the **name** column from the **user's** table where the **city** column is 'Sydney' and the **credits** column is greater than 3000.

For straightforward tasks such as generating SELECT, INSERT, UPDATE, or DELETE statements, ChatGPT can quickly provide you with the necessary SQL code, speeding up the development process.

Twenty SQL Prompts

Here are some **useful SQL prompts** that can help you create your own SQL prompts.

ChatGPT Prompt Template:

1. Generate an SQL query to retrieve all **[customer names]** and their corresponding **[orders]** from the '**[Customers]**' and '**[Orders]**' tables.
2. Create an SQL query to calculate the **[average salary]** of **[employees]** in the '**[Employees]**' table.
3. Write an SQL query to find the total number of **[products]** in the '**[Products]**' table with a **[quantity]** greater than **[50]**.
4. Generate an SQL query to display the **[top 5 highest-earning customers]** from the '**[Transactions]**' table.
5. Create an SQL query to list the **[names of employees]** who belong to the '**[Sales]**' department and have been with the company for more than **[2 years]**.
6. Write an SQL query to retrieve the **[unique categories]** of **[products]** available in the '**[Inventory]**' table.

7. Generate an SQL query to find the **[total revenue generated]** from each **[product category]** in the '**[Sales]**' table.
8. Create an SQL query to **[update]** the '**[Stock]**' column of a specific **[product]** in the '**[Products]**' table.
9. Write an SQL query to **[delete records]** of **[customers]** who have not placed any **[orders]** from the '**[Customers]**' table.
10. Generate an SQL query to **[join]** the '**[Employees]**' and '**[Departments]**' tables to display the **[names of employees]** along with their corresponding **[department names]**.

SQL has various dialects depending on the database management system (DBMS) in use (e.g., MySQL, PostgreSQL, SQL Server). ChatGPT may not be aware of the specific syntax or functions unique to a particular DBMS.

Add Comments, Debug and Fix Codes

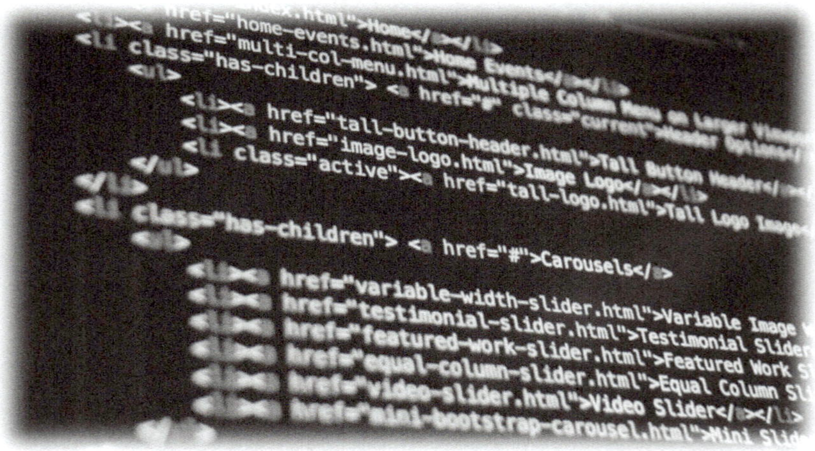

ChatGPT can **explain complex code sections** or **programming concepts** in simple English. This makes it a **valuable tool** for developers who may be new to a programming language or need help understanding a particular **code snippet**.

By simply **describing the code section to ChatGPT**, it can be **explained in easy-to-understand language**.

Another way **ChatGPT** can help developers is by **adding comments to code** that does not already have any. Adding comments can be **time-consuming**, but they can be **extremely helpful** for other developers who need to understand the code in the future.

ChatGPT can **analyse code** and determine which sections might benefit from **additional comments**, and then **generate those comments in plain English**.

This can be especially **useful for developers** who are working on large or **complex codebases** and need **assistance** in identifying areas for improvement. With **ChatGPT's help**, developers can **streamline their code** and create **more efficient applications**.

it's important to note that **understanding code** requires a **strong foundation** in programming concepts and terminology. If you're unfamiliar with these concepts, it may be helpful to **review some introductory programming materials** or seek out guidance from a mentor or tutor.

ChatGPT can analyse the code and identify areas where it could be optimised for better performance or readability to a reasonable extent. ChatGPT can generate comments that describe the purpose of a particular block of code, helping both the original developer and others to understand its function at a glance.

Explaining the Program Code

When it comes to **explaining code**, it's important to use clear language and break down **complex concepts into smaller, more digestible pieces**. This is where ChatGPT comes in - it can help **developers, students and teachers explain code** in a way that's **easy** for anyone to **understand**.

ChatGPT Prompt Template:

> **Create Explain the following [name of the programming language] code [Paste the code here]**

Customised ChatGPT Prompt Created from the Template:

> **Explain the following [Java] code** [*import java.util.ArrayList;*
>
> *import java.util.Collections;*
>
> *public class SortArrayListDescending {*
>
> *public static void main(String[] args) {*

```
        ArrayList<String> list = new ArrayList<>();
        list.add("apple");
        list.add("banana");
        list.add("cherry");
        list.add("date");
        list.add("elderberry");
        Collections.sort(list, Collections.reverseOrder());
        System.out.println("Sorted ArrayList (descending order):");
        for (String str : list) {
            System.out.println(str);
        }
    }
}]
```

ChatGPT Video Output URL and QR Code:

https://tinyurl.com/ExplainCode

ChatGPT Output:

This is a Java program that demonstrates how to sort an ArrayList of strings in descending order using the **Collections.sort()** method.

First, an ArrayList of strings is created and initialized with a few sample values. Then, the **Collections.sort()** method is called with the ArrayList and **Collections.reverseOrder()** as arguments. This sorts the ArrayList in descending order.

Finally, a for-each loop is used to iterate over the sorted ArrayList and print each element on a separate line to the console.

In summary, this Java program shows how to sort an ArrayList of strings in descending order using the **Collections.sort()** method with **Collections.reverseOrder()**.

Adding Inline Comments to Existing Code

Adding inline comments to existing code is an **essential practice** that can enhance the **readability** and **maintainability** of software applications.

Inline comments, also known as **code comments**, are short notes inserted within the code to elucidate its **purpose**, **function**, or **behaviour**.

These comments can **serve as a guide** for the developer to remember their **own code's logic** or for others who might need to re-use and modify the code later on for **further development**.

By offering clear explanations of each section of code, **inline comments** can assist developers in **swiftly pinpointing and rectifying issues** in their applications.

ChatGPT Prompt Template:

> **Add inline comments to explain the following [name of the programming language] code [Paste the code here].**

Customised ChatGPT Prompt Created from the Template:

Add inline comments to explain the following [Java] code

```
[import java.util.ArrayList;

import java.util.Collections;


public class SortArrayListDescending {
   public static void main(String[] args) {
       ArrayList<String> list = new ArrayList<>();
      list.add("apple");
      list.add("banana");
      list.add("cherry");
      list.add("date");
      list.add("elderberry");


      Collections.sort(list, Collections.reverseOrder());


      System.out.println("Sorted ArrayList (descending
order):");
      for (String str : list) {
         System.out.println(str);
```

```
    }
  }
}].
```

ChatGPT Video Output URL and QR Code:

https://tinyurl.com/InlineCommentsCode

ChatGPT Output:

```
import java.util.ArrayList;
import java.util.Collections;

public class SortArrayListDescending {
  public static void main(String[] args) {

    // Create a new ArrayList of Strings
    ArrayList<String> list = new ArrayList<>();

    // Add some elements to the ArrayList
    list.add("apple");
    list.add("banana");
```

```
        list.add("cherry");
        list.add("date");
        list.add("elderberry");

        // Sort the ArrayList in descending order using Collections.sort() method
        Collections.sort(list, Collections.reverseOrder());

        // Print the sorted ArrayList
        System.out.println("Sorted ArrayList (descending order):");
        for (String str : list) {
            // Print each element in the ArrayList
            System.out.println(str);
        }
    }
}
```

Debugging and Fixing Codes

Debugging and **fixing code** can be a daunting task, particularly for novice programmers just embarking on their programming journey. ChatGPT emerges as a potent tool to assist students in **debugging** and **correcting** their code. ChatGPT can provide valuable recommendations to students grappling with **coding blunders**.

Here are some ways in which ChatGPT can be used for **debugging** and **rectifying code**:

1. **Real-time Error Correction**: ChatGPT can be used to provide real-time feedback on the code being written by the students. As soon as an error is detected, ChatGPT can provide suggestions on how to correct it. This will not only save time but also help students learn from their mistakes as they are writing the code.

2. **Contextual Help**: ChatGPT can analyse the code and provide contextual help based on the specific problem that the student is trying to solve. This will help students understand the concepts behind the code and how it relates to the problem they are trying to solve.

3. **Step-by-Step Guidance**: ChatGPT can provide step-by-step guidance on how to solve a specific coding problem. This can help students break down complex problems into smaller, more manageable parts, and understand the logic behind each step.

4. **Code Optimization**: ChatGPT can analyse the code and provide suggestions on how to optimise it for better performance. This can help students write more efficient and effective code, which is essential for real-world programming.

5. **Learning from Examples**: ChatGPT can be used to provide examples of correct code that students can learn from. This will help students understand the best practices for writing clean, efficient, and well-structured code.

By providing real-time feedback, contextual help, step-by-step guidance, code optimisation, and examples, ChatGPT can help students become better programmers and learn the best practices for writing high-quality code.

ChatGPT Prompt Template:

Please assist me in resolving the problem by providing an updated code solution and a clear explanation of the

issue and the steps taken to fix it. Here is the code [paste the code]

Customised ChatGPT Prompt Created from the Template:

Please assist me in resolving the problem by providing an updated code solution and a clear explanation of the issue and the steps taken to fix it.

Here is the code [*num1 = float(input("Enter the first number: "))*

num2 = (input("Enter the second number: "))

num3 = float(input("Enter the third number: "))

sum = num1 + num2 + num3

*print("The sum is:", sum)***]**

ChatGPT Video Output URL and QR Code:

https://tinyurl.com/DebugProgCode

ChatGPT Output:

The issue with this code is that the second number is not being converted to a float before addition, as it is being stored as a string from the **input()** function. This will cause a **TypeError** when trying to add it with the other two numbers. To fix this, you need to convert the second input to a float before adding it to the other two numbers. Here is the updated code:

num1 = float(input("Enter the first number: "))

num2 = float(input("Enter the second number: "))

num3 = float(input("Enter the third number: "))

sum = num1 + num2 + num3

print("The sum is:", sum)

In this code, we have converted the second input to a float using the **float()** function before adding it to the other two numbers. This will ensure that the addition operation works correctly without any **TypeError** issues.

Convert Programs Across Different Languages

Converting program codes from one language to another using ChatGPT has several potential benefits, including:

1. **Improved cross-platform compatibility:** Converting code to another language can make it more compatible with different platforms and operating systems. For example, a program originally written in a language that is only supported on Windows can be converted to a language that is supported on both Windows and Mac OS.

2. **Increased flexibility:** Converting code to another language can increase the flexibility of the program by allowing it to

be used in different contexts. For example, a program originally written for a specific device or application can be converted to a language that is more widely supported, making it more accessible and adaptable.

3. **Easier maintenance:** Converting code to another language can make it easier to maintain over time. For example, if a programming language falls out of favour or becomes less supported, converting the code to another language can ensure that it remains viable and can be updated or modified as needed.

4. **Improved performance:** Converting code to another language can improve the performance of the program. For example, a program written in a scripting language that is converted to a compiled language can run faster and use less memory.

5. **Access to new features:** Converting code to another language can provide access to new features and capabilities that are not available in the original language. For example, a program originally written in an older language can be converted to a newer language that has more advanced features, such as support for multi-threading or improved security.

Converting program codes from one language to another using ChatGPT can be **useful** for improving the performance, flexibility, and maintainability of code.

However, it is important to note that **code conversion** is not always a **straightforward process**, and may require **significant testing and debugging** to ensure that the converted code works correctly.

ChatGPT Prompt Template:

Please convert this Java code into Python [insert Java code here]

Customised ChatGPT Prompt Created from the Template:

Please convert this Java code into Python [import java.util.ArrayList;

```
import java.util.Collections;

public class SortArrayListDescending {

    public static void main(String[] args) {

        // Create an ArrayList of Strings

        ArrayList<String> list = new ArrayList<>();

        list.add("apple");

        list.add("banana");
```

```
        list.add("cherry");

        list.add("date");

        list.add("elderberry");

        // Sort the ArrayList in descending order using Collections.sort() method

        Collections.sort(list, Collections.reverseOrder());

        // Print the sorted ArrayList

        System.out.println("Sorted ArrayList (descending order):");

        for (String str : list) {
            System.out.println(str);

        }

    }

}

]
```

ChatGPT Video Output URL and QR Code:

https://tinyurl.com/JavaToPythonConv

ChatGPT Output:

```
Create # Create a list of strings

lst = ["apple", "banana", "cherry", "date", "elderberry"]


# Sort the list in descending order

lst.sort(reverse=True)


# Print the sorted list

print("Sorted List (descending order):")

for item in lst:

    print(item)
```

Check the generated code for consistency and accuracy. You must test the generated code using your preferred IDE (Integrated Development Environment).

CHAPTER 12

CREATE TABULAR FORMAT OUTPUTS

12. Create Tabular Format Outputs

Australia: Growth of the Population by State, 2010 to 2030

Source: ABS 2008 Series B Projections

State/Territory	2010	2020	2030	Growth Rate(%) Per Annum, 2010 to 2030
		Population'000		
NSW	7,121.3	7,925.0	8,690.3	0.10
Vic	5,439.0	6,208.9	6,951.0	0.12
Qld	4,465.0	5,447.7	6,424.2	0.18
SA	1,633.2	1,793.3	1,940.0	0.09
WA	2,245.6	2,717.1	3,185.3	0.17
Tas	505.2	537.2	559.8	0.05
NT	227.2	263.1	299.7	0.14
ACT	352.0	393.2	431.0	0.10
Australia	21,991.0	25,288.1	28,484.2	0.13

Creating a **tabular format** using ChatGPT is easy. Whether you need to present data, **compare different elements**, or organise content, ChatGPT can assist you in **generating clear** and organised tables.

Here is an example that can help to get **well-versed** in using ChatGPT for **tabular format** output.

ChatGPT Prompt Template:

Provide the top **[number]** countries **[datapoint 1]** and **[datapoint 2]** in table format.

Customised ChatGPT Prompt Created from the Template:

Provide the top 4 countries' GDP and population in table format.

ChatGPT Video Output URL and QR Code:

https://tinyurl.com/TabularOut

ChatGPT Output:

Rank	Country	GDP (Trillion USD)	Population
1	United States	$21.43	331.00
2	China	$14.34	1441.00

3	Japan	$5.08	126.00
4	Germany	$3.86	83.00

Ten Table Output Generation Prompts

Here are some **example prompts** that can be customised for getting tabular output:

1. List the leading **[number]** nations in terms of **[datapoint 1]** and **[datapoint 2]** in tabular representation.
2. Showcase the primary **[number]** countries by **[datapoint 1]** and **[datapoint 2]** in a table.
3. Display the foremost **[number]** nations ranking for **[datapoint 1]** and **[datapoint 2]** in table form.
4. Present the top-ranking **[number]** countries based on **[datapoint 1]** and **[datapoint 2]** in a structured table.
5. Highlight the key **[number]** nations excelling in **[datapoint 1]** and **[datapoint 2]** within a table.

6. Enumerate the dominant **[number]** countries in **[datapoint 1]** and **[datapoint 2]** using a tabulated format.
7. Illustrate the superior **[number]** nations regarding **[datapoint 1]** and **[datapoint 2]** in a clear table.
8. Detail the principal **[number]** countries measured by **[datapoint 1]** and **[datapoint 2]** in a laid-out table.
9. Tabulate the premier **[number]** nations considering **[datapoint 1]** and **[datapoint 2]**.
10. Outline the standout **[number]** countries in relation to **[datapoint 1]** and **[datapoint 2]** in a systematic table.

ChatGPT can format text in a tabular manner to some extent, although it won't be as flexible or visually appealing as a table generated by specialised software or libraries. Tabular output can be useful for presenting data in a more organised and readable way.

CHAPTER 13

CREATE A POWERPOINT PRESENTATION OUTLINE

13. Create a PowerPoint Presentation Outline

ChatGPT **simplifies** the process of **generating PowerPoint outlines** for presentations on a wide range of topics.

With its natural language processing capabilities, you can get ChatGPT to **quickly outline** the **key points, structure**, and **content flow** of your presentation.

You can either use the ChatGPT to **create a PowerPoint presentation outline** on a **particular topic** or use **your text content** to quickly generate a PowerPoint outline.

Here are a **few examples** of how you can easily use ChatGPT to generate PowerPoint presentation outlines.

ChatGPT Prompt Template:

Please generate [number of slides] slides PowerPoint presentation outline on [topic] with individual slide content

Customised ChatGPT Prompt Created from the Template:

Please generate **[10]** slides PowerPoint presentation outline on **[Using AI Chatbot for marketing]** with individual slide content and slide notes

ChatGPT Video Output URL and QR Code:

https://tinyurl.com/GPT-PPTOutline

ChatGPT Output:

Create **Slide 1: Title Slide**

- Title: Leveraging AI Chatbots for Marketing

- Subtitle: Enhancing Customer Engagement and Conversion
- Your Name/Organisation
- Date

Slide Notes: Introduce the topic and the importance of AI chatbots in modern marketing. Highlight the agenda of the presentation and set the stage for discussing the benefits and strategies of using AI chatbots.

Slide 2: Introduction to AI Chatbots

- Definition of AI chatbots
- Importance of AI chatbots in modern marketing
- Statistics on increasing customer expectations for instant responses

Slide Notes: Define AI chatbots and their role in revolutionizing marketing. Emphasize the growing demand for instant and personalized customer interactions, driving the need for AI-driven solutions.

Slide 3: Benefits of AI Chatbots in Marketing

- Improved customer engagement
- 24/7 availability for customer queries
- Personalized interactions at scale
- Data-driven insights for better targeting

Slide Notes: Explore the advantages of AI chatbots in marketing, focusing on how they enhance customer engagement, provide round-the-clock support, deliver personalized experiences, and offer valuable insights for refining strategies.

Slide 4: Use Cases for Marketing AI Chatbots

- Lead generation and qualification
- Customer support and issue resolution
- Product recommendations and cross-selling
- Feedback collection and sentiment analysis

Slide Notes: Discuss various applications of AI chatbots in marketing, showcasing how they can assist in lead generation, customer support, sales, and gathering customer feedback to gauge sentiment.

Slide 5: AI Chatbot Implementation Process

- Identifying marketing goals
- Choosing a suitable AI chatbot platform
- Designing conversational flows
- Integration with CRM and other tools

Slide Notes: Outline the steps involved in implementing AI chatbots for marketing purposes. From setting goals and selecting the right platform to designing engaging conversations and integrating with existing tools.

Slide 6: Designing Effective Conversations

- Crafting engaging greetings
- Providing clear options and responses
- Using natural language processing for better understanding
- Implementing fallback mechanisms for unrecognized queries

Slide Notes: Delve into the art of crafting effective chatbot conversations. Offer tips for creating engaging greetings, designing clear response options, utilizing natural language processing, and handling unexpected user queries gracefully.

Slide 7: Real-life Success Stories

- Example 1: Company X's 30% increase in lead conversion
- Example 2: Company Y's improved customer satisfaction scores
- Example 3: Company Z's enhanced user experience leading to increased sales

Slide Notes: Present real-life success stories of businesses that have benefited from AI chatbot implementation. Highlight quantitative results, such as increased conversion rates, improved satisfaction scores, and higher sales.

Slide 8: Overcoming Challenges

- Ensuring data privacy and security
- Handling complex customer inquiries
- Monitoring and maintaining the chatbot's performance
- Balancing automation with human touch

Slide Notes: Address potential challenges and concerns associated with AI chatbots. Discuss strategies for maintaining data privacy, managing complex queries, ensuring consistent performance, and finding the right balance between automation and human intervention.

Slide 9: Best Practices for AI Chatbot Marketing

- Regularly updating the chatbot knowledge base
- Training the chatbot with real customer interactions
- Continuous monitoring and optimization
- Collecting user feedback for improvement

Slide Notes: Provide a set of best practices for successful AI chatbot marketing. Emphasize the importance of keeping the chatbot's knowledge up to date, training it with real interactions, ongoing optimization, and the significance of user feedback.

Slide 10: Future of AI Chatbots in Marketing

- Evolving AI technologies and capabilities
- Integration with voice assistants and smart devices
- Predictions for increased AI adoption in marketing
- Encouraging the audience to explore AI chatbots for their marketing strategies

Slide Notes: Conclude the presentation by discussing the future potential of AI chatbots in marketing. Touch upon advancements in AI and integration with emerging technologies.

You can use the generated presentation outline to create a PowerPoint presentation using Microsoft PowerPoint or Google Docs.

Ten PowerPoint Presentation Outline Prompts

Here are some **example prompts** that can be customised for creating a **PowerPoint presentation outline** that can further be used to create a **PowerPoint presentation**:

1. Generate an outline for a PowerPoint presentation with **[number of slides]** slides focused on **[topic]**, detailing each slide's content.
2. Create an outline for **[number of slides]** slides on **[topic]** for a PowerPoint presentation, specifying content for each slide.
3. I'd like an outline for a **[number of slides]** slide PowerPoint presentation on **[topic]**. Please provide a content breakdown for each slide.
4. Please write an overview for a PowerPoint comprising **[number of slides]** slides about **[topic]**, indicating the content for each.
5. I'd appreciate an outline for a **[number of slides]** slide presentation on **[topic]** with descriptions for each slide.

6. Could you devise a structure for a **[number of slides]** slide PowerPoint on **[topic]**, enumerating content for each?
7. Please generate a PowerPoint presentation outline having **[number of slides]** slides concerning **[topic]**, detailing the subject matter for each slide.
8. I need a plan for a **[number of slides]** slide PowerPoint on **[topic]**. Can you outline what each slide should cover?
9. Kindly put together an outline suitable for a **[number of slides]** slide PowerPoint presentation centred on **[topic]**, elaborating on the content for every slide.
10. I'd like to see an outline for a **[number of slides]** slide presentation on **[topic]** in PowerPoint. Please indicate the proposed content for each slide.

CHAPTER 14

SIMPLIFY AND ADAPT TEACHING RESOURCES

14. Simplify and Adapt Teaching Resources

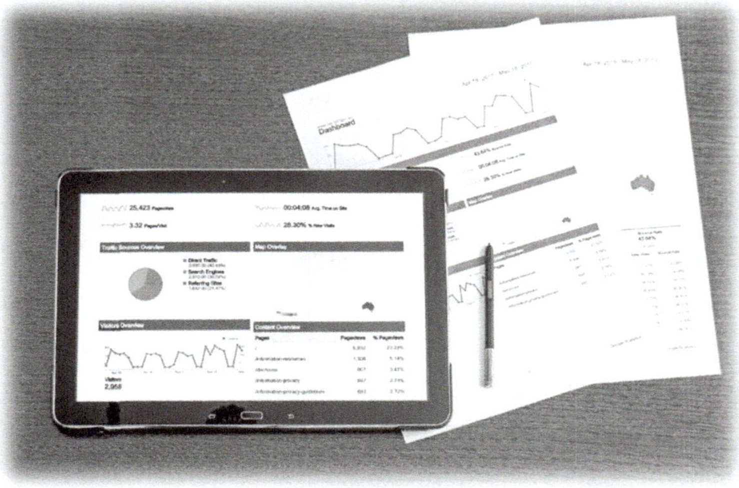

As an educator, you might **encounter situations** where you need to **simplify or adapt** teaching **materials** for **different educational levels**. ChatGPT can help to **adjust the complexity of text-based** resources.

Here is **an example** that can help you understand how to use ChatGPT to **adapt resources** to different **difficulty levels or age** groups:

ChatGPT Prompt Template:

Please simplify the following resource for **[teaching level or age group] [paste the content]**

Customised ChatGPT Prompt Created from the Template:

Please simplify the following resource for [year 10 learners] [*Human genome sequencing is a powerful and sophisticated scientific process that involves decoding the entire genetic makeup of a human being. It's like deciphering the complete instruction manual for building and operating a human body.*

At its core, every living organism, including humans, carries genetic information in the form of DNA. DNA is made up of a sequence of smaller units called nucleotides, often referred to by the letters A, T, C, and G. These letters are like the alphabet of genetics, and the unique sequence of these letters in your DNA is what makes you different from everyone else.

Genome sequencing is the method by which scientists determine the exact order of these nucleotides in a person's DNA. This process involves cutting the DNA into tiny fragments, reading the sequence of letters in these fragments, and then using powerful computers to put all the pieces back together in the right order.

The information obtained from genome sequencing is incredibly valuable. It can provide insights into an individual's genetic predisposition to certain diseases, help identify genetic mutations that cause disorders, and even guide personalized medical treatments. It's a fundamental tool for advancing our understanding of genetics, human health, and biology as a whole.

The field of genome sequencing has made remarkable progress over the years, with significant improvements in speed and cost-effectiveness. As a postgraduate student, you're positioned to explore the cutting-edge technologies and methodologies involved in genome sequencing, contributing to advancements in medical research, personalized medicine, and beyond.

]

ChatGPT Video Output URL and QR Code:

https://tinyurl.com/SimplifyTeaching

ChatGPT Output:

Imagine that your body is like a super complex puzzle, and the pieces of this puzzle are called 'genes.' These genes are like the instructions that make you who you are and how your body works.

Scientists have this amazing process called 'genome sequencing.' It's like they're reading the super tiny letters in your genes to understand what makes you unique. These letters are like the building blocks of life and they're called A, T, C, and G.

Genome sequencing figures out the order of these letters in your genes. It's like solving a big puzzle! Scientists cut the genes into tiny pieces, read the order of the letters, and then use powerful computers to put them in the right order again.

This special information from genome sequencing is really important. It helps scientists learn about diseases you might be prone to, find mistakes in genes that cause problems, and even help doctors give you personalized treatments.

Genome sequencing has come a long way and it's getting faster and cheaper. If you're studying more about this, you could be part of the exciting discoveries in medicine and biology. You'll learn about cool technologies and methods that help us understand our bodies better and make the world healthier."

Twenty Simplify or Adapt Prompts

Here are some **example prompts** that can be customised to simplify or **change the difficulty level** of resources:

1. Kindly adapt the given material for **[teaching level or age group]**: **[paste the content]**.
2. Can you rework the below content to suit **[teaching level or age group]**? **[paste the content]**.
3. Modify the following information for **[teaching level or age group]**: **[paste the content]**.
4. Please adjust the content to make it appropriate for **[teaching level or age group]**: **[paste the content]**.
5. Make the following resource more accessible for **[teaching level or age group]**. **[paste the content]**.
6. I'd like the content below to be refined for **[teaching level or age group]**: **[paste the content]**.
7. Tailor the given material to better suit **[teaching level or age group]**: **[paste the content]**.
8. Refine the resource material to better resonate with the specific requirements of **[teaching level or age group]**. **[paste the content]**.

9. Taking into account the distinctive needs of **[teaching level or age group]**, restructure the following content for improved accessibility. **[paste the content]**.
10. Given the unique learning dynamics of **[teaching level or age group]**, please transform the content below to ensure greater receptivity: **[paste the content]**.
11. To better cater to the nuances of **[teaching level or age group]**, kindly rearrange and improve the subsequent resource: **[paste the content]**.
12. Recognising the distinct learning patterns of **[teaching level or age group]**, could you adapt the following material to be more congruent? **[paste the content]**.
13. In order to optimise the learning experience for **[teaching level or age group]**, please recalibrate and modify the content presented below: **[paste the content]**.
14. With a focus on the specific developmental stages of **[teaching level or age group]**, rework the ensuing material for better clarity and engagement: **[paste the content]**.
15. Endeavouring to ensure tailored content delivery for **[teaching level or age group]**, could you fine-tune the material below for optimal alignment? **[paste the content]**.

16. In order to provide targeted learning for **[teaching level or age group]**, please critically assess and adapt the following resource to ensure maximum impact: **[paste the content]**.
17. Aiming for a more bespoke educational experience for **[teaching level or age group]**, please reorient and adjust the content presented below: **[paste the content]**.
18. Please rephrase the subsequent material to cater to **[teaching level or age group]**: **[paste the content]**.
19. Adapt the content below to make it suitable for **[teaching level or age group]**: **[paste the content]**.
20. Provide a more straightforward version of the following for **[teaching level or age group]**: **[paste the content]**.

ChatGPT can rephrase complex sentences to make them easier to understand, which is particularly useful for audiences that may not be familiar with the topic. Creating simplified content manually can be time-consuming. ChatGPT can generate outlines or entire sections quickly.

Create Resources to Suit Multiple Cohorts

You can create teaching materials to suit **various student groups** simultaneously.

For instance, if you want to **create** a teaching resource centred around the theme of **positive psychology** for **enhancing mental health**, you can tailor it for **Year 10, Year 12, and undergraduate students**.

Here is an **example prompt** that shows how to **create resources** for **3 types of cohorts**.

ChatGPT Prompt Template:

Generate **[number of words]** words teaching resource on **[topic]** separately and respectively for **[grade/level]**, **[grade/level]**, and **[grade/level]** students.

Customised ChatGPT Prompt Created from the Template:

Generate [800] words teaching resource on [What is positive psychology and how to use it to improve [mental health] separately and respectively for [Year 11], [Year 12] and [Postgraduate] students

ChatGPT Video Output URL and QR Code:

https://tinyurl.com/MultiCohortResource

ChatGPT Output:

Teaching Resource: Harnessing Positive Psychology for Enhanced Mental Health

Positive psychology, a science focused on understanding and promoting well-being, offers valuable insights and strategies to elevate mental health.

This comprehensive teaching resource is tailored for [Year 11], [Year 12], and [Postgraduate] students.

By exploring the principles and practices of positive psychology, students across different levels can learn how to apply them effectively to improve their mental well-being.

Year 11: Introduction to Positive Psychology and Mental Health

Understanding Positive Psychology: In [Year 11], you're beginning to delve deeper into psychological concepts. Positive psychology focuses on shifting the emphasis from solely addressing mental illness to nurturing strengths, resilience, and overall well-being.

Key Concepts:

- Positive Emotions: Explore how cultivating positive emotions like gratitude, joy, and contentment can enhance mental health.
- Strengths Identification: Learn to identify and leverage your personal strengths for better self-awareness and confidence.

Practical Application:

- Gratitude Journaling: Engage in daily journaling to reflect on moments of gratitude and positivity.
- Strengths Exploration: Identify your top strengths and consider how they can be utilised in various aspects of life.
- Setting Growth Goals: Set goals that promote personal growth and encourage a positive mindset.

Year 12: Applying Positive Psychology to Mental Health Challenges

Deeper Dive into Positive Psychology: As [Year 12] students, you're becoming more attuned to psychological complexities.

Key Concepts:

- Resilience Building: Learn strategies to enhance emotional resilience, allowing you to bounce back from setbacks.
- Positive Relationships: Understand the impact of nurturing meaningful connections on mental well-being.
- Self-Compassion: Discover the importance of self-compassion in managing stress and building mental resilience.

Practical Application:

- Resilience Toolkit: Develop a toolkit of coping strategies to effectively manage stress and adversity.
- Relationship Building: Engage in activities that promote positive interactions and forge deeper connections.
- Self-Care Rituals: Create self-care routines that prioritize your mental well-being and foster self-compassion.

Postgraduate: Advanced Applications of Positive Psychology for Mental Health

Professional and Personal Integration: As postgraduate students, you're examining concepts from both academic and practical perspectives. Positive psychology offers advanced insights for personal and professional growth.

Key Concepts:

- Flourishing at Work: Explore how positive psychology interventions can enhance workplace satisfaction and productivity.
- Mindfulness and Well-Being: Dive into mindfulness practices that promote emotional regulation and overall mental well-being.
- Positive Interventions: Learn evidence-based interventions for improving mental health and fostering a positive outlook.

Practical Application:

- Positive Leadership: Apply positive psychology principles to leadership roles, cultivating a positive work environment.
- Mindfulness Practice: Incorporate mindfulness techniques into daily routines for improved stress management.
- Well-Being Action Plan: Develop a personalized well-being plan incorporating positive interventions for holistic mental health.

Conclusion: Empowering Mental Health Through Positive Psychology

From [Year 11] to [Postgraduate] studies, the principles of positive psychology provide invaluable tools to enhance mental well-being. The understanding of positive emotions, strengths identification, resilience-building, and other concepts equip students to navigate challenges, cultivate positive relationships, and achieve personal and professional flourishing.

Twenty Resources Creation for Multiple Cohorts Prompts

Here are some **example prompts** that can be customised for creating **resources for multiple cohorts in one go**:

1. Create Create a **[number of words]**-word educational material focusing on **[topic]** specifically tailored for students in **[grade/level]**, **[grade/level]**, and **[grade/level]**.
2. Produce a **[number of words]**-word learning guide on **[topic]**, individually designed for **[grade/level]**, **[grade/level]**, and **[grade/level]** students.
3. Develop a **[number of words]**-word instructional resource on **[topic]**, distinctively for **[grade/level]**, **[grade/level]**, and **[grade/level]** students.

4. Craft a **[number of words]**-word educational content on **[topic]**, separately aimed at **[grade/level]**, **[grade/level]**, and **[grade/level]** students.
5. Compose a **[number of words]**-word teaching aid on **[topic]**, uniquely for **[grade/level]**, **[grade/level]**, and **[grade/level]** students.
6. Formulate a **[number of words]**-word study material on **[topic]**, respectively for **[grade/level]**, **[grade/level]**, and **[grade/level]** students.
7. Construct a **[number of words]**-word lesson plan on **[topic]**, individually suited for **[grade/level]**, **[grade/level]**, and **[grade/level]** students.
8. Formulate a **[number of words]**-word educational toolkit on **[topic]**, distinctly for **[grade/level]**, **[grade/level]**, and **[grade/level]** students.
9. Design a **[number of words]**-word learning module on **[topic]**, specifically for **[grade/level]**, **[grade/level]**, and **[grade/level]** students.
10. Draft a **[number of words]**-word educational outline on **[topic]**, respectively targeting **[grade/level]**, **[grade/level]**, and **[grade/level]** students.
11. Author a **[number of words]**-word educational syllabus on **[topic]**, each section tailored for **[grade/level]**, **[grade/level]**, and **[grade/level]** students.

12. Generate a **[number of words]**-word teaching blueprint on **[topic]**, distinctly crafted for **[grade/level]**, **[grade/level]**, and **[grade/level]** students.
13. Prepare a **[number of words]**-word study guide on **[topic]**, each part aimed at **[grade/level]**, **[grade/level]**, and **[grade/level]** students.
14. Compile a **[number of words]**-word educational article on **[topic]**, separately for **[grade/level]**, **[grade/level]**, and **[grade/level]** students.
15. Curate a **[number of words]**-word learning resource on **[topic]**, individually intended for **[grade/level]**, **[grade/level]**, and **[grade/level]** students.
16. Author a **[number of words]**-word educational workbook on **[topic]**, specifically for **[grade/level]**, **[grade/level]**, and **[grade/level]** students.
17. Create a **[number of words]**-word teaching manual on **[topic]**, each chapter for **[grade/level]**, **[grade/level]**, and **[grade/level]** students.
18. Write a **[number of words]**-word study outline on **[topic]**, distinctly for **[grade/level]**, **[grade/level]**, and **[grade/level]** students.
19. Create a **[number of words]**-word educational brief on **[topic]**, each section designed for **[grade/level]**, **[grade/level]**, and **[grade/level]** students.

20. Develop a **[number of words]**-word learning pamphlet on **[topic]**, respectively for **[grade/level]**, **[grade/level]**, and **[grade/level]** students.

CHAPTER 15

MERGE DOCUMENTS AND REMOVE DUPLICATE CONTENT

15. Merge Documents and Remove Duplicate Content

ChatGPT can also **merge** documents, **remove duplicate** information, and even **rewrite it to suit different cohorts**. In other words, ChatGPT can help you create a **cohesive and well-tailored merged document** that efficiently delivers information to **different levels** of students while maintaining **accuracy** and **clarity**.

However, please review ChatGPT-generated output for **fact-checking** and **removing biases**, so that the **final output document** meets your desired **expectations**.

Here is an example of how to merge 3 documents about the **"benefits of brushing teeth"**.

ChatGPT Video Output URL and QR Code:

https://tinyurl.com/MergeRemoveDocs

ChatGPT Multi-prompt Example Conversation for Merging Three Documents:

Prompt: I want you to merge 3 documents and remove any duplicate information. Please ask me to provide a separate document.

ChatGPT: Of course, I can help you with that. Please provide the three separate documents that you would like me to merge. Once you've provided the documents, I'll start the process of merging them and removing any duplicate information.

Prompt (Input document one text): Dental hygiene is essential for a variety of reasons. First, it helps prevent cavities, gum disease, and bad breath. It also promotes overall health and well-being. While brushing once a day is better than nothing, more is needed to keep your mouth healthy. You need to brush twice a day for two minutes each time. This may seem like a lot, but it's pretty easy. There are plenty of ways to ensure you're brushing your teeth twice daily. You can set a reminder on your phone, put a note in your bathroom, or set a rule for yourself that you must brush your teeth before leaving the house in the morning and before you go to bed at night.

Whatever method you choose, ensure that you're making dental hygiene a priority. Your mouth will thank you for it!

ChatGPT: Thank you for providing the first document. Before we proceed, could you please provide the second and third documents as well? This will allow me to effectively merge the information while removing any duplicates.

Prompt (Input document two text): Our mouths are constantly filled with bacteria and germs that are growing and spreading. Brushing your teeth twice a day will ensure that this bad bacterium is destroyed or removed. If you brush your teeth in the morning and go the entire day without brushing again, the build-up of bacteria will start damaging the enamel of your teeth and weaken their gums and roots, allowing decay to occur. The presence of this bad bacteria also contributes to foul breath. It Reduces Saliva We produce more saliva when we're awake than when we sleep. Why is this important? Because saliva helps build up a barrier against plaque and bacteria and prevents cavities from occurring. Therefore, brushing your teeth in the evening or just before you go to sleep assists with reducing bacteria and saliva when you're sleeping. This reduces terrible breath in the morning by decreasing the acids that build up while you're asleep. It Protects Your Gums Brushing your teeth just once isn't enough to maintain a happy mouth. The reality is that the less you brush your teeth, the more damage you expose your gums to. Plaque, bacteria and tartar are detrimental to the health of your gums and can cause infections and bleeding. It Improves Your Overall Health Our medical knowledge has dramatically increased over the years and dentists, and general medical practitioners now know that there are plenty of diseases directly related to poor oral health. Poor oral health can lead to heart disease, diabetes and osteoporosis. It's also been linked to preterm labour and low birth weight in pregnant women. Hopefully, you'll now understand just how important brushing twice daily is. This, in combination with annual dental check-ups, will ensure that you keep smiling and enjoy healthy teeth.

ChatGPT: Thank you for providing the second document as well. Could you please provide the third and final document? Once I have all three documents, I will be able to proceed with merging the information and removing any duplicate content.

Prompt (Input document three text): Why Should I Brush My Teeth? Why do we brush our teeth? The simple answer is to prevent cavities. We need to remove plaque, the transparent layer of bacteria that coats the teeth. We have heard it over and over again: the best way to do this is by brushing our teeth twice a day and flossing at least once a day. Brushing also stimulates the gums, which helps to keep them healthy and prevent gum disease. Why is this important? Besides complicating your social life, neglecting to brush your teeth can land you with more than just a couple of cavities. It could stop your heart. Gum disease has been linked to an increased prevalence of numerous other conditions such as heart disease, stroke, diabetes, and bronchitis. But how? Because your mouth is full of bacteria, if you have poor dental hygiene those bacteria can potentially make their way into your bloodstream and thus infect distant parts of your body.

ChatGPT: Thank you for providing all three documents. I will now proceed with merging the information and removing any duplicate content. Here's the merged content:

ChatGPT Merged Output: Dental Hygiene and the Importance of Brushing Your Teeth

Dental hygiene is essential for a variety of reasons. First and foremost, it helps prevent cavities, gum disease, and bad breath. Moreover, maintaining proper dental hygiene contributes to overall health and well-being. While brushing your teeth once a day is better than neglecting it altogether, it's insufficient to maintain optimal oral health. To effectively care for your mouth, it's recommended to brush your teeth twice a day for two minutes each time.

Our mouths are inhabited by a continuous presence of bacteria and germs that propagate and spread. Brushing your teeth twice a day plays a pivotal role in eradicating or removing harmful bacteria. If brushing is limited to the morning only, the accumulated bacteria can damage tooth enamel, weaken gums and roots, and lead to decay. This harmful bacterial presence is also a significant factor in causing bad breath.

Regular brushing not only combats bacteria but also reduces saliva production. Saliva serves as a protective barrier against plaque and bacteria, thwarting the formation of cavities. Brushing your teeth before sleeping helps reduce bacteria and saliva production during sleep, minimizing morning breath by mitigating acid accumulation.

Maintaining dental hygiene doesn't solely protect your teeth; it safeguards your gums as well. Inadequate brushing exposes gums to harm from plaque, bacteria, and tartar, potentially leading to infections and bleeding.

Beyond oral health, proper dental care has implications for overall well-being. Scientific advancements reveal links between poor oral health and systemic diseases like heart disease, diabetes, and osteoporosis. Additionally, pregnant women with inadequate oral health face risks of preterm labour and low birth weight.

In essence, brushing your teeth twice daily is crucial. This practice, coupled with regular dental check-ups, ensures not only a radiant smile but also sustains healthy teeth and gums. Remember, neglecting dental hygiene can lead to complications, as poor oral health can contribute to serious medical conditions. By brushing and caring for your teeth, you're promoting a healthier life.

Sources: Document 1, Document 2, Document 3

Please review the merged document, and if you're satisfied with the result, you can let me know. If you'd like any further adjustments or have any additional instructions, feel free to inform me.

Five Merge and Remove Duplicate Prompts

Here are some **example prompts** that can be customised for **merging and removing duplicate content** from the resources:

1. Could you consolidate **[number of files]** documents, ensuring there's no repetitive content?
2. Is it possible to amalgamate **[number of files]** files and eliminate any redundant data?
3. Are you able to unify **[number of files]** documents and remove any duplicate content?
4. Can you integrate **[number of files]** files into a single document without any repetitive information?
5. Can you merge **[number of files]** documents and remove any repeated data?

Note: Please follow the ChatGPT instructions after you have entered the prompt asking to merge documents. ChatGPT will ask you for a **"text version of each document"** that requires **merging** and **removal** of duplicate content.

Create Flashcard Learning Resources

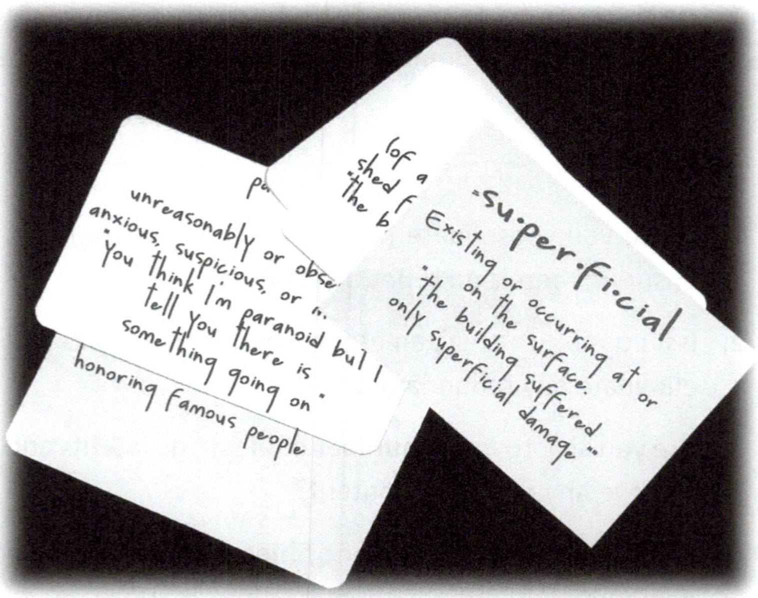

You can create **flashcard learning resources** for almost any subject using ChatGPT.

Flashcards can be used by the students to **memorise or revise** their learning **resources**. Flashcards serve as an **effective educational tool** that students can **utilise to enhance** their **learning experience**.

By **actively engaging** with flashcards, students can **reinforce** their **memory** and understanding of the **subject matter**, making it **easier** for them to **recall information** during **exams**.

Here is an example of how to create flashcards.

ChatGPT Prompt Template:

> **Create [number] flashcards on the topic of [topic] for [subject/unit] students studying [educational program] at [educational level]**

Customised ChatGPT Prompt Created from the Template:

> **Create [20] flashcards on the topic of [cardiovascular terms] for [biology] students studying [medical science] at [University level]**

ChatGPT Video Output URL and QR Code:

https://tinyurl.com/TeachingFlashcards

ChatGPT Output:

Flashcard 1:

Term: Cardiovascular System

Definition: The complex network of the heart, blood vessels, and blood responsible for circulating oxygen, nutrients, and waste products throughout the body.

Flashcard 2:

Term: Atria

Definition: The upper chambers of the heart that receive blood from the body (right atrium) and lungs (left atrium).

Flashcard 3:

Term: Ventricles

Definition: The lower chambers of the heart are responsible for pumping blood to the body (left ventricle) and lungs (right ventricle).

Flashcard 4:

Term: Systole

Definition: The phase of the cardiac cycle when the heart contracts to pump blood out.

Flashcard 5:

Term: Diastole

Definition: The phase of the cardiac cycle when the heart relaxes to fill with blood.

Flashcard 6:

Term: Cardiac Output

Definition: The amount of blood pumped by the heart in one minute, calculated by heart rate multiplied by volume.

Flashcard 7:

Term: Str e Volume

Definition: The volume of blood pumped by a ventricle in a single heartbeat.

Flashcard 8:

Term: Blood Pressure

Definition: The force of blood against the walls of arteries, measured in millimetres of mercury (mmHg).

Flashcard 9:

Term: Hypertension

Definition: Persistent high blood pressure, a risk factor for cardiovascular diseases.

Flashcard 10:

Term: Atherosclerosis

Definition: The gradual buildup of fatty deposits (plaque) in artery walls, leading to reduced blood flow and potential blockages.

Flashcard 11:

Term: Coronary Arteries

Definition: Blood vessels that supply oxygen-rich blood to the heart muscle.

Flashcard 12:

Term: Myocardial Infarction

Definition: A heart attack caused by a blockage in a coronary artery, leading to tissue damage.

Flashcard 13:

Term: Arrhythmia

Definition: Abnormal heart rhythm, potentially affecting the heart's pumping efficiency.

Flashcard 14:

Term: Angina Pectoris

Definition: Chest pain or discomfort caused by reduced blood flow to the heart muscle.

Flashcard 15:

Term: Cardiomyopathy

Definition: A disease that weakens the heart muscle, affecting its ability to pump blood effectively.

Flashcard 16:

Term: Congestive Heart Failure

Definition: A condition where the heart is unable to pump blood efficiently, leading to fluid buildup in the lungs and other tissues.

Flashcard 17:

Term: Thrombosis

Definition: Formation of a blood clot within a blood vessel, potentially causing obstruction.

Flashcard 18:

Term: Embolism

Definition: A blood clot or other foreign substance that travels through the bloodstream and blocks a blood vessel.

Flashcard 19:

Term: Valvular Heart Disease

Definition: Conditions affecting heart valves, leading to impaired blood flow or valve function.

Flashcard 20:

Term: Endocarditis

Definition: Inflammation of the inner lining of the heart chambers and valves, often caused by bacterial infection.

ChatGPT can generate flashcards that are specifically designed to simplify and reinforce complex concepts. By breaking down intricate ideas into more digestible terms or questions, the platform aids in making these concepts easier to understand and remember. This approach is particularly useful for students or professionals who are grappling with complicated subject matter and are looking for effective ways to internalise this information. Although the flashcards generated by ChatGPT will likely require some level of human review to ensure accuracy and relevance, having a foundational base to start from can significantly streamline the process of creating these educational tools. This initial set of flashcards can serve as a draft that can be further refined, saving valuable time and effort.

Twenty Flashcard Prompts

Here are some **example prompts** that can be **adapted** for **creating flashcards** using ChatGPT on the topic of your choice:

1. Create **[number]** study aids covering the topic of **[topic]** for students in the **[subject/unit]** program at **[educational level]**.
2. Develop **[number]** educational flashcards specifically designed for **[educational level]** students from this content **[paste the content].**
3. Produce **[number]** flashcards to assist **[educational level]** students in mastering **[topic]** as part of their **[subject/unit]** curriculum in the **[educational program]**.
4. Design **[number]** flashcards with a focus on **[topic]**, tailored for students enrolled in the **[subject/unit]** program at **[educational level]**.
5. Formulate **[number]** flashcards aimed at enhancing the understanding of **[topic]** among **[educational level]** students in the **[subject/unit]** program.
6. Prepare **[number]** flashcards to reinforce understanding of **[topic]** among **[educational level]**

students enrolled in the **[subject/unit]** program. Use this content **[paste the content].**

7. Design **[number]** flashcards that cover **[topic]**, aligning with the curriculum of **[subject/unit]** students in the **[educational program]** at **[educational level]**.
8. Generate **[number]** flashcards focusing on the topic of **[topic]**, intended for **[educational level]** students studying **[subject/unit]** in the **[educational program]**.
9. Craft **[number]** flashcards using this content **[paste the content].**
10. Formulate **[number] flashcards** aimed at aiding **[educational level]** students in comprehending **[topic]** within their **[subject/unit]** coursework in the **[educational program]**. Use this content **[paste the content]**
11. Formulate **[number]** sets of educational flashcards strategically designed to elevate the comprehension of **[topic]** among **[educational level]** students engaged in the **[subject/unit]** program.
12. Develop **[number]** comprehensive study materials dedicated to **[topic]** for students enrolled in the **[subject/unit]** program at **[educational level]**.
13. Craft **[number]** sets of educational flashcards utilizing the provided content **[paste the content]**.

14. Design **[number]** sets of educational flashcards with a strong emphasis on **[topic]**, custom-crafted to cater to the specific learning needs of students in the **[subject/unit]** program at **[educational level]**.
15. Create **[number]** sets of specialised educational flashcards meticulously tailored to meet the needs of **[educational level]** students. Use the provided content **[paste the content]**.
16. Formulate **[number]** sets of educational flashcards aimed at providing invaluable assistance to **[educational level]** students in grasping the essence of **[topic]** within the context of their **[subject/unit]** coursework in the **[educational program]**. Utilise the provided content **[paste the content]**.
17. Prepare **[number]** sets of educational flashcards geared towards reinforcing the understanding of **[topic]** among **[educational level]** students actively enrolled in the **[subject/unit]** program. Leverage the provided content **[paste the content]**.
18. Produce **[number]** sets of educational flashcards to facilitate **[educational level]** students' mastery of **[topic]** as an integral part of their **[subject/unit]** curriculum within the **[educational program]**.
19. Create **[number]** sets of educational flashcards comprehensively covering **[topic]**, meticulously aligned with the curriculum standards of

[subject/unit] students in the **[educational program]** at **[educational level]**.

20. Generate **[number]** sets of educational flashcards with a singular focus on the intricacies of **[topic]**, designed specifically for **[educational level]** students pursuing **[subject/unit]** studies in the **[educational program]**.

Automated flashcard generation using ChatGPT may reduce the need for purchasing pre-made flashcards or educational resources, potentially saving money. Digital flashcards generated by ChatGPT can be easily shared and accessed from anywhere, making it convenient for group studies or remote learning.

CHAPTER 16

CHATGPT FOR PROFESSIONAL DEVELOPMENT

16. ChatGPT for Professional Development

ChatGPT is a versatile tool that can assist **teachers and other professionals** in **numerous ways** in the area of **professional development.**

One of its **primary applications** is in creating a set of **questions** and sample **responses** for job **interviews**. By utilising **ChatGPT**, individuals can prepare for interviews by simulating **potential questions** and formulating **suitable answers**. This not only boosts their **confidence** but also enhances their prospects of securing the desired **position**.

Furthermore, **ChatGPT** is invaluable for **crafting** or **updating resumes** and **cover letters**, especially for those transitioning between careers or re-entering the job market after a hiatus.

Create Job Interview Questions

Preparing for a job interview is a **vital** step towards securing a job. ChatGPT can be used to **generate questions and sample answers** to assist both the **interviewer and interviewee**.

On the other hand, If you are the one **conducting** the interview, it's **essential** to devise a set of questions that are **specifically tailored** to the job tasks and **responsibilities**. This will aid you in **better evaluating** the applicant's **qualifications** and appropriateness for the position.

It's also **vital** to be ready to **address any queries** the candidate might have about the **company or the role** they are applying for.

Executing a comprehensive and impartial interview procedure can assist in ensuring that the **optimal** candidate is selected for the job.

ChatGPT possesses the capability to **generate a comprehensive list of frequently asked questions (FAQs)** tailored to a particular subject or field.

This list can serve as a **valuable resource** for individuals seeking **quick answers** to **common queries**. But the utility of this feature goes beyond merely listing questions;

ChatGPT can also **formulate well-crafted**, informative **responses** to each of those **questions**.

Here is an example of a prompt for creating interview questions.

ChatGPT Prompt Template:

> Create a list of **[number of questions]** questions with answers for a job interview for the position of **[teaching level]** [subject].

Customised ChatGPT Prompt Created from the Template:

> **Create a list of [10] questions with answers for a job interview for the position of [University] [Physics teacher]**

ChatGPT Video Output URL and QR Code:

https://tinyurl.com/GPTJobInterviewQuestions

ChatGPT Output:

Question: Could you elaborate on your teaching philosophy and how it aligns with instructing physics at the university level?

Answer: My teaching philosophy revolves around nurturing a profound comprehension of physics through interactive exploration, critical analysis, and practical applications. I believe in fostering an environment where students become adept problem solvers and independent thinkers.

Question: How do you plan to engage and intellectually challenge advanced physics students at the university level?

Answer: I intend to design intricate problem-solving tasks, initiate collaborative research initiatives, and facilitate thought-provoking dialogues on cutting-edge physics topics. This approach will stimulate curiosity and provide substantial intellectual stimulation.

Question: Adapting to diverse learning styles and academic backgrounds is crucial in a university setting. How will you tailor your teaching approach to accommodate such diversity?

Answer: I will combine dynamic lectures with hands-on experiments and leverage technology for personalized learning experiences. Additionally, fostering peer mentorship will establish a supportive learning network that embraces a wide range of learning preferences.

Question: Can you illustrate a scenario where you effectively conveyed a complex physics concept to university students? How did you ensure clarity and engagement?

Answer: While teaching quantum mechanics, I employed interactive simulations and relatable analogies. By linking these abstractions to real-world applications, I enabled students to grasp intricate principles with enthusiasm.

Question: Assessing student learning and ensuring mastery of intricate physics theories is vital. How do you plan to evaluate their understanding of both theoretical and applied aspects?

Answer: My assessment strategy includes comprehensive assignments such as problem sets, research papers, and presentations. This holistic approach gauges students' grasp of not only theories but also their practical applications.

Question: Remaining updated with physics research is essential. How do you intend to incorporate the latest advancements into your teaching?

Answer: I regularly participate in conferences, collaborate with fellow physicists, and engage in ongoing research. I believe in infusing these fresh insights into my teaching, demonstrating the current relevance of physics.

Question: Fostering critical thinking and scientific inquiry is pivotal. How will you nurture these skills among university-level physics students?

Answer: I encourage students to dissect real-world scenarios, formulate hypotheses, and design experiments to validate their theories. This approach equips them with essential problem-solving skills vital in the realm of physics.

Question: Balancing interaction in large lecture-style classes is challenging. How do you sustain engagement and interactivity while managing substantial student numbers?

Answer: I employ interactive techniques like concept mapping, peer discussions, and real-time polling to cultivate active student participation and bolster comprehension, even within large lecture halls.

Question: Collaboration across disciplines is enriching. How do you envision contributing to interdisciplinary collaborations and fostering cross-disciplinary interactions?

Answer: Actively seeking opportunities for cross-disciplinary projects and joint seminars will encourage dialogue between diverse fields. By guiding students to connect physics concepts with other domains, I aim to cultivate a holistic understanding.

Question: Can you recount an instance where your teaching inspired a university physics student to pursue a career in related fields?

Answer: One student, initially uncertain of their career direction, discovered an affinity for astrophysics through a gravitational waves project. Nurturing their independent research led to a national conference presentation, igniting their passion for physics and its boundless possibilities.

Create, Rewrite, or Update Your Resume

You can write a new resume or **revamp your existing resume** by using **ChatGPT** in a few minutes.

You can also **rewrite/customise certain sections** of your resume to **suit the job you are applying for** to **increase your chance of getting an interview**.

Updating and optimising your **resume** for any specific job you are applying for is **easy**.

Here is an example of **ChatGPT prompts** that can help you **customise or update your resume** when applying for a new job.

ChatGPT Prompt Template:

> Rewrite my resume for a **[job title]** position at **[company].** Please refer to my current resume and the provided job description. Here is my current resume [*Paste your current resume and the job description*]

Customised ChatGPT Prompt Created from the Template:

Rewrite my resume for a [Senior Lecturer of Economics] position at [UOW, Wollongong]. Please refer to my current resume and the provided job description. Here is my current resume [*George Warren Address: 456 Oak Street, Melbourne, VIC 3000 Phone: (03) 5555 7890 | Email:* george.warren@email.com

Objective: Dedicated and passionate Assistant Lecturer with a decade of experience at Monash University, Melbourne. Seeking to further contribute my expertise in Economics, innovative teaching methods, and commitment to student success to advance the academic excellence and reputation of a respected educational institution.

Professional Experience:

Assistant Lecturer of Economics Monash University, Melbourne, VIC | 05/2013 - Present

- *Instruct and facilitate engaging lectures and tutorials for undergraduate and postgraduate students.*
- *Design curriculum, develop course materials, and create assessments aligned with learning outcomes.*
- *Mentor and guide students, providing academic advice and support, and facilitating academic growth.*

- *Conduct research in the field of Economics, publishing articles in reputable journals and presenting findings at conferences.*
- *Collaborate with colleagues on academic projects, contributing to departmental research initiatives.*
- *Utilise innovative teaching methods, including case studies, simulations, and technology integration, to enhance student engagement and comprehension.*
- *Assist in curriculum development and program review, ensuring alignment with industry trends and academic standards.*

Key Achievements:

- *Recognized for outstanding teaching and awarded the "Excellence in Teaching" accolade three times.*
- *Led a research project on "Sustainable Economic Development" that received a grant and commendation from the university.*
- *Published multiple articles in peer-reviewed Economics journals, contributing to the academic discourse.*
- *Successfully supervised numerous undergraduate and postgraduate research projects, nurturing students' research skills.*

Teaching Assistant Monash University, Melbourne, VIC | 02/2010 - 05/2013

- *Assisted senior faculty members in delivering lectures and tutorials for Economics courses.*
- *Provided support to students during office hours, addressing questions and clarifying concepts.*
- *Graded assignments and exams, providing timely and constructive feedback to enhance learning outcomes.*

Education:

Master of Economics Monash University, Melbourne, VIC | Graduated: 2009

Bachelor of Commerce (Honours) - Economics Monash University, Melbourne, VIC | Graduated: 2008

Skills:

- *Expertise in Economics theories, models, and empirical analysis.*
- *Proficient in curriculum design and course development.*
- *Strong research and analytical skills.*
- *Effective communication and presentation abilities.*

- *Innovative teaching methods and technology integration.*
- *Collaborative team player.*
- *Data analysis using statistical software (STATA, R).*

Professional Memberships:

- *Member of the Economic Society of Australia (ESA).*
- *Member of the Australian Association for Research in Education (AARE).*

References: Available upon request.

]

ChatGPT Video Output URL and QR Code:

https://tinyurl.com/Resume-Rewrite

ChatGPT Output:

George Warren

Address: 456 Oak Street, Melbourne, VIC 3000

Phone: (03) 5555 7890 | Email: george.warren@email.com

Objective:

Passionate and accomplished Senior Lecturer with a decade of impactful experience at Monash University, Melbourne. Eager to leverage my proven expertise in Economics, innovative teaching methodologies, and dedication to academic excellence to contribute to the growth and reputation of the esteemed University of Wollongong.

Professional Experience:

Assistant Lecturer of Economics

Monash University, Melbourne, VIC | 05/2013 - Present

Championed dynamic lectures and tutorials, engaging both undergraduate and postgraduate students in advanced Economics concepts.

Formulated comprehensive curricula, tailored course materials, and developed assessments that aligned with strategic learning objectives.

Guided and mentored students, offering academic guidance, fostering growth, and nurturing their potential.

Showcased a strong research portfolio, publishing impactful articles in esteemed journals and delivering influential conference presentations.

Collaborated extensively on pioneering academic projects, significantly contributing to the institution's research endeavours.

Pioneered innovative pedagogies, integrating cutting-edge technology, simulations, and interactive case studies to elevate student comprehension and participation.

Contributed significantly to curriculum enhancement and program refinement, ensuring alignment with industry trends and academic benchmarks.

Successfully supervised and guided a multitude of undergraduate and postgraduate research projects, nurturing and honing students' research capabilities.

Teaching Assistant

Monash University, Melbourne, VIC | 02/2010 - 05/2013

Collaborated closely with senior faculty members in delivering impactful lectures and tutorials for diverse Economics courses.

Provided unwavering support to students during dedicated office hours, addressing inquiries and clarifying intricate concepts.

Played a pivotal role in grading assignments and exams, offering timely and constructive feedback to drive enhanced learning outcomes.

Key Achievements:

Honoured with the prestigious "Excellence in Teaching" award on three occasions, reflecting outstanding dedication to student learning and engagement.

Spearheaded a groundbreaking research initiative on "Sustainable Economic Development," securing substantial funding and university recognition.

Established a notable presence in the academic community, with multiple publications in peer-reviewed Economics journals, enriching scholarly discourse.

Education:

Master of Economics

Monash University, Melbourne, VIC | Graduated: 2009

Bachelor of Commerce (Honours) - Economics

Monash University, Melbourne, VIC | Graduated: 2008

Skills:

- Expertise in advanced Economics theories, models, and empirical analysis.
- Proficiency in crafting tailored curricula and shaping engaging course structures.
- Strong aptitude for comprehensive research and advanced analytical methodologies.
- Persuasive communication and adept presentation capabilities.
- Champion of innovative teaching practices and seamless technology integration.
- Collaborative and adaptable team player.
- Advanced proficiency in data analysis using statistical software (STATA, R).
- Skilled in the application of behavioural and experimental economics.
- Expert in developing and evaluating economic policies and strategies.
- Skilled in the application of behavioural and experimental economics.

Professional Memberships:

- Proud member of the esteemed Economic Society of Australia (ESA).
- Active participant in the Australian Association for Research in Education (AARE).

References:

Available upon request.

Here is another example prompt to help you update your resume's section for any particular reason such as updating or applying for a new job.

ChatGPT Prompt Template:

Update the **[name of resume section]** section of my resume to make it sound **[tone]** and **[feel]**. Here is my current resume **[Paste your current resume and the job description]**.

Customised ChatGPT Prompt Created from the Template:

Update the [experience] section of my resume to make it sound [professional] and [action-oriented]. Here is my current resume [

George Warren Address: 456 Oak Street, Melbourne, VIC 3000

Phone: (03) 5555 7890 | Email: george.warren@email.com

Objective: Dedicated and passionate Assistant Lecturer with a decade of experience at Monash University, Melbourne. Seeking to further contribute my expertise in Economics, innovative teaching methods, and commitment to student success to advance the academic excellence and reputation of a respected educational institution.

Professional Experience:

Assistant Lecturer of Economics Monash University, Melbourne, VIC | 05/2013 - Present

- *Instruct and facilitate engaging lectures and tutorials for undergraduate and postgraduate students.*
- *Design curriculum, develop course materials, and create assessments aligned with learning outcomes.*

- *Mentor and guide students, providing academic advice and support, and facilitating academic growth.*
- *Conduct research in the field of Economics, publishing articles in reputable journals and presenting findings at conferences.*
- *Collaborate with colleagues on academic projects, contributing to departmental research initiatives.*
- *Utilise innovative teaching methods, including case studies, simulations, and technology integration, to enhance student engagement and comprehension.*
- *Assist in curriculum development and program review, ensuring alignment with industry trends and academic standards.*

Key Achievements:

- *Recognized for outstanding teaching and awarded the "Excellence in Teaching" accolade three times.*
- *Led a research project on "Sustainable Economic Development" that received a grant and commendation from the university.*
- *Published multiple articles in peer-reviewed Economics journals, contributing to the academic discourse.*

- *Successfully supervised numerous undergraduate and postgraduate research projects, nurturing students' research skills.*

Teaching Assistant Monash University, Melbourne, VIC | 02/2010 - 05/2013

- *Assisted senior faculty members in delivering lectures and tutorials for Economics courses.*
- *Provided support to students during office hours, addressing questions and clarifying concepts.*
- *Graded assignments and exams, providing timely and constructive feedback to enhance learning outcomes.*

Education:

Master of Economics Monash University, Melbourne, VIC | Graduated: 2009

Bachelor of Commerce (Honours) - Economics Monash University, Melbourne, VIC | Graduated: 2008

Skills:

- *Expertise in Economics theories, models, and empirical analysis.*

- *Proficient in curriculum design and course development.*
- *Strong research and analytical skills.*
- *Effective communication and presentation abilities.*
- *Innovative teaching methods and technology integration.*
- *Collaborative team player.*
- *Data analysis using statistical software (STATA, R).*

Professional Memberships:

- *Member of the Economic Society of Australia (ESA).*
- *Member of the Australian Association for Research in Education (AARE).*

References: Available upon request.]

ChatGPT Video Output URL and QR Code:

https://tinyurl.com/Resume-Update

Using ChatGPT to update your resume offers a streamlined approach, enabling you to efficiently generate job-specific content. It maintains a consistent tone while offering creative phrasing, thereby enhancing the professionalism and readability of your resume.

ChatGPT Output:

George Warren Address: 456 Oak Street, Melbourne, VIC 3000

Phone: (03) 5555 7890 | Email: george.warren@email.com

Objective: Dedicated and passionate Assistant Lecturer with a decade of experience at Monash University, Melbourne. Seeking to further contribute my expertise in Economics, innovative teaching methods, and commitment to student success to advance the academic excellence and reputation of a respected educational institution.

Professional Experience: Assistant Lecturer of Economics Monash University, Melbourne, VIC | 05/2013 - Present

- Deliver engaging and impactful lectures and tutorials to both undergraduate and postgraduate students, fostering a dynamic learning environment.
- Lead curriculum design, resource development, and aligned assessment creation to ensure optimal learning outcomes.
- Mentor and guide students, offering tailored academic advice and unwavering support for their educational journey.
- Drive empirical research in Economics, resulting in publications in reputable journals and dynamic presentations at prestigious conferences.
- Collaborate seamlessly with peers on multifaceted academic projects, contributing significantly to departmental research endeavours.
- Innovatively integrate teaching methodologies, such as case studies, simulations, and technology, to heighten student engagement and comprehension.
- Contribute strategically to curriculum enhancement and program evaluation, aligning academic standards with industry trends.

Key Achievements:

- Earned the esteemed "Excellence in Teaching" award on three occasions, showcasing an unwavering commitment to student growth and learning.
- Spearheaded and secured funding for a groundbreaking research initiative on "Sustainable Economic Development," garnering commendation from the university.
- Published multiple insightful articles in peer-reviewed Economics journals, positively influencing the academic discourse.

- Mentored and guided a multitude of undergraduate and postgraduate research projects, nurturing a generation of skilled researchers.

Teaching Assistant Monash University, Melbourne, VIC | 02/2010 - 05/2013

- Collaborated seamlessly with senior faculty members, assisting in the delivery of engaging lectures and tutorials for a range of Economics courses.
- Provided adept support to students during dedicated office hours, addressing queries and elucidating complex concepts.
- Played an integral role in meticulously grading assignments and exams, offering timely, constructive feedback to enhance learning outcomes.

Education:

Master of Economics Monash University, Melbourne, VIC | Graduated: 2009 Bachelor of Commerce (Honours) - Economics Monash University, Melbourne, VIC | Graduated: 2008

Skills:

- Demonstrated expertise in advanced Economics theories, models, and empirical analysis.
- Proficiently designed and developed tailored curricula and engaging course structures.
- Possesses strong research and analytical acumen, evidenced by impactful research contributions.

- Communicate persuasively and present with finesse, enhancing comprehension and engagement.
- Pioneered innovative teaching methodologies, effectively integrating technology for optimal learning experiences.
- Collaborative team player, adept at fostering interdisciplinary cooperation.
- Utilise advanced data analysis techniques using statistical software (STATA, R).

Professional Memberships:

- Active participant and proud member of the esteemed Economic Society of Australia (ESA).
- Engaged member of the Australian Association for Research in Education (AARE).

References: Available upon request.

Create a Cover Letter for a Job Advertisement

Creating a **cover letter** and **addressing the performance criteria** of the job you are applying for can be a **time-consuming task**. ChatGPT can help to **write a cover letter** meeting all the **job requirements**.

Here is an **example ChatGPT prompt** for writing a **cover letter** for a job application.

ChatGPT Prompt Template:

> Write a **[tone 1]** and **[tone 2]** cover letter in **[number of words]** words long highlighting my qualifications, experiences, and skills for **[job title]** at **[company]** using my resume. **[paste your resume here]**.

Customised ChatGPT Prompt Created from the Template:

> **Write a [professional] and [persuasive] cover letter that is [150] words long highlighting my qualifications, experiences, and skills for [Senior Lecturer] at [UOW] using my resume. [paste your resume here]**

ChatGPT Video Output URL and QR Code:

https://tinyurl.com/Job-CoverLetter

ChatGPT Output:

[Your Name]

[Your Address]

[City, State, ZIP Code]

[Your Phone Number]

[Your Email Address]

[Date]

[Recipient's Name]

[Recipient's Title]

[University Name]

[University Address]

[City, State, ZIP Code]

Dear [Recipient's Name],

I am writing to express my strong interest in the Senior Lecturer position at the University of UOW, as advertised. With a decade of proven expertise and accomplishments in academia, I am excited about the prospect of contributing to the esteemed institution's academic excellence and further enhancing its reputation.

My extensive experience as an Assistant Lecturer of Economics at Monash University has equipped me with a deep understanding of effective pedagogy, curriculum development, and research. I have a track record of delivering engaging lectures and tutorials, implementing innovative teaching methodologies, and nurturing student growth. My dedication to mentorship, exemplified by receiving the "Excellence in Teaching" award thrice, underscores my commitment to student success.

Moreover, my research contributions, including published articles in peer-reviewed journals and successful grant-funded projects, demonstrate my ability to contribute to the university's academic discourse and research initiatives. My proficiency in curriculum design, data analysis, and collaboration enhances my potential to enrich the department's curriculum program development.

I am confident that my qualifications, skills, and dedication align well with the requirements of the Senior Lecturer. I look forward to the opportunity to discuss how my background can contribute to your institution's growth.

I eagerly await the chance to discuss my candidacy further.

Sincerely,

[Your Full Name]

Twenty Cover Letter Prompts

1. [**Draft a professional and confident cover letter**] in 150 words [**highlighting my qualifications, experiences, and skills**] for the [**Science Teacher position at XYZ University**] using my resume. **[Paste your resume here]**
2. [**Create a persuasive and approachable cover letter**] in 180 words [**showcasing my qualifications, experiences, and skills**] for the [**Senior Lecturer role at LMN College**] using my resume. **[Paste your resume here]**
3. [**Compose a friendly and goal-oriented cover letter**] in 170 words [**underscoring my qualifications, experiences, and skills**] for the [**Head Teacher position at Tamworth High School**] using my resume. **[Paste your resume here]**
4. [**Write a concise and determined cover letter**] in 160 words [**highlighting my qualifications, experiences, and skills**] for the [**Geography Teacher at DEF Middle School**] using my resume. **[Paste your resume here]**
5. [**Craft a dynamic and visionary cover letter**] in 190 words [**illuminating my qualifications, experiences, and skills**] for the [**Maths Teacher position at MNO College**] using my resume. **[Paste your resume here]**

6. [**Develop an engaging and innovative cover letter**] in 180 words [**showcasing my qualifications, experiences, and skills**] for the [**Economics Professor role at UVW University**] using my resume. **[Paste your resume here]**

7. [**Formulate a sincere and empathetic cover letter**] in 150 words [**emphasising my qualifications, experiences, and skills**] for the [**Clinical Nursing Teacher position at HealthFirst Hospital**] using my resume. **[Paste your resume here]**

8. [**Construct an organised and detail-oriented cover letter**] in 170 words [**highlighting my qualifications, experiences, and skills**] for the [**Sport Science Teacher role at GHI Primary School**] using my resume. **[Paste your resume here]**

9. [**Write a compelling and results-driven cover letter**] in 190 words [**showcasing my qualifications, experiences, and skills**] for the [**Social Science Teacher position at JKL Community College**] using my resume. **[Paste your resume here]**

10. **[Write a passionate and dedicated** cover **letter]** in 155 words **[outlining my qualifications, experiences, and skills]** for the **[Head of Environmental Science Department at GreenEarth Polytechnic]** using my resume. **[Paste your resume here]**

11. **[Draft an articulate and impactful cover letter]** in 175 words **[detailing my qualifications, experiences, and skills]** for the **[Criminal Law Teacher role at LawFirst College]** using my resume. **[Paste your resume here]**
12. **[Construct a vibrant and persuasive cover letter]** in 185 words [emphasising **my qualifications, experiences, and skills]** for the **[Marketing Teacher position at OnlineGrowth University]** using my resume. **[Paste your resume here]**
13. **[Compose a** strategic **and assertive cover letter]** in 160 words **[highlighting my qualifications, experiences, and skills]** for the **[Graphic Design Teacher position at GlobalTrade Business College]** using my resume. **[Paste your resume here]**
14. **[Design a proactive** and **forward-thinking cover letter] in 165 words [presenting my qualifications, experiences, and skills] for the [Data Science Teacher role at ABC Analytics] using my resume. [Paste your resume here]**
15. **[Craft a compelling and dynamic cover letter]** in 190 words **[underscoring my qualifications, experiences, and skills]** for the **[Software Engineering Teacher position at ABC Technology Institute]** using my resume. **[Paste your resume here]**
16. **[Compose a heartfelt and genuine cover letter]** in 160 words **[focusing on my qualifications,**

experiences, and skills] for the **[Pediatrician Teacher role at KidsCare College]** using my resume. **[Paste your resume here]**

17. **[Design a structured and meticulous cover letter]** in 175 words **[accentuating my qualifications, experiences, and skills]** for the **[Marketing Professor role at XYZ College]** using my resume. **[Paste your resume here]**

18. **[Craft a dedicated and assertive cover letter]** in 155 words **[emphasizing my qualifications, experiences, and skills]** for the **[Sustainability Teacher position at Genx Earth Community College]** using my resume. **[Paste your resume here]**

19. **[Formulate a genuine and impactful cover letter]** in 165 words **[detailing my qualifications, experiences, and skills]** for the **[Finance Teacher role at UVW Training Institute]** using my resume. **[Paste your resume here]**

20. **[Design a structured and engaging cover letter]** in 175 words **[focusing on my qualifications, experiences, and skills]** for the **[Business Teacher position at STU Business School]** using my resume. **[Paste your resume here]**

CHAPTER 17

BONUS 1165 CHATGPT CUSTOMISABLE PROMPTS

17. Bonus 1165 ChatGPT Customisable Prompts

This section includes **bonus ChatGPT prompt templates** for **easy access**. I have categorised the **prompt templates** to make it **quick for the readers** to be able to find and use them. You can choose to access and use them in any order you prefer.

I've also provided a **weblink and QR code** to facilitate the swift and straightforward downloading of **1165 ChatGPT prompts in PDF format**, categorised across twenty-four areas, ideal for educational and professional development purposes.

PDF Download Link for 1165 ChatGPT Prompts

Please find the weblink and QR code for downloading 1,165 ChatGPT prompts in PDF format for quick and easy access.

These teaching and learning prompts span across twenty-four different categories, including teaching, learning, and professional development.

PDF download link and QR code:

https://tinyurl.com/PromptsPDFDownload

Sixty Lesson Plan Prompts

You can **customise** the following prompts to create a **lesson plan** for your chosen **topic**, number of **sessions and cohort level**:

1. Develop a **[no. of weeks]**-week lesson plan that employs project-based learning to explore **[topic]** with **[teaching level]** students, divided into **[no. of subtopics]** project phases. Include **[no. of activities]** real-world problem-solving tasks and **[no. of learning outcomes]** project milestones to assess student progress.
2. Construct a **[no. of weeks]**-week lesson plan that utilises a Socratic seminar approach to delve into **[topic]** for **[teaching level]** students, broken down into **[no. of subtopics]** discussion themes. Incorporate **[no. of activities]** guided questions and **[no. of learning outcomes]** reflective essays to encourage critical dialogue.
3. Develop a **[no. of weeks]**-week lesson plan that leverages storytelling to introduce **[topic]** to **[teaching level]** students, segmented into **[no. of subtopics]** narrative arcs. Include **[no. of activities]** storyboarding exercises and **[no. of learning**

outcomes] character analyses to foster empathy and understanding.

4. Create a **[no. of weeks]**-week lesson plan that employs a case-study method to examine **[topic]** with **[teaching level]** students, divided into **[no. of subtopics]** real-world scenarios. Include **[no. of activities]** role-playing exercises and **[no. of learning outcomes]** case analyses to cultivate problem-solving skills.

5. Design a **[no. of weeks]**-week lesson plan that utilises a thematic approach to explore **[topic]** with **[teaching level]** students, broken down into **[no. of subtopics]** thematic units. Incorporate **[no. of activities]** interdisciplinary projects and **[no. of learning outcomes]** thematic assessments to encourage holistic learning.

6. Generate a **[no. of weeks]**-week lesson plan that employs a spiral curriculum to revisit **[topic]** with **[teaching level]** students, segmented into **[no. of subtopics]** learning cycles. Include **[no. of activities]** review quizzes and **[no. of learning outcomes]** cumulative assessments to reinforce learning.

7. Formulate a **[no. of weeks]**-week lesson plan that leverages a flipped mastery model to teach **[topic]** to **[teaching level]** students, divided into **[no. of subtopics]** mastery units. Include **[no. of activities]** self-paced assignments and **[no. of learning**

outcomes] mastery checks to foster student autonomy.

8. Craft a **[no. of weeks]**-week lesson plan that employs a station rotation model to cover **[topic]** with **[teaching level]** students, broken down into **[no. of subtopics]** learning stations. Incorporate **[no. of activities]** interactive kiosks and **[no. of learning outcomes]** station assessments to facilitate differentiated learning.
9. Devise a **[no. of weeks]**-week lesson plan that utilises a peer teaching model to explore **[topic]** with **[teaching level]** students, segmented into **[no. of subtopics]** peer-led units. Include **[no. of activities]** teaching scripts and **[no. of learning outcomes]** peer evaluations to foster collaborative learning.
10. Formulate a **[no. of weeks]**-week lesson plan that employs a microlearning approach to delve into **[topic]** for **[teaching level]** students, divided into **[no. of subtopics]** bite-sized modules. Include **[no. of activities]** quick quizzes and **[no. of learning outcomes]** micro-assessments to ensure rapid skill acquisition.
11. Create a **[number]**-week lesson plan for **[teaching level]** students on **[topic]**, covering **[number]** subtopics.

12. Design a lesson plan for **[teaching level]** students on **[topic]**, outlining **[number]** lessons and activities that build upon one another over **[number]** weeks.

13. Craft an engaging and effective lesson plan for **[teaching level]** students on **[topic]**, focused on deepening their understanding of **[number]** related concepts over **[number]** weeks.

14. Create a structured lesson plan for **[teaching level]** students on **[topic]**, with a particular emphasis on developing their critical thinking and problem-solving skills over **[number]** weeks.

15. Develop a lesson plan that allows **[teaching level]** students to explore the intricacies of **[topic]** in depth, building their knowledge and understanding over **[number]** weeks. Assemble an interactive **[no. of weeks]**-week syllabus that navigates **[topic]** for **[teaching level]** learners, featuring **[no of subtopics]** distinct areas of focus. Curate **[no of activities]** hands-on tasks and **[no of learning outcomes]** objectives to cultivate analytical abilities and skill mastery each week.

16. Construct an all-encompassing **[no. of weeks]**-week lesson plan that encompasses **[no. of subtopics]** facets of **[topic]** tailored for **[teaching level]** students. Integrate captivating exercises and quantifiable

weekly goals to deepen subject matter comprehension.

17. Draft an in-depth **[no. of weeks]**-week educational lesson plan that acquaints **[teaching level]** students with **[topic]** via **[no. of subtopics]** thematic units. Incorporate **[no. of activities]** experiential learning tasks and **[no. of learning outcomes]** weekly objectives to facilitate a rich and effective educational journey.
18. Devise a methodical **[no. of weeks]**-week lesson plan that investigates **[topic]** with **[teaching level]** students, dissecting it into **[no. of subtopics]** modules. Formulate **[no. of activities]** interactive exercises and **[no. of learning outcomes]** weekly targets aimed at enhancing cognitive skills and practical abilities.
19. Create a lively and stimulating **[no. of weeks]**-week educational lesson plan that scrutinises **[no. of subtopics]** elements of **[topic]** for **[teaching level]** students. Enumerate **[no. of activities]** participatory tasks and **[no. of learning outcomes]** weekly milestones to track and ensure student advancement.
20. Devise an exhaustive **[no. of weeks]**-week instructional lesson plan that probes into **[topic]** with **[teaching level]** students, segmented into **[no. of subtopics]** units. Embed **[no. of activities]** collaborative projects and **[no. of learning outcomes]**

weekly benchmarks to solidify foundational knowledge and skill sets.

21. Curate a **[no. of weeks]**-week lesson plan focussing on an immersive experience that uses virtual reality to explore **[topic]** with **[teaching level]** students, divided into **[no of subtopics]** interactive modules. Include **[no of activities]** VR-based tasks and **[no of learning outcomes]** real-world applications to sharpen critical thinking and skills.

22. Generate a **[no. of weeks]**-week lesson plan for a gamified course that turns **[topic]** into a series of challenges for **[teaching level]** students, featuring **[no. of subtopics]** game levels. Include **[no of activities]** in-game quests and **[no of learning outcomes]** achievement badges to measure and encourage learning.

23. Create a **[no. of weeks]**-week lesson plan focussed on a flipped classroom model that allows **[teaching level]** students to self-explore **[topic]** through **[no. of subtopics]** online modules. Include **[no. of activities]** peer-teaching assignments and **[no. of learning outcomes]** self-assessment tools to create an autonomous learning environment.

24. Develop a **[no. of weeks]**-week lesson plan about a podcast series that delves into **[topic]** with **[teaching level]** students, broken down into **[no. of subtopics]** episodes. Script **[no. of activities]** interactive listening

exercises and **[no. of learning outcomes]** discussion points for each episode to foster critical thinking and skill development.

25. Generate a **[no. of weeks]**-week lesson plan about the "Choose Your Own Adventure" course that allows **[teaching level]** students to select their path through **[no. of subtopics]** aspects of **[topic]**. Offer **[no. of activities]** decision-based scenarios and **[no. of learning outcomes]** branching outcomes to ensure personalised learning experiences.

26. Create a **[no. of weeks]**-week lesson plan for a cross-disciplinary project that integrates **[topic]** with other subjects like art or science for **[teaching level]** students, divided into **[no. of subtopics]** interdisciplinary units.

27. Create lesson plan with **[no. of activities]** collaborative cross-subject tasks and **[no. of learning outcomes]** holistic assessments to build a well-rounded understanding for **[no. of weeks]**-week immersive journey into **[topic]** for **[teaching level]** students, segmented into **[no of subtopics]** thematic clusters.

28. Develop **[no. of weeks]**-week lesson plan for a blended learning experience that traverses **[no. of subtopics]** dimensions of **[topic]**, tailored for **[teaching level]** students.

29. Generate a **[no. of weeks]**-week lesson plan for flipped classroom model that introduces **[teaching level]** students to **[topic]** through **[no. of subtopics]** lenses. Integrate **[no. of activities]** peer-led workshops and **[no. of learning outcomes]** weekly micro-goals to create a learner-centric environment.
30. Create a **[no. of weeks]**-week lesson plan for an experiential learning cycle that delves into **[topic]** with **[teaching level]** students, broken down into **[no. of subtopics]** learning stations. Incorporate **[no. of activities]** real-world challenges and **[no. of learning outcomes]** weekly success criteria to stimulate critical thinking and skill application.
31. Formulate a **[no. of weeks]**-week lesson plan for a modular course that dissects **[no. of subtopics]** facets of **[topic]** for **[teaching level]** students. Include **[no. of activities]** virtual field trips and **[no. of learning outcomes]** weekly reflective journals to monitor and assess student growth.
32. Produce a **[no. of weeks]**-week lesson plan on inquiry-based exploration that tackles **[topic]** with **[teaching level]** students, divided into **[no. of subtopics]** investigative units. Include **[no. of activities]** student-led research projects and **[no. of learning outcomes]** weekly self-assessments to foster autonomy and mastery.

33. Develop a **[number]**-week curriculum for **[teaching level]** learners focused on **[topic]**, segmented into **[number]** key areas.
34. Devise a pedagogical training plan for **[teaching level]** students centred around **[topic]**, featuring a sequence of **[number]** interconnected lessons spread over **[number]** weeks.
35. Produce a **[number]**-week teaching plan for **[teaching level]** students, focusing on **[topic]** and incorporating **[number]** interconnected lessons.
36. Curate a **[no. of weeks]**-week lesson plan that employs a self-directed learning model to explore **[topic]** with **[teaching level]** students, segmented into **[no. of subtopics]** learner-chosen units. Include **[no. of activities]** research projects and **[no. of learning outcomes]** self-assessment rubrics to foster student autonomy.
37. Design a **[no. of weeks]**-week lesson plan that utilises a team-based learning approach to delve into **[topic]** for **[teaching level]** students, broken down into **[no. of subtopics]** team challenges. Incorporate **[no. of activities]** team-building exercises and **[no. of learning outcomes]** team assessments to cultivate collaborative skills.
38. Generate a **[no. of weeks]**-week lesson plan that employs a concept mapping technique to introduce

[topic] to **[teaching level]** students, divided into **[no. of subtopics]** conceptual units. Include **[no. of activities]** mind-mapping tasks and **[no. of learning outcomes]** concept quizzes to enhance understanding.

39. Construct a **[no. of weeks]**-week lesson plan that leverages a service-learning approach to explore **[topic]** with **[teaching level]** students, segmented into **[no. of subtopics]** community projects. Include **[no. of activities]** volunteer opportunities and **[no. of learning outcomes]** reflective journals to encourage civic engagement.

40. Develop a **[no. of weeks]**-week lesson plan that utilises a debate format to examine **[topic]** with **[teaching level]** students, broken down into **[no. of subtopics]** debate topics. Incorporate **[no. of activities]** argumentation exercises and **[no. of learning outcomes]** debate assessments to foster critical thinking.

41. Create a **[no. of weeks]**-week lesson plan that employs a simulation model to teach **[topic]** to **[teaching level]** students, divided into **[no. of subtopics]** simulated scenarios. Include **[no. of activities]** role-playing games and **[no. of learning outcomes]** simulation debriefs to enhance experiential learning.

42. Formulate a **[no. of weeks]**-week lesson plan that leverages a problem-based learning approach to explore **[topic]** with **[teaching level]** students, segmented into **[no. of subtopics]** problem-solving units. Include **[no. of activities]** case studies and **[no. of learning outcomes]** problem-solving assessments to cultivate analytical skills.
43. Craft a **[no. of weeks]**-week lesson plan that utilises a jigsaw classroom model to delve into **[topic]** for **[teaching level]** students, broken down into **[no. of subtopics]** jigsaw pieces. Incorporate **[no. of activities]** group presentations and **[no. of learning outcomes]** peer assessments to foster cooperative learning.
44. Develop a **[no. of weeks]**-week lesson plan that employs a blended learning model to cover **[topic]** with **[teaching level]** students, divided into **[no. of subtopics]** online and in-person units. Include **[no. of activities]** digital assignments and **[no. of learning outcomes]** blended assessments to facilitate flexible learning.
45. Curate a **[no. of weeks]**-week lesson plan that leverages a scaffolding approach to introduce **[topic]** to **[teaching level]** students, segmented into **[no. of subtopics]** scaffolded units. Include **[no. of activities]** guided practice and **[no. of learning outcomes]**

independent tasks to ensure gradual skill development.

46. Design a **[no. of weeks]**-week lesson plan that utilises a storytelling approach to explore **[topic]** with **[teaching level]** students, divided into **[no. of subtopics]** narrative arcs. Include **[no. of activities]** storyboarding tasks and **[no. of learning outcomes]** narrative assessments to foster creative thinking.

47. Generate a **[no. of weeks]**-week lesson plan that employs a case study method to delve into **[topic]** for **[teaching level]** students, broken down into **[no. of subtopics]** case scenarios. Incorporate **[no. of activities]** case analyses and **[no. of learning outcomes]** case evaluations to cultivate analytical skills.

48. Create a **[no. of weeks]**-week lesson plan that leverages a thematic approach to introduce **[topic]** to **[teaching level]** students, segmented into **[no. of subtopics]** thematic units. Include **[no. of activities]** thematic projects and **[no. of learning outcomes]** thematic assessments to encourage interdisciplinary learning.

49. Formulate a **[no. of weeks]**-week lesson plan that utilises a peer teaching model to explore **[topic]** with **[teaching level]** students, divided into **[no. of subtopics]** peer-led sessions. Include **[no. of activities]** peer evaluations and **[no. of learning**

outcomes] peer feedback to foster collaborative learning.

50. Construct a **[no. of weeks]**-week lesson plan that employs a flipped mastery model to delve into **[topic]** for **[teaching level]** students, broken down into **[no. of subtopics]** mastery units. Incorporate **[no. of activities]** mastery quizzes and **[no. of learning outcomes]** mastery checkpoints to ensure individualised learning.

51. Develop a **[no. of weeks]**-week lesson plan that leverages a project-based learning approach to introduce **[topic]** to **[teaching level]** students, segmented into **[no. of subtopics]** project phases. Include **[no. of activities]** project milestones and **[no. of learning outcomes]** project evaluations to cultivate real-world skills.

52. Craft a **[no. of weeks]**-week lesson plan that utilises a station rotation model to explore **[topic]** with **[teaching level]** students, divided into **[no. of subtopics]** learning stations. Include **[no. of activities]** station tasks and **[no. of learning outcomes]** station assessments to facilitate differentiated instruction.

53. Create a **[no. of weeks]**-week lesson plan that employs a microlearning approach to delve into **[topic]** for **[teaching level]** students, broken down into **[no. of subtopics]** micro-lessons. Incorporate **[no. of activities]** micro-assessments and **[no. of**

learning outcomes] micro-goals to ensure focused learning.

54. Make a **[no. of weeks]**-week lesson plan that leverages a dialogue circle method to introduce **[topic]** to **[teaching level]** students, segmented into **[no. of subtopics]** dialogue sessions. Include **[no. of activities]** dialogue prompts and **[no. of learning outcomes]** dialogue reflections to foster social-emotional learning.

55. Produce a **[no. of weeks]**-week lesson plan that utilises a role-playing approach to explore **[topic]** with **[teaching level]** students, divided into **[no. of subtopics]** role scenarios. Include **[no. of activities]** role evaluations and **[no. of learning outcomes]** role reflections to encourage empathy and perspective-taking.

56. Construct a **[no. of weeks]**-week lesson plan that leverages a concept mapping technique to introduce **[topic]** to **[teaching level]** students, segmented into **[no. of subtopics]** concept nodes. Include **[no. of activities]** concept exercises and **[no. of learning outcomes]** concept evaluations to encourage conceptual understanding.

57. Develop a **[no. of weeks]**-week lesson plan that utilises a simulation model to explore **[topic]** with **[teaching level]** students, divided into **[no. of subtopics]** simulation scenarios. Include **[no. of**

activities] simulation tasks and **[no. of learning outcomes]** simulation assessments to facilitate experiential learning.

58. Craft a **[no. of weeks]**-week lesson plan that employs a problem-based learning approach to delve into **[topic]** for **[teaching level]** students, broken down into **[no. of subtopics]** problem sets. Incorporate **[no. of activities]** problem-solving tasks and **[no. of learning outcomes]** problem evaluations to cultivate problem-solving skills.
59. Make a **[no. of weeks]**-week lesson plan that leverages a team-based learning model to introduce **[topic]** to **[teaching level]** students, segmented into **[no. of subtopics]** team challenges. Include **[no. of activities]** team tasks and **[no. of learning outcomes]** team assessments to foster teamwork and collaboration.
60. Produce a **[no. of weeks]**-week lesson plan that employs a flipped mastery model to delve into **[topic]** for **[teaching level]** students, broken down into **[no. of subtopics]** mastery units. Incorporate **[no. of activities]** mastery quizzes and **[no. of learning outcomes]** mastery checkpoints to ensure individualised learning.

Sixty Assessment Activity Prompts

Here are some **assessment prompts** that can be customised for creating **various types of assessment** activities:

1. Design a quiz featuring **20 crossword puzzles** that test knowledge on **[your chosen topic]**, providing hints for each clue.
2. Develop a quiz with **15 questions** where students must identify different terms related to **[topic of your choice]**.
3. Generate a quiz containing **20 questions** that require students to interpret terminologies related to **[topic of your choice]**.
4. Produce a quiz that includes **25 Likert scale questions** to gauge students' attitudes or perceptions about **[topic of your choice]**.
5. Compose a quiz featuring **30 vocabulary questions** that test student's understanding of key terms related to **[topic of your choice]**.
6. Compose a quiz with **20 calculation questions** that require students to solve mathematical problems based on **[topic of your choice]**.
7. Create a quiz containing **15 code snippet questions** that test students' ability to read or write code related to **[topic of your choice]**.

8. Build a quiz that includes **20 role-play questions** where students must respond to simulated scenarios related to **[topic of your choice]**.
9. Create a quiz featuring **25 debate questions** that ask students to argue for or against a statement related to **[topic you select]**.
10. Curate a test with **20 analogy questions** that require students to identify relationships between concepts related to **[topic you select]**.
11. Construct a test featuring **15 classification questions** that ask students to categorise items based on certain criteria related to **[topic you select]**.
12. Devise a test with **30 error identification questions** that ask students to find and correct mistakes in a given text related to **[topic you select]**.
13. Generate an assessment with **20 priority ranking questions** that require students to rank items in order of importance, based on **[topic you select]**.
14. Produce an assessment featuring **25 situational judgement questions** that test students' decision-making skills in scenarios related to **[your chosen subject]**.
15. Compose an exam with **20 ethical dilemma questions** that challenge students to consider moral implications related to **[your preferred topic]**.
16. Formulate a quiz featuring 15 multiple-choice queries centred around **[your chosen topic]**.
17. Develop a quiz containing 20 true-or-false questions based on **[topic of your choice]**.

18. Generate a quiz with 25 fill-in-the-blank questions that explore **[topic of your choice]**.
19. Produce a quiz that includes 25 short-answer questions delving into **[topic of your choice]**.
20. Compose a quiz with 30 multiple-choice questions derived from the following text: **[paste the content here]**.
21. Assemble a quiz featuring 35 true-or-false questions inspired by the following content: **[paste the content here]**.
22. Create a quiz with 40 fill-in-the-blank questions that are based on this material: **[paste the content here]**.
23. Build a quiz with 20 short-answer questions that are based on the following content: **[paste the content here]**.
24. Formulate a test that offers 10 multiple-choice items related to **[topic you select]**.
25. Design a test with 35 yes-or-no questions that focus on **[topic you select]**.
26. Curate a test with 25 sentence-completion questions that cover **[topic you select]**.
27. Create a test with 10 brief-response questions that examine **[topic you select]**.
28. Develop a test with 10 multiple-choice items using this source material: **[insert the material here]**.
29. Formulate a test with 15 yes-or-no questions that are based on the following material: **[insert the material here]**.

30. Construct a test with 40 sentence-completion questions based on this material: **[insert the material here]**.
31. Devise a test with 30 brief-response questions that utilise the following material: **[insert the material here]**.
32. Create an assessment featuring 20 fill-in-the-blank tasks that reference this material: **[insert the material here]**.
33. Develop an assessment with 20 concise-answer tasks that are based on the following content: **[insert the material here]**.
34. Generate a quiz that includes 10 option-based questions on **[your chosen subject]**.
35. Produce a quiz with 45 true-false questions that delve into **[your chosen subject]**.
36. Compose a quiz featuring 25 sentence-completion tasks that explore **[your chosen subject]**.
37. Assemble a quiz with 25 succinct replies to challenges that focus on **[your chosen subject]**.
38. Draft an exam that offers 30 sentence-finishing tasks related to **[your preferred topic]**.
39. Design an exam with 10 short-answer segments that cover **[your preferred topic]**.
40. Curate an exam with 40 selection-based queries using this content: **[provide the content here]**.
41. Develop a quiz featuring **20 match the following questions** that explore **[your chosen topic].**

42. Produce a quiz containing **15 questions** that allow students to identify correct synonyms related to **[topic of your choice]**.
43. Formulate a quiz with **20 matching questions** that challenge students to pair terms with definitions based on **[topic of your choice]**.
44. Design a quiz that includes **30 scenario-based questions** that simulate real-world situations related to **[topic of your choice]**.
45. Generate a quiz with **25 ranking questions** that ask students to order items according to specific criteria in the context of **[topic of your choice]**.
46. Produce a quiz featuring **20 multiple-response questions** that allow for more than one correct answer, based on the following content: **[paste the content here]**.
47. Develop a quiz with **15 sequence questions** that require students to place events in the correct order, inspired by the following content: **[paste the content here]**.
48. Create a quiz containing **10 antonym questions** based on this material: **[paste the content here]**.
49. Build a quiz that includes **20 multiple-choice questions** and **10 true-false questions** based on the following content: **[paste the content here]**.
50. Create a quiz featuring **15 true-or-false questions** that incorporate real-world scenarios related to **[topic you select]**.

51. Curate a test with **20 case study questions** that delve into real or hypothetical scenarios related to **[topic you select]**.
52. Construct a test featuring **25 multiple-choice questions** that cover **[topic you select]**, using this source material: **[insert the material here]**.
53. Compose a **quiz featuring 10 questions** that require short essay answers, focusing on **[topic you select]**.
54. Generate an assessment with **20 close questions** that require students to fill in missing words from a passage, referencing this material: **[insert the material here]**.
55. Produce an assessment featuring **15 short answer questions** and **20 long answer questions** related to **[your chosen subject]**.
56. Formulate a test that includes **5 case study questions** and **10 multiple-choice questions**, centred on **[topic you select]**.
57. Design an exam that includes **30 simulation based questions** where students must make decisions based on **[your preferred topic]**.
58. Create an exam with **25 long-answer questions** that require detailed responses, using this content: **[provide the content here]**.
59. Draft an exam that offers **20 multiple-choice questions** with feedback explanations for each answer choice related to **[your preferred topic]**.

60. Formulate an exam with **15 true-or-false questions** that provide immediate feedback, using this content: **[provide the content here]**.

Seventy Brainstorming and Research Prompts

Here are some **prompts** that can be **further customised for either brainstorming** or **researching** using ChatGPT:

1. Can you formulate a set of questions that delve into the **[socio-economic impacts]** of **[topic]** on **[vulnerable communities]**?
2. Could you generate a list of questions that explore the role of **[topic 1]** in accelerating **[topic 2]**?
3. Can you suggest various **[perspectives]** from which to examine the **[ethical implications]** of **[artificial intelligence]**?
4. Could you recommend different **[lenses]** through which to study the **[impact]** of **[topic]** on **[job displacement]**?

5. Can you compile a list of **[keywords and phrases]** that focus on the **[technological advancements]** in **[topic]**?
6. Could you generate a set of **[keywords and phrases]** that can be used to research the **[policy implications]** of transitioning to **[topic]**?
7. Can you provide a curated list of **[primary source documents]** that offer insights into the **[diplomatic relations]** during **[World War II]**?
8. Could you suggest some **[scholarly articles]** that discuss the **[role of women]** in **[topic]**?
9. Can you identify some **[subtopics]** within **[artificial intelligence]** that focus on its **[application in the area]**?
10. Could you suggest some **[subtopics]** that explore the **[limitations and challenges]** of implementing **[artificial intelligence]** in **[legal systems]**?
11. Would you recommend various **[approaches]** for examining the **[effects]** of **[topic 1]** on **[topic 2]**?
12. Can you assemble a collection of **[key terms and expressions]** centred on the **[innovations]** in **[renewable energy storage]**?
13. Could you produce a list of **[search terms and phrases]** useful for studying the **[regulatory consequences]** of moving towards **[industry type]**?

14. Can you pinpoint specific **[areas of study]** within **[major topic]** that are relevant to **[subtopic]**?
15. Would you propose some **[focused topics]** that look into the **[barriers and issues]** of using **[artificial intelligence]** in **[judicial systems]**?
16. Could you list some **[specific areas]** in **[field of study or technology]** that are geared towards **[specific application or industry]**?
17. Would you identify a few **[focused themes]** that discuss the **[obstacles and complexities]** of integrating **[technology or methodology]** into **[industry or system]**?
18. Can you suggest different **[methodologies]** to investigate the **[ramifications]** of **[technology or phenomenon]** on **[specific impact area]**?
19. Would you compile an assortment of **[relevant words and phrases]** that highlight **[breakthroughs or innovations]** in **[field or technology]**?
20. Could you assemble a set of **[research keywords and idioms]** that are pertinent for understanding the **[policy outcomes or implications]** of adopting **[technology or practice]**?
21. Can you put together a compilation of **[primary literature or source type]** that provides insights into **[specific aspect]** during **[historical event or period]**?

22. Could you recommend **[books or publications]** that offer a deep dive into the **[cultural aspects]** of **[specific community or region]**?
23. Can you identify **[key debates or controversies]** within the field of **[academic discipline or industry]**?
24. Would you suggest **[strategies or techniques]** for analysing the **[environmental impact]** of **[specific technology or industry]**?
25. Can you provide a list of **[experts or thought leaders]** who are influential in the field of **[specific subject or industry]**?
26. Could you compile **[case studies or examples]** that illustrate the **[success or failure]** of **[particular initiatives or projects]**?
27. Would you assemble a set of **[statistical data or metrics]** that can help evaluate the **[performance or effectiveness]** of **[specific program or policy]**?
28. Can you curate a collection of **[artworks or literary pieces]** that reflect the **[cultural or social themes]** of a **[specific era or movement]**?
29. Could you generate a list of **[questions or topics]** for a panel discussion on the **[ethical or moral dilemmas]** in **[specific field or situation]**?

30. Would you identify **[software tools or platforms]** that are essential for **[specific task or project]** in **[industry or field of study]**?

31. Can you suggest **[courses or training programs]** that can enhance skills in **[specific area or discipline]**?

32. Could you recommend **[podcasts or webinars]** that focus on **[emerging trends]** in **[specific industry or field]**?

33. Can you list **[best practices or guidelines]** for achieving **[specific goals or outcomes]** in **[particular setting or industry]**?

34. Would you suggest **[innovative methods or tools]** for **[data collection or analysis]** in **[research area or project]**?

35. Can you identify **[key performance indicators (KPIs)]** that are crucial for **[business or project success]** in **[specific industry]**?

36. Could you compile a set of **[interview questions or prompts]** that can help assess **[skills or competencies]** for a **[job role or position]**?

37. Would you assemble a list of **[resources or materials]** that can aid in **[self-study or professional development]** in **[specific subject or skill]**?

38. Can you curate a selection of **[films or documentaries]** that offer insights into **[social issues or historical events]**?
39. Could you generate **[survey questions or metrics]** that can measure **[customer satisfaction or user experience]** for a **[product or service]**?
40. Would you identify **[networking opportunities or events]** that are beneficial for professionals in **[specific field or industry]**?
41. Can you suggest **[investment opportunities or strategies]** for growing **[personal or business finances]**?
42. Could you recommend **[mobile apps or software]** that can improve **[productivity or well-being]** in a **[work or personal setting]**?
43. Can you provide **[sample projects or portfolios]** that demonstrate **[expertise or creativity]** in **[specific field or medium]**?
44. Could you generate **[discussion topics or themes]** for a **[workshop or seminar]** focused on **[specific issue or skill development]**?
45. Would you list **[websites or online platforms]** that offer **[credible information or resources]** on **[specific subject or industry]**?

46. Can you suggest **[volunteer opportunities or internships]** that provide experience in **[specific field or role]**?
47. Could you recommend **[travel destinations or cultural experiences]** that offer insights into **[specific culture or history]**?
48. Would you identify **[grants or scholarships]** that can support **[educational or research pursuits]** in **[specific field or subject]**?
49. Can you compile **[exercise routines or wellness practices]** that contribute to **[specific health goals or well-being]**?
50. Can you recommend **[blogs or vlogs]** that offer **[tips or tutorials]** on **[specific skill or interest area]**?
51. Could you curate a bibliography of **[academic papers or articles]** that delve into the **[psychological aspects]** of **[specific behaviour or phenomenon]**?
52. Would you assemble a list of **[online courses]** that are beneficial for **[career advancement]** in **[specific industry]**?
53. Can you identify **[key historical events or milestones]** that have shaped the **[current landscape]** of **[specific field or discipline]**?

54. Could you suggest **[simulation software or tools]** that are crucial for **[research or experimentation]** in **[specific scientific field]**?

55. Would you compile a set of **[ethical guidelines or principles]** that are generally accepted in the field of **[specific discipline or industry]**?

56. Can you recommend **[conferences or symposiums]** that are must-attend events for professionals in **[specific field or industry]**?

57. Could you generate a list of **[textbooks or reference materials]** that are considered foundational in **[specific academic subject]**?

58. Would you identify **[peer-reviewed journals or publications]** that are reputable sources for research in **[specific field or subject]**?

59. Can you curate a selection of **[YouTube channels or educational platforms]** that offer quality content on **[specific subject or skill]**?

60. Could you suggest **[mentorship programs or career advisors]** that can guide **[specific career path or industry]**?

61. Would you compile a list of **[certifications or accreditations]** that are recognised in **[specific industry or field]**?

62. Can you recommend **[workshops or bootcamps]** that offer intensive training in **[specific skill or technique]**?

63. Could you identify **[awards or accolades]** that are prestigious in the field of **[specific discipline or industry]**?

64. Would you suggest **[crowdfunding platforms or investors]** that are known for supporting **[innovative projects or startups]** in **[specific field]**?

65. Can you compile a list of **[social media influencers or thought leaders]** who are shaping public opinion in **[specific subject or industry]**?

66. Could you recommend **[online forums or communities]** where professionals in **[specific field]** can exchange ideas and knowledge?

67. Would you identify **[research grants or funding opportunities]** that are available for **[specific type of research or project]**?

68. Can you suggest **[internship programs or entry-level positions]** that offer valuable experience in **[specific industry or field]**?

69. Could you compile a list of **[essential readings or literature]** that provide a comprehensive understanding of **[specific topic or issue]**?

70. Would you recommend **[podcast episodes or radio shows]** that discuss **[current trends or developments]** in **[specific field or industry]**?

Sixty Conversational Prompts

Here are sixty **conversational ChatGPT prompt templates** that can help you create your own customised conversational prompts to **stimulate engaging** and **thought-provoking** conversations:

1. What **[traits or principles]** do you value in a **[companion or life partner]**? Discuss a meaningful **[bond or connection]** you've had and its influence on you.
2. What **[food style or dish]** do you relish the most? Ever tried an unusual or foreign **[meal]**? What was it like?
3. How do you feel about **[recent news or developments]**? What actions do you think could bring about positive change for this **[concern]**?

4. What **[gadget or application]** can you not live without? How has it enriched your daily life? Any reservations about **[technology's]** societal role?
5. What's your go-to **[entertainment source or platform]**? Could you share a recent pick? How do you think **[this entertainment medium]** influences public opinion?
6. What's your top **[athletic pursuit or game]**, and what attracts you to it? Ever been to a live **[match or competition]**? Share your impressions.
7. What **[worldview or ethical stance]** guides you? How has it changed over time? How do you derive **[significance]** or **[direction]** in your existence?
8. How would you define your **[aesthetic or fashion choices]**? Describe a **[garment or adornment]** that epitomises your style. What's your take on the **[fashion sector]** and its societal implications?
9. Are you into **[artistic creation or appreciation]**? What **[form or genre]** resonates with you? Discuss a memorable **[art piece]** and its significance to you.
10. What **[scientific theory or breakthrough]** do you find most compelling? Could you break down its scientific basis? How does **[science]** shape societal norms?
11. How do you navigate your **[individual hurdle or subject matter]**? What are your viewpoints on

[associated themes or issues]? Do you have **[concrete objectives or strategies]** for tackling this **[obstacle or subject]** in the future?

12. What's your perspective on **[online learning or e-learning platforms]**? Have you had any standout experiences? How do you think **[this mode of education]** is reshaping traditional classrooms?
13. What **[academic subject or course]** has had a lasting impact on you? Could you share a **[concept or theory]** that you found enlightening? How do you think **[this subject]** prepares students for real-world challenges?
14. What **[extracurricular activity or club]** do you find most enriching? Can you recommend a **[project or event]** you've been part of? How does **[this activity]** complement academic learning?
15. What **[study techniques or learning hacks]** do you employ for effective learning? Can you share a **[tip or strategy]**? How do you think **[these techniques]** enhance educational outcomes?
16. What **[educational podcast or YouTube channel]** do you find beneficial? Could you recommend a **[specific episode or video]**? How does **[this medium]** supplement traditional learning?
17. What **[educational technology or tool]** do you wish was more widely used? How would it address a

current **[educational gap or challenge]**? What steps could schools take to implement it?

18. What **[historical figure or author]** should be more widely taught in schools? Why? How would their inclusion enrich **[cultural or historical understanding]**?

19. What **[ethical or civic topics]** do you think should be included in the curriculum? How would these topics prepare students for **[citizenship and community engagement]**?

20. What **[game or interactive educational software]** do you find most instructive? How does it make learning **[fun or engaging]**? What does it teach about **[cognitive skills or problem-solving]**?

21. What **[foreign language or cultural studies]** do you think should be mandatory? How would it broaden students' **[worldview or employability]**?

22. What **[financial literacy or life skills]** topics are missing from the current curriculum? How would their inclusion better prepare students for **[adulthood or financial independence]**?

23. What **[artistic medium or creative outlet]** do you think enhances cognitive development? Could you share an **[art project or performance]** that was particularly impactful?

24. What **[scientific experiment or field trip]** had a lasting impression on you? How did it deepen your understanding of **[science and its real-world applications]**?

25. What **[debate topic or critical thinking exercise]** do you find most stimulating? How does it challenge your **[assumptions or viewpoints]**? What skills does it help develop? What **[language learning app or platform]** do you find most effective? Can you share a **[feature or exercise]** that has helped you the most?

26. How do you feel about **[immersion techniques]** for language learning? Have you ever tried a **[language immersion program]**? What was your experience?

27. What **[grammar rule or language structure]** did you find most challenging to grasp? How did you finally **[understand or master]** it?

28. What **[cultural nuances or idioms]** in your target language intrigued you the most? How do you think understanding these adds depth to your **[language proficiency]**?

29. What **[listening exercises or audio resources]** do you use to improve your comprehension skills? Can you recommend a **[podcast or audiobook]** in your target language?

30. What **[writing exercises or platforms]** do you find beneficial for improving your language skills? Have you tried **[language exchange or pen-pal programs]**?

31. What **[flashcard system or memory technique]** do you find most effective for vocabulary building? How has it improved your **[speaking or writing skills]**?

32. How do you tackle **[pronunciation or accent challenges]** in your target language? Have you used any **[tools or methods]** that you found particularly helpful?

33. What **[language learning community or forum]** do you participate in? How has the **[community]** helped you overcome challenges?

34. What **[real-world scenarios or role-playing exercises]** do you find most useful for practising your language skills? How do these **[scenarios]** prepare you for actual conversations?

35. What **[reading materials, such as books or articles]**, do you find most beneficial for language learning? Can you recommend a **[must-read]** in your target language?

36. What **[language learning challenges or competitions]** have you participated in? How did they **[motivate or accelerate]** your learning?

37. What **[language learning myths or misconceptions]** did you have before starting? How have your views **[changed or evolved]**?
38. How do you integrate **[language learning into your daily routine]**? Do you have any **[habits or rituals]** that make learning more seamless?
39. What **[career opportunities or personal growth]** do you see as a result of learning a new language? How has language learning **[impacted your worldview or interpersonal skills]**? What **[scientific theory or principle]** do you find most captivating?
40. Can you share a **[real-world application or experiment]** that demonstrates its significance?
41. How do you view the role of **[ethics in scientific research]**? Can you cite an example where **[ethical considerations]** had a major impact on a **[study or discovery]**?
42. What **[recent scientific breakthrough]** has caught your attention? How do you think it will **[affect society or the environment]** in the long run?
43. What **[science podcast or YouTube channel]** do you find most enlightening? Could you recommend a **[specific episode or video]** that deepened your understanding of a scientific topic?
44. What **[data analysis techniques or statistical methods]** do you find most useful in interpreting

scientific results? Can you share a **[case study or research paper]** that employed these methods effectively?

45. What **[laboratory techniques or experimental setups]** do you find most intriguing? Have you ever conducted a **[lab experiment]** that yielded surprising results?
46. What **[scientific instrument or technology]** do you wish was more accessible for research? How would it solve a current **[scientific challenge or limitation]**?
47. What **[historical scientist or researcher]** do you think deserves more recognition? How has their work contributed to **[modern scientific understanding]**?
48. What **[environmental or conservation issues]** do you think should be prioritised in scientific research? How could science help in **[mitigating or solving]** these issues?
49. What **[science fiction concept or technology]** do you wish were real? How would it **[change our lives or solve a current problem]**?
50. What **[citizen science project or community-driven research]** have you participated in or would like to? How does it contribute to **[scientific knowledge or public awareness]**?

51. What **[interdisciplinary approaches, like bioinformatics or neuroeconomics]**, do you find most promising for future scientific research? Can you cite a **[study or project]** that successfully employed such an approach?
52. What **[ethical or philosophical questions]** do you think science alone cannot answer? How should these be addressed in **[research or public discourse]**?
53. What **[science education initiative or outreach program]** do you admire? How does it **[promote scientific literacy or engage the public]**?
54. What **[scientific mystery or unanswered question]** do you hope will be solved in your lifetime? What would be the **[implications or applications]** of solving it?
55. What **[nursing software or electronic health record system]** do you wish was more user-friendly? How would that improve **[documentation or patient management]**?
56. What **[historical nurse or healthcare provider]** do you think deserves more recognition? How has their work shaped **[modern nursing practices]**?
57. What **[public health issues or community care]** do you think should be a focus in nursing education? How could this **[enhance healthcare outcomes or social awareness]**?

58. What **[simulation training or hands-on exercises]** do you find most beneficial for nursing students? How do these **[prepare them for real-world challenges]**?

59. What **[mentorship program or professional development]** opportunities have you found most rewarding? How have these **[advanced your career or skill set]**?

60. What **[interdisciplinary collaboration, such as with doctors or social workers]**, do you find most effective in-patient care? Can you cite a **[successful case or outcome]**?

One Hundred Multilingual Translation Prompts

Here are some prompts to **inspire translation ideas** beneficial for both **language learners** and **instructors**:

1. Can you **[interpret]** this **[Source Language]** idiom into **[Target Language]**? **[Idiom to Interpret]**
2. **[Adapt]** this **[Source Language]** joke into **[Target Language]** while keeping its humour intact: **[Joke to Adapt]**
3. **[Localise]** this **[Source Language]** website content into **[Target Language]**: **[Website Content to Localise]**
4. **[Translate]** this **[Source Language]** advertising slogan into **[Target Language]**: **[Slogan to Transcreate]**
5. **[Rephrase]** this **[Source Language]** technical manual into **[Target Language]** using simpler terms: **[Technical Manual to Rephrase]**
6. **[Summarise]** this **[Source Language]** academic paper into a **[Target Language]** abstract: **[Academic Paper to Summarise]**

7. **[Annotate]** this **[Source Language]** religious text with **[Target Language]** footnotes: **[Religious Text to Annotate]**

8. **[Mirror-translate]** this **[Source Language]** palindrome into a **[Target Language]** palindrome: **[Palindrome to Mirror-Translate]**

9. **[Adapt]** this **[Source Language]** children's story into **[Target Language]**, making it culturally relevant: **[Children's Story to Adapt]**

10. **[Rework]** this **[Source Language]** poem into **[Target Language]**, using a different poetic form: **[Poem to Rework]**

11. **[Transmute]** this **[Source Language]** scientific article into **[Target Language]** layman's terms: **[Scientific Article to Transmute]**

12. **[Translate]** this **[Source Language]** classical text into **[Target Language]**, maintaining its archaic tone: **[Classical Text to Translate]**

13. **[Translate]** this **[Source Language]** fairy tale into **[Target Language]**, adding modern elements: **[Fairy Tale to Translate]**

14. **[Translate]** this **[Source Language]** epic into **[Target Language]**, altering its narrative style: **[Epic to Translate]**

15. **[Convert]** this **[Source Language]** philosophical text into **[Target Language]**, preserving its complex ideas: **[Philosophical Text to Convert]**
16. **[Translate]** this **[Source Language]** screenplay into **[Target Language]**, adapting its cultural references: **[Screenplay to Translate]**
17. **[Adapt]** this **[Source Language]** gardening guide into **[Target Language]**, considering local flora: **[Gardening Guide to Adapt]**
18. **[Convert]** this **[Source Language]** nautical manual into **[Target Language]**, keeping maritime terms intact: **[Nautical Manual to Convert]**
19. **[Translate]** this **[Source Language]** travel guide into **[Target Language]**, updating place names and attractions: **[Travel Guide to Translate]**
20. Reinterpret the following sentence from **[Source Language]** to **[Target Language]**: **[Sentence to Reinterpret]**
21. Provide a **[Target Language]** rendition of this phrase: **[Phrase to Rendition]**
22. Translate this paragraph from **[Source Language]** into **[Target Language]**: **[Paragraph to Translate]**
23. Adapt this **[Source Language]** cooking guide into **[Target Language]**: **[Cooking Guide to Adapt]**

24. Maintain the artistic elements and translate this **[Source Language]** poem into **[Target Language]**
25. Please offer a **[Target Language]** version of this sentence: **[Sentence to Version]**
26. Translate this dialogue from **[Source Language]** into **[Target Language]**: **[Dialogue to Translate]**
27. Convert this famous quote from **[Source Language]** into **[Target Language]**: **[Quote to Render]**
28. Adapt this **[Source Language]** haiku into a **[Target Language]** form: **[Haiku to Adapt]**
29. Transform these **[Source Language]** song lyrics into **[Target Language]**: **[Lyrics to Transform]**
30. Make this **[Source Language]** news report more globally accessible by translating it into **[Target Language]**.
31. Can you translate this **[Source Language]** narrative into **[Target Language]**, preserving its cultural subtleties?
32. Can you reword this well-known **[Source Language]** expression in **[Target Language]**? **[Expression to Reword]**
33. Retain the essence while translating this **[Source Language]** poem into **[Target Language]**.

34. Convert this phrase in **[Target Language]**: **[Phrase to Convert]**
35. Can you translate this **[Source Language]** recipe into **[Target Language]**? **[Recipe to Translate]**
36. Translate this **[Source Language]** traditional tune into **[Target Language]**, keeping its cultural richness.
37. Adapt this **[Source Language]** food formula into **[Target Language]**: **[Food Formula to Adapt]**
38. Translate while capturing the essence and charm of this **[Source Language]** epic in **[Target Language]**.
39. Convey this **[Source Language]** folk melody into **[Target Language]**, retaining its heritage.
40. Translate this **[Source Language]** limerick into **[Target Language]**, keeping its whimsical nature.
41. Transform this **[Source Language]** exchange of words into **[Target Language]**: **[Exchange of Words to Transform]**
42. Summarise this **[Source Language]** article in a paragraph using **[Target Language]**: **[Article to Summarise]**
43. Adapt this **[Source Language]** fable into a **[Target Language]** short story: **[Fable to Adapt]**
44. Translate this **[Source Language]** text with **[Target Language]** explanations: **[Text to Translate]**

45. Rephrase this **[Source Language]** sentence using **[Target Language]** synonyms: **[Sentence to Rephrase]**
46. Adapt this **[Source Language]** dialogue into **[Target Language]**: **[Dialogue to Adapt]**
47. Translate this **[Source Language]** text into **[Target Language]**, providing cultural context: **[Text to Translate]**
48. Compose a **[Target Language]** poem inspired by this **[Source Language]** poem: **[Poem to Inspire]**
49. Narrate this **[Source Language]** children's book in **[Target Language]**: **[Book to Narrate]**
50. Translate this **[Source Language]** cipher into **[Target Language]**: **[Cipher to Translate]**
51. Translate this **[Source Language]** text into **[Target Language]** script: **[Text to Translate]**
52. Paraphrase this **[Source Language]** passage in **[Target Language]**: **[Passage to Paraphrase]**
53. Rewrite this **[Source Language]** instruction manual into **[Target Language]**: **[Manual to Rewrite]**
54. Recreate this **[Source Language]** comic strip in **[Target Language]**: **[Comic Strip to Recreate]**

55. Translate this **[Source Language]** website into **[Target Language]**: **[Website to Translate]**
56. Provide a **[Target Language]** translation for the **[Source Language]** country name: **[Country Name to Translate]**
57. Convert this **[Source Language]** geographical description into **[Target Language]**: **[Description to Convert]**
58. Can you translate this **[Source Language]** idiom related to geography into **[Target Language]**? **[Idiom to Translate]**
59. Please translate this **[Source Language]** travel itinerary into **[Target Language]**: **[Itinerary to Translate]**
60. Translate this **[Source Language]** poem about a famous landmark into **[Target Language]** while preserving its rhyme and rhythm.
61. Provide a **[Target Language]** translation for the **[Source Language]** weather report: **[Weather Report to Translate]**
62. Convert this **[Source Language]** dialogue about a geographical expedition into **[Target Language]**: **[Dialogue to Convert]**
63. Can you translate this **[Source Language]** quote about nature into **[Target Language]**? **[Quote to Translate]**

64. Please translate this **[Source Language]** song lyrics about a city into **[Target Language]**: **[Lyrics to Translate]**
65. Translate this **[Source Language]** news article about climate change into **[Target Language]** to make it accessible to a wider audience.
66. Convert this **[Source Language]** travel blog into **[Target Language]** while retaining its cultural nuances.
67. Can you provide a **[Target Language]** translation for this **[Source Language]** proverb about the sea? **[Proverb to Translate]**
68. Translate this **[Source Language]** poem about mountains into **[Target Language]**, maintaining its poetic flow.
69. Translate this **[Source Language]** dialogue about a road trip into **[Target Language]**: **[Dialogue to Translate]**
70. Please provide a **[Target Language]** translation for the **[Source Language]** phrase about the desert: **[Phrase to Translate]**
71. Convert this **[Source Language]** recipe for a regional dish into **[Target Language]**: **[Recipe to Convert]**

72. Translate this **[Source Language]** folklore about a lake into **[Target Language]**, capturing its mythos and charm.

73. Translate this **[Source Language]** folk song about a forest into **[Target Language]**, preserving its cultural significance.

74. Transform this **[Source Language]** culinary recipe from a coastal region into **[Target Language]**: **[Recipe to Transform]**

75. Convey the essence of this **[Source Language]** traditional melody about a valley into **[Target Language]**, safeguarding its cultural importance.

76. Translate this **[Source Language]** poem about the sky into **[Target Language]**, retaining its poetic flow. **[Poem to Translate]**

77. Convert this **[Source Language]** conversation about a hiking trail into **[Target Language]**: **[Dialogue to Convert]**

78. Convert this **[Source Language]** description of a **[famous landmark]** into **[Target Language]**: **[Description to Convert]**

79. Can you translate this **[Source Language]** saying about **[geographical feature, e.g., mountains, rivers]** into **[Target Language]**? **[Saying to Translate]**

80. Please translate this **[Source Language]** travel itinerary for a trip to **[Destination]** into **[Target Language]**: **[Itinerary to Translate]**

81. Translate this **[Source Language]** poem about **[a natural phenomenon]** into **[Target Language]** while preserving its rhyme and rhythm.

82. Provide a **[Target Language]** translation for this **[Source Language]** weather report for **[Location]**: **[Weather Report to Translate]**

83. Convert this **[Source Language]** dialogue about **[an outdoor activity]** into **[Target Language]**: **[Dialogue to Convert]**

84. Can you translate this **[Source Language]** quote about **[a specific season]** into **[Target Language]**? **[Quote to Translate]**

85. Translate this **[Source Language]** limerick about **[a type of weather]** into **[Target Language]**: **[Limerick to Translate]**

86. Please translate these **[Source Language]** song lyrics about **[a region]** into **[Target Language]**: **[Lyrics to Translate]**

87. Translate this **[Source Language]** news article about **[a natural disaster]** into **[Target Language]** to make it accessible to a wider audience.

88. Convert this **[Source Language]** travel blog about **[a place of interest]** into **[Target Language]** while retaining its cultural nuances.

89. Can you provide a **[Target Language]** translation for this **[Source Language]** proverb about **[a specific body of water]**? **[Proverb to Translate]**

90. Translate this **[Source Language]** poem about **[a celestial body]** into **[Target Language]**, maintaining its poetic flow.

91. Translate this **[Source Language]** dialogue about **[a famous festival in a particular location]** into **[Target Language]**: **[Dialogue to Translate]**

92. Please provide a **[Target Language]** translation for the **[Source Language]** phrase about **[a specific climate zone]**: **[Phrase to Translate]**

93. Convert this **[Source Language]** recipe for **[a traditional meal from a high-altitude region]** into **[Target Language]**: **[Recipe to Convert]**

94. Translate this **[Source Language]** folklore about **[a river or a stream]** into **[Target Language]**, capturing its mythos and charm.

95. Translate this **[Source Language]** folk song about **[a historical figure related to a specific location]** into **[Target Language]**, preserving its cultural significance.

96. Transform this **[Source Language]** culinary recipe from **[a region famous for its beaches]** into **[Target Language]**: **[Recipe to Transform]**
97. Translate this **[Source Language]** poem about **[an ocean or sea]** into **[Target Language]**, retaining its poetic flow. **[Poem to Translate]**
98. Convert this **[Source Language]** conversation about **[a specific type of terrain]** into **[Target Language]**: **[Dialogue to Convert]**
99. Provide a **[Target Language]** translation for the **[Source Language]** name of **[a large body of water, e.g., lake, ocean, sea]**: **[Name to Translate]**
100. Convert this **[Source Language]** description of **[an exotic location]** into **[Target Language]**: **[Description to Convert]**

Since ChatGPT is designed to produce text that sounds like it's written by a human, it could offer more nuanced translations when dealing with casual or conversational language

Fifty Summarisation Prompts

Here are some ChatGPT **prompts for summarisation** that can be **customised** for your own **summarisation tasks**:

1. **[Summarise]** the **[causes and consequences]** of the **[First World War]**.
2. **Condense]** the **[fundamental theories and applications]** of **[quantum computing]**.
3. **[Outline]** the **[major figures and their contributions]** to the **[Civil Rights Movement]** in the **[United States]**.
4. **[Summarise]** the **[key discoveries and their implications]** in the **[field of neuroscience]**.
5. **[Provide]** a **[concise overview]** of the **[major works and themes]** in **[Postcolonial literature]**.
6. **[Distill]** the **[core tenets and practices]** of **[ethical hacking]** and its **[role in cybersecurity]**.
7. **[Summarise]** the **[main theories and models]** in **[educational psychology]**.
8. **[Compile]** a **[summary]** of the **[key milestones]** in the **[development of artificial intelligence]**.
9. **[Condense]** the **[major events and figures]** of the **[American Revolution]**.
10. **[Provide]** a **[brief overview]** of the **[key concepts and methodologies]** in **[environmental science]**.
11. **[Summarise]** the **[main theories and principles]** of **[cognitive psychology]**.

12. **[Outline]** the **[key events and their significance]** in the **[history of jazz music]**.
13. **[Compile]** a **[summary]** of the **[major theories and principles]** in **[linguistics]**.
14. **[Distill]** the **[core ideas and practices]** of **[agile project management]**.
15. **[Summarise]** the **[key elements and themes]** of **[Impressionist painting]**.
16. **[Provide]** a **[concise overview]** of the **[major works and contributions]** to **[feminist theory]**.
17. **[Condense]** the **[fundamental principles and applications]** of **[blockchain technology]**.
18. **[Outline]** the **[key figures and their contributions]** to **[modern dance]**.
19. **[Compile]** a **[summary]** of the **[major theories and principles]** in **[sociology]**.
20. **[Distill]** the **[core tenets and practices]** of **[organic chemistry]**.
21. **[Summarise]** the **[main theories and models]** in **[urban planning]**.
22. **[Provide]** a **[brief overview]** of the **[key concepts and methodologies]** in **[data science]**.
23. **[Condense]** the **[major]** of the **[French Enlightenment]**.
24. **[Outline]** the **[key events and their significance]** in the **[history of opera]**.
25. **[Compile]** a **[summary]** of the **[major theories and principles]** in **[anthropology]**.
26. **[Distill]** the **[core ideas and practices]** of **[sustainable agriculture]**.

27. **[Compile]** a **[summary]** of the **[key theories and practices]** in **[forensic science]**.
28. **[Sketch]** an **[overview]** of the **[major figures and their works]** in **[Classical music]**.
29. **[Summarise]** the **[main theories and models]** in **[landscape architecture]**.
30. **[Provide]** an **[overview]** of the **[key concepts and practices]** in **[cybersecurity]**.
31. **[Break Down]** the **[major events and figures]** of the **[Meiji Restoration]** in **[Japan]**.
32. **[Compile]** a **[summary]** of the **[major theories and principles]** in **[criminology]**.
33. **[Summarise]** an **[overview]** of the **[key events and their significance]** in the **[history of jazz]**.
34. **[Summarise]** on the **[key theories and applications]** of **[virtual reality]** in **[healthcare]**.
35. **[Provide]** a **[concise summary]** of the **[major contributions]** to **[game theory]**.
36. **[Summarise]** the **[key elements and themes]** of **[Cubist art]**.
37. **[Break Down]** the **[main theories and models]** in **[speech therapy]**.
38. **[Generate]** a **[summary]** of the **[major developments]** in **[renewable energy technologies]** over the past few decades.
39. **[Dissect]** the **[core tenets and practices]** of **[alternative medicine]**.

40. **[Compile]** a **[summary]** of the **[major scientific discoveries and advancements]** in the **[field of astronomy]**.
41. **[Provide]** a **[summary]** of the **[key principles and techniques]** of **[molecular gastronomy]** in **[culinary arts]**.
42. **[Summarise]** the **[key ideas and tenets]** of **[Confucianism]** and its **[impact on East Asian cultures]**.
43. **[Generate]** a **[summary]** of the **[major milestones]** in **[robotics]** and their **[impact on industries]**.
44. **[Summarise]** the **[major contributions]** of the **[Impressionism movement]** to **[visual arts]**.
45. **[Provide]** a **[summary]** of the **[key principles and techniques]** of **[digital marketing]**.
46. **[Generate]** a **[summary]** of the **[major developments]** in **[nanotechnology]** and their **[potential applications]**.
47. **[Provide]** a **[summary]** of the **[key principles and practices]** of **[sustainable tourism]**.
48. **[Summarise]** the **[major events and outcomes]** of the **[Mexican Revolution]**.
49. **[Provide]** a **[summary]** of the **[fundamental principles and techniques]** in **[data science]**.
50. **[Summarise]** the **[key theories and applications]** of **[machine learning algorithms]** in **[finance]**.

Fifty Proofreading and Feedback Prompts

Here are some **prompts** that can be **customised** for **proofreading** and **obtaining feedback on students' work** from ChatGPT:

PROOFREADING

1. Correct writing style **[Insert the student's written content, such as an essay, poem, or story, here]** to meet academic standards.
2. Proofread **[Insert the student's written content, such as an essay, poem, or story, here]** for better readability and flow.
3. Optimise **[Insert the student's written content, such as an essay, poem, or story, here]** for clarity and coherence.
4. Audit **[Insert the student's written content, such as an essay, poem, or story, here]** for grammatical accuracy.
5. Refine **[Insert the student's written content, such as an essay, poem, or story, here]** by enriching vocabulary.

6. Streamline **[Insert the student's written content, such as an essay, poem, or story, here]** for concise expression.
7. Revise **[Insert the student's written content, such as an essay, poem, or story, here]** for consistent tone and style.
8. Rectify **[Insert the student's written content here]** to eliminate any inaccuracies.
9. Improve **[Insert the student's written content, such as an essay, poem, or story, here]** the final draft quality.
10. Clarify **[Insert the student's written content here]** by rephrasing ambiguous sentences.
11. Standardise **[Insert the student's written content here]** according to the required citation style.
12. Correct formatting issues **[Insert the student's written content here].**
13. Fix grammar and punctuation **[Insert the student's written content, such as an essay, poem, or story, here]** for improved clarity and logical coherence.
14. Examine **[Insert the student's written content here]** for grammatical precision and correctness.
15. Suggest improvements to **[Insert the student's written content, such as an essay, poem, or story, here]** by expanding the lexical range.
16. Provide language and grammar suggestions **[Insert the student's written content, such as an essay, poem, or story, here]** for brevity and succinctness.

17. Modify **[Insert the student's written content, such as an essay, poem, or story, here]** to maintain a uniform tone.
18. Amend **[Insert the student's content, such as an essay, poem, or story, here]** to correct any factual errors.
19. Edit [**Insert the student's written content here**] for narrative flow and pacing.
20. Scrutinise and fix [**Insert the student's written content here**] for syntactical coherence.
21. Assess and update [**Insert the student's written content here**] for thematic consistency.
22. Update [**Insert the student's written content here**] for proper use of literary devices.
23. Update [**Insert the student's written content here**] for adherence to the assignment guidelines.
24. Analyse and fix language [**Insert the student's written content here**] for effective use of dialogue.
25. Review and correct logical structure and argumentation in this assignment [**Insert the student's written content here**]
26. Validate [**Insert the student's written content here**] for credible sourcing and citations.
27. Fix and update [**Insert the student's written content here**] for originality and plagiarism concerns.
28. Appraise [**Insert the student's written content here**] for emotional impact and reader engagement.

29. Evaluate [**Insert the student's written content here**] for appropriate use of technical jargon or terminology.
30. Check [**Insert the student's written content here**] for clarity in the introduction and conclusion.
31. Check [**Insert the student's written content here**] for proper formatting and layout.
32. Scrutinise [**Insert the student's written content here**] for balanced viewpoints and arguments.
33. Check [**Insert the student's written content here**] for unanswered questions or loose ends.
34. Examine [**Insert the student's written content here**] for nuanced character development (if applicable).
35. Check [**Insert the student's written content here**] for effective use of rhetorical devices.

SEEKING FEEDBACK

36. Provide feedback on **[Formatting and Referencing]**, ensuring academic integrity and proper citation in **[Insert student's written content here]**.
37. Offer Constructive Critique on the overall composition of **[Insert student's written content here]** tailored for **[teaching level]**.
38. Assess **[Cohesive Flow]**, recommending paragraph and transitional elements for a unified narrative in **[Insert student's written content here]**.
39. Provide feedback on **[Structural Integrity]**, recommending paragraph divisions or reordering for

better flow in **[Insert student's written content here]**.

40. Analyse and Comment on **[specific types of errors, e.g., punctuation or syntax]** in **[Insert student-written content here]**.
41. Review the **[Conclusion]**, offering strategies to encapsulate and emphasise the main arguments effectively in **[Insert student's written content here]**.
42. Provide feedback about **[Linguistic Elements]**, focusing on enhancing the clarity and precision of language in **[Insert student's written content here]**.
43. Review **[Lexical Choices]**, proposing synonyms or rephrasing for enhanced impact in **[Insert student's written content here]**.
44. Examine the **[Thesis]**, offering refinements to make it more compelling and narrowly focused. Thesis content: **[Insert student's written content here]**.
45. Evaluate **[Evidential Support]**, ensuring relevance and effectiveness in bolstering the argument in **[Insert student's written content here]**.
46. Examine the **[Introduction]**, proposing captivating hooks and a clear topic statement for **[Insert student's written content here]**.
47. Scrutinise **[Thematic Elements]**, advising on paragraph construction and evidential support for the thesis based on **[Insert student's written content here]**.

48. Critique the **[Core Argument]**, focusing on the robustness and clarity of the thesis statement in **[Insert student's written content here]**.
49. Assess **[Overall Impact]**, offering insights on how to craft a compelling and coherent piece in **[Insert student's written content here]**.
50. Analyse **[Linguistic Style]**, providing tips to enhance the clarity and exactness of **[Insert student's written content here]**.

Fifty Essay Prompts

Here are some **prompt templates** you can use to create a **draft essay** with **ChatGPT**. You'll need to insert the **essay topic** into these **example prompts** and **customise** them for **optimised output**:

1. Investigate the impact of [**essay topic**] on cultural diversity. Discuss how it influences cultural preservation, assimilation, or appropriation.
2. Examine the role of [**essay topic**] in shaping public policy. Discuss its influence on legislation, governance, and public opinion.
3. Analyse the influence of [**essay topic**] on consumer behaviour. Discuss how it shapes purchasing decisions and market trends.
4. Explore the impact of [**essay topic**] on digital privacy. Discuss how it affects individual rights and data security.
5. Examine the role of [**essay topic**] in the development of artificial intelligence. Discuss its ethical, practical, and technological implications.

6. Assess the legal ramifications of [**essay topic**]. Identify at least three legal issues or challenges and discuss their implications.
7. Explore the role of [**essay topic**] in the advancement of medical research. Discuss its ethical and practical implications, including potential benefits and risks.
8. Investigate the impact of [**essay topic**] on mental health. Identify at least three ways it affects mental well-being and provide evidence to support your claims.
9. Analyse the influence of [**essay topic**] on social justice issues. Discuss how it intersects with issues like inequality, discrimination, and human rights.
10. Examine the impact of [**essay topic**] on the development of renewable energy. Discuss its technological, economic, and environmental implications.
11. Investigate the role of [**essay topic**] in shaping historical events. Analyse how it has contributed to or influenced key moments in history, and discuss its lasting effects.
12. Explore the role of [**essay topic**] in the gig economy. Discuss its impact on job security, benefits, and worker rights.

13. Scrutinise the gender dynamics involved in [**essay topic**]. Discuss how gender roles and expectations shape the issue and provide at least three examples.
14. Examine the role of [**essay topic**] in shaping personal identity. Discuss how it influences self-perception and social interactions.
15. Investigate the impact of [**essay topic**] on intergenerational relationships. Discuss how it affects family dynamics and social structures.
16. Examine the impact of [**essay topic**] on educational outcomes. Discuss how it affects academic performance, opportunities, and the overall educational experience.
17. Explore the philosophical questions raised by [**essay topic**]. Discuss at least three major questions and their implications for society or individuals.
18. Dissect the underlying assumptions behind [**essay topic**]. Identify at least three assumptions and evaluate their validity.
19. Deconstruct the power structures that influence [**essay topic**]. Identify key players or institutions and their roles in shaping the issue.
20. Investigate the environmental sustainability of [**essay topic**]. Assess its long-term impact on the environment and propose sustainable alternatives.

21. Examine the role of [**essay topic**] in the evolution of language. Discuss how it influences language use, development, and preservation.

22. Discuss the psychological effects of [**essay topic**]. Examine how [**essay topic**] influences human behaviour, emotions, and cognition, and consider both positive and negative effects.

23. Analyse the portrayal of [**essay topic**] in popular media. Discuss how [**essay topic**] is depicted in movies, TV shows, literature, or other forms of media, and consider its impact on public perception.

24. Investigate the connection between [**essay topic**] and global trends. Examine how [**essay topic**] is influenced by urbanisation, globalisation, or technological advancements.

25. Investigate the role of [**essay topic**] in the rise of virtual communities. Discuss its impact on social interactions and community building in the digital age.

26. Examine the influence of [**essay topic**] on the future of work. Discuss how it's shaping remote work, automation, and job satisfaction.

27. Analyse the impact of [**essay topic**] on mental resilience. Discuss how it affects coping mechanisms and emotional well-being.

28. Explore the ethical dilemmas associated with [**essay topic**]. Discuss the moral questions it raises and how they can be addressed.

29. Scrutinise the impact of [**essay topic**] on public health. Discuss its role in healthcare policies, prevention strategies, and community health.

30. Investigate the role of [**essay topic**] in the development of smart cities. Discuss its implications for urban planning, sustainability, and citizen engagement.

31. Examine the influence of [**essay topic**] on the global food supply chain. Discuss its impact on food security, sustainability, and ethical consumption.

32. Analyse the impact of [**essay topic**] on the evolution of social norms. Discuss how it shapes cultural attitudes, behaviours, and expectations.

33. Explore the role of [**essay topic**] in the advancement of gender equality. Discuss its impact on gender roles, representation, and opportunities.

34. Investigate the influence of [**essay topic**] on the development of virtual reality. Discuss its applications in education, healthcare, and entertainment.

35. Examine the role of [**essay topic**] in the rise of citizen journalism. Discuss its impact on media ethics, credibility, and public discourse.

36. Analyse the impact of [**essay topic**] on the preservation of indigenous cultures. Discuss its role in cultural heritage, language, and traditions.

37. Explore the influence of [**essay topic**] on the development of blockchain technology. Discuss its applications and implications for data security and transparency.

38. Investigate the role of [**essay topic**] in the fight against climate change. Discuss its impact on renewable energy, conservation efforts, and policy-making.

39. Examine the impact of [**essay topic**] on the gig economy. Discuss its implications for worker rights, job security, and economic stability.

40. Evaluate the impact of [**essay topic**] on the mental health of adolescents. Discuss its role in shaping self-esteem, coping mechanisms, and social skills.

41. Examine the influence of [**essay topic**] on the evolution of language. Discuss its impact on dialects, slang, and communication in a digital age.

42. Analyse the role of [**essay topic**] in the advancement of telemedicine. Discuss its implications for healthcare accessibility and quality of care.
43. Investigate the impact of [**essay topic**] on the future of transportation. Discuss its role in the development of electric vehicles, public transit, and urban planning.
44. Explore the influence of [**essay topic**] on the ethics of artificial intelligence. Discuss its implications for data privacy, algorithmic bias, and human rights.
45. Scrutinise the role of [**essay topic**] in the growth of eSports. Discuss its impact on traditional sports, entertainment, and youth culture.
46. Examine the impact of [**essay topic**] on the rise of citizen science. Discuss its implications for scientific research, public engagement, and education.
47. Analyse the influence of [**essay topic**] on the development of sustainable fashion. Discuss its impact on consumer behaviour, waste reduction, and ethical production.
48. Investigate the role of [**essay topic**] in the advancement of space tourism. Discuss its ethical, economic, and technological implications.
49. Evaluate the influence of [**essay topic**] on the development of renewable energy storage solutions.

Discuss its implications for sustainability and energy independence.

Twenty-Five Sentiment Analysis Prompts

Here are some **ChatGPT prompts** to help you do **sentiment analysis:**

1. Determine the sentiment conveyed in the following **[text/article/review]**.
2. Examine the prevailing emotional tone in this **[text/article/review]**. Would you categorise it as buoyant, sombre, or ambivalent?
3. Scrutinise the emotional timbre of the following **[text/article/review]**. Does it evoke specific feelings?
4. Utilising a scale from 1 to 10, quantify the emotional resonance of the following **[text/article/review]**. (1 = deeply negative, 10 = profoundly positive)
5. Expose the latent emotional layers within the provided **[text/article/review]**.

6. Assign an emotional valence score ranging from 1 to 10 for the sentiment expressed in the ensuing **[text/article/review]**. (1 = deeply cynical, 10 = highly sanguine)

7. Decode the emotional subtext embedded in the given **[text/article/review]**.

8. Investigate the sentiment dynamics portrayed in the subsequent **[text/article/review]**.

9. Using a numerical scale, pinpoint the emotional intensity of the sentiment in the ensuing **[text/article/review]**. (1 = markedly negative, 10 = notably positive)

10. Critically evaluate the sentiment conveyed in the forthcoming **[text/article/review]**. Is it congruent with the topic?

11. Delineate the range of emotions encapsulated in the given **[text/article/review]**.

12. Ascertain the emotional texture of the given **[text/article/review]**. Is it complex or straightforward?

13. Conduct a qualitative analysis of the sentiment expressed in this **[text/article/review]**.

14. Appraise the emotional landscape depicted in this **[text/article/review]**.

15. Gauge the emotional undertones in the following **[text/article/review]** using sentiment analysis techniques.
16. Probe into the sentiment nuances in the subsequent **[text/article/review]**. Are there mixed emotions?
17. Assess the overarching emotional tone in this **[text/article/review]**. Would you term it as favourable, unfavourable, or balanced?
18. Dissect the emotional nuances present in the given **[text/article/review]**.
19. What sentiment dominates the narrative in this **[text/article/review]**?
20. On a scale of 1 to 10, how would you evaluate the emotional weight carried by the subsequent **[text/article/review]**? (1 = extremely bleak, 10 = exceedingly buoyant)
21. Perform a sentiment breakdown of the following **[text/article/review]**, identifying key phrases that contribute to the overall sentiment.
22. Perceive the emotional palette of the ensuing **[text/article/review]**. Is it monochromatic or diverse in sentiment?
23. Utilise machine learning algorithms to predict the sentiment in the following **[text/article/review]**.

24. Perform a lexical analysis to identify the frequency of positive and negative words in the given **[text/article/review]**. Please reveal the overall sentiment.
25. Conduct a thematic sentiment analysis on the subsequent **[text/article/review]**.

Twenty Java Program Prompts

Here are some **useful Java program prompts** that can help you create your own prompts for creating Java:

1. Develop **[JAVA]** code that utilises **[multithreading]** to perform multiple calculations simultaneously.
2. Write **[JAVA]** code that integrates with a **[RESTful API]** to fetch real-time weather data and display it.
3. Compose a **[JAVA method]** that reverses a **[linked list]** without using any additional memory.
4. Craft **[JAVA]** code that reads **[XML files]** and converts them into **[JSON format]**.

5. Implement **[JAVA]** code that uses **[cryptography]** to encrypt and decrypt a given **[text message]**.
6. Assemble a **[JAVA]** that performs **[automated unit testing]** on a set of predefined functions.
7. Construct **[JAVA]** code that utilises **[machine learning algorithms]** to classify a set of data into different categories.
8. Formulate **[JAVA]** code that applies **[regular expressions]** to validate a **[credit card number]**.
9. Generate a **[JAVA GUI application]** that allows users to draw and save **[basic shapes]** like circles and rectangles.
10. Create **[JAVA]** code that performs **[file compression and decompression]** using **[ZIP algorithms]**.
11. Develop a **[JAVA Web Application]** using **[Spring Boot]** that allows users to manage a **[to-do list]** online.
12. Create a **[JAVA Android App]** that uses **[Google Maps API]** to show nearby **[restaurants]**.
13. Implement a **[JAVA Swing Application]** that simulates a **[simple calculator]** with basic arithmetic operations.

14. Write a **[JAVA Servlet]** that handles **[HTTP requests and responses]** for a basic web service.
15. Construct a **[JAVA JPA Application]** that performs **[CRUD operations]** on a **[MySQL database]**.
16. Design a **[JAVA program]** that uses **[JavaFX]** for creating a **[media player]**.
17. Build a **[JAVA Network Program]** that implements a **[simple chat server]** using **[sockets]**.
18. Develop a **[JAVA program]** that uses **[JDBC]** to connect to a **[PostgreSQL database]** and perform queries.
19. Create a **[JAVA program]** that uses **[Apache Kafka]** for **[message queuing]** in a distributed system.
20. Implement a **[JAVA program]** that uses **[JSP and Servlets]** to create a **[login and registration form]**.

Twenty JavaScript Prompts

Here are some **useful JavaScript prompts** that can help you create your own prompts for creating JavaScript:

1. Write a **[JavaScript]** function that performs **[data validation]** on a **[web form]**, ensuring all fields meet specified criteria.
2. Construct **[JavaScript]** code that integrates with a **[third-party API]** like **[Google Maps]** to display location-based data.
3. Assemble a **[JavaScript]** program that uses **[WebGL]** to render **[3D graphics]** on a web page.
4. Formulate **[JavaScript]** code that uses **[Service Workers]** to enable **[offline functionality]** for a web application.
5. Create a **[JavaScript]** function that encrypts and decrypts **[text]** using a **[symmetric encryption algorithm]**.
6. Generate **[JavaScript]** code that uses **[Drag and Drop API]** to allow users to **[rearrange items]** on a web page.

7. Build a **[JavaScript]** program that uses **[IndexedDB]** to store **[large amounts of structured data]** locally.
8. Write **[JavaScript]** code that leverages **[Web Audio API]** to play, pause, and manipulate **[audio files]**.
9. Develop a **[JavaScript]** function that uses **[CSS Variables]** to dynamically change the **[theme]** of a web page.
10. Craft a **[JavaScript]** program that uses **[Intersection Observer API]** to trigger **[lazy loading]** of images.
11. Write a **[JavaScript]** script that uses **[WebSockets]** to enable **[real-time communication]** between clients and a server.
12. Compose **[JavaScript]** code that leverages **[Canvas API]** to create **[interactive drawings]** or **[animations]** on a web page.
13. Develop a **[JavaScript]** function that uses **[Geolocation API]** to fetch and display the user's **[current location]**.
14. Implement **[JavaScript]** code that uses **[Fetch API]** to make **[asynchronous requests]** and update the DOM without reloading the page.
15. Create a **[JavaScript]** program that uses **[Local Storage]** to save **[user preferences]** and load them upon revisit.

16. Develop **[JavaScript]** code that uses **[MediaStream API]** to capture **[video and audio]** from the user's device.
17. Construct **[JavaScript]** code that uses **[Pointer Events]** to handle **[multi-touch gestures]** on mobile devices.
18. Generate a **[JavaScript]** function that uses **[WebRTC]** to facilitate **[peer-to-peer video conferencing]**.
19. Design a **[JavaScript]** program that uses **[Notifications API]** to send **[desktop notifications]** to the user.
20. Write **[JavaScript]** code that leverages **[Accelerometer and Gyroscope APIs]** to detect **[device orientation and motion]**.

Twenty PHP Prompts

Here are some **useful PHP prompts** that can help you create your own prompts for coding using PHP:

1. Write **[PHP]** logic to **[summate]** two **[input numbers]** and **[output]** the **[calculation]**.
2. Craft **[PHP]** syntax to **[authenticate]** a **[user-submitted email]** via **[regex patterns]**.
3. Develop a **[PHP subroutine]** that **[ingests]** a **[numerical array]** and **[isolates]** the **[maximum value]**.
4. Compose **[PHP]** code to **[establish a connection]** with a **[MySQL data source]** and **[fetch]** all **[data rows]** from a **[designated table]**.
5. Author **[PHP]** script to **[transfer]** an **[image asset]** and **[archive]** it in a **[server-defined directory]**.
6. Construct a **[PHP algorithm]** that **[synthesizes]** a **[randomised alphanumerical password]** with a **[predetermined character count]**.
7. Implement **[PHP]** logic to **[iterate]** over a **[string dataset]** and **[render]** each **[text element]** in **[capital letters]**.

8. Devise **[PHP]** code to **[compute]** the **[factorial value]** of a **[specified integer]** through **[recursive calls]**.
9. Assemble a **[PHP user interface]** that **[solicits]** **[demographic details]** like **[name and age]**, then **[outputs]** an **[age-appropriate greeting]**.
10. Formulate **[PHP]** code to **[facilitate]** **[elementary cart operations]** in a **[web-based marketplace]**, such as **[item addition and deletion]**.
11. Construct **[PHP]** logic to **[aggregate]** two **[user-supplied integers]** and **[display]** the **[resultant sum]**.
12. Fabricate **[PHP]** code to **[verify]** a **[user-input email address]** using **[regex validation]**.
13. Forge a **[PHP method]** that **[accepts]** a **[numeric array]** and **[returns]** the **[peak value]**.
14. Synthesize **[PHP]** code to **[initiate a link]** to a **[MySQL database]** and **[pull]** all **[entries]** from a **[selected table]**.
15. Generate **[PHP]** script to **[handle]** an **[image upload]** and **[store]** it in a **[server-specified folder]**.
16. Create a **[PHP algorithm]** to **[produce]** a **[random string password]** of a **[set length]** using **[letters and numbers]**.
17. Draft **[PHP]** code to **[cycle]** through a **[string array]** and **[output]** each **[string]** in **[uppercase format]**.

18. Compose **[PHP]** code to **[determine]** the **[factorial]** of a **[given integer]** using **[recursive methodology]**.
19. Design a **[PHP form]** that **[collects]** **[user's name and age]** and **[generates]** a **[custom greeting]** based on **[age criteria]**.
20. Author **[PHP]** code to **[enable]** **[basic cart features]** for an **[e-commerce platform]**, including **[addition and removal of products]**.

Twenty SQL Prompts

Here are some **useful SQL prompts** that can help you create your **own SQL queries** using ChatGPT:

1. Construct an SQL command to **[fetch]** all **[client names]** along with their **[associated purchases]** from the **[Clientele]** and **[Purchases]** tables.
2. Devise an SQL query to **[compute]** the **[median wage]** for **[staff members]** within the **[Workforce]** table.

3. Formulate an SQL query to **[count]** the **[items]** in the **[Merchandise]** table that have a **[stock level]** exceeding **[50 units]**.
4. Craft an SQL query to **[showcase]** the **[top 5 spenders]** from the **[Financials]** table.
5. Compose an SQL query to **[enumerate]** the **[employee names]** who are part of the **[Marketing]** division and have a **[tenure]** longer than **[24 months]**.
6. Author an SQL query to **[isolate]** the **[distinct product types]** found in the **[Warehouse]** table.
7. Create an SQL query to **[ascertain]** the **[cumulative income]** per **[product class]** in the **[Earnings]** table.
8. Design an SQL query to **[modify]** the **['Inventory']** column for a particular **[merchandise]** in the **[Goods]** table.
9. Write an SQL query to **[purge entries]** for **[clients]** who have **[zero transactions]** in the **[ClientBase]** table.
10. Generate an SQL query to **[merge]** the **['Staff']** and **[Divisions]** tables to **[reveal]** the **[employee names]** and their **[respective department titles]**.
11. Construct an SQL query to **[aggregate]** **[customer names]** and their **[lifetime purchase values]** from the

[Customers] table, grouping them by **[membership status]**.

12. Generate an SQL query to **[compute]** the **[weighted average salary]** of **[employees]** in the **[Staff]** table, factoring in their **[years of service]**.
13. Formulate an SQL query to **[identify]** **[products]** in the **[Inventory]** table that have a **[stock-to-sales ratio]** greater than **[2.0]**.
14. Devise an SQL query to **[rank]** the **[top 10 customers]** by **[annual spending]** from the **[Financials]** table, partitioned by **[customer segment]**.
15. Create an SQL query to **[list]** **[employees]** in the **[HR]** table who have **[multiple skill sets]** and a **[performance rating]** above **[4.0]**.
16. Provide an SQL query to **[extract]** **[unique product families]** from the **[Catalogue]** table, filtering by **[seasonal availability]**.
17. Draft an SQL query to **[calculate]** the **[quarterly revenue]** for each **[product line]** in the **[Sales]** table, using a **[window function]**.
18. Author an SQL query to **[update]** the **[Stock]** column in the **[Products]** table, applying a **[10% discount]** to **[items with low turnover]**.

19. Craft an SQL query to **[purge records]** from the **[CustomerBase]** table where **[last activity date]** is older than **[one year]** and **[account balance]** is zero.
20. Develop an SQL query to **[correlate]** the **['Employees']** and **[ProjectAssignments]** tables, displaying **[employee names]**, **[project names]**, and **[hours allocated]**.

Twenty Debugging Prompts

Here are some **useful debugging prompts** that can help you to fix your **own codes**. You can **adapt them** to suit your needs:

JAVA Debugging Prompts

1. Investigate the **[infinite loop]** issue in the **[method name]**. **[paste your code]**
2. Debug the **[exception handling]** in **[class name]** to find out why it's not catching exceptions. **[paste your code]**
3. Examine the **[type casting]** errors in the **[method name]**. **[paste your code]**

4. Identify why the **[JVM]** is throwing an **OutOfMemoryError** in your application. **[paste your code]**
5. Resolve the **[dependency issues]** in your **[Maven project]**. **[paste your code]**

JavaScript Debugging Prompts

1. Debug the **[event listener]** to find out why it's not triggering the expected function. **[paste your code]**
2. Investigate why the **[Promise]** is always going into the **catch block**. **[paste your code]**
3. Examine the **[closure]** to find out why it's not preserving the variable state. **[paste your code]**
4. Debug the **[asynchronous function]** to find out why it's blocking the main thread. **[paste your code]**
5. Identify why the **[React component]** is not re-rendering when the state changes. **[paste your code]**

SQL Debugging Prompts

1. Debug the **[indexing]** to find out why queries are running slowly on **[table name]**. **[paste your code]**
2. Investigate why the **[primary key]** constraint is failing on **[table name]**. **[paste your code]**

3. Examine the **[subquery]** to find out why it's returning **duplicate records. [paste your code]**
4. Debug the **[transaction]** to find out why it's not committing. **[paste your code]**
5. Investigate why the **[stored function]** is not returning the expected value. **[paste your code]**

PHP Debugging Prompts

1. Debug the **[regular expression]** in **[PHP script]** to find out why it's not matching patterns. **[paste your code]**
2. Examine the **[header function]** to find out why it's not redirecting to the expected page. **[paste your code]**
3. Investigate why the **[POST variables]** are not being received in the **[PHP script]**. **[paste your code]**
4. Debug the **[file upload]** feature to find out why files are not being uploaded. **[paste your code]**
5. Examine the **[cookie handling]** in your **[PHP application]** to find out why cookies are not being set. **[paste your code]**

Thirty Program Code Conversion Prompts

Here are some **useful program code conversion prompts** that can help you to fix your **own codes**:

Java to Python

1. Convert the **[JAVA class]** implementing **[Singleton pattern]** to Python. **[paste your code]**
2. Translate the **[JAVA method]** for **[file I/O]** into Python. **[paste your code]**
3. Convert **[JAVA JDBC code]** for a database connection to Python using **[SQLAlchemy]**. **[paste your code]**

Python to JavaScript

1. Translate the **[Python Flask API]** to a **[Node.js Express API]**. **[paste your code]**
2. Convert **[Python list comprehensions]** to **[JavaScript map/filter]**. **[paste your code]**
3. Translate **[Python decorators]** to **[JavaScript higher-order functions]**. **[paste your code]**

JavaScript to TypeScript

1. Convert **[JavaScript ES6 classes]** to **[TypeScript classes]** with type annotations. **[paste your code]**
2. Translate **[JavaScript promises]** to **[TypeScript async/await]**. **[paste your code]**
3. Convert **[JavaScript object destructuring]** to **[TypeScript object destructuring]**. **[paste your code]**

SQL to NoSQL (MongoDB)

1. Translate **[SQL queries]** for **[JOIN operations]** to **[MongoDB aggregation pipeline]**. **[paste your code]**
2. Convert **[SQL triggers]** to **[MongoDB triggers]**. **[paste your code]**
3. Translate **[SQL stored procedures]** to **[MongoDB functions]**. **[paste your code]**

PHP to Node.js

1. Convert **[PHP session handling]** to **[Node.js session management]**. **[paste your code]**
2. Translate **[PHP form validation]** to **[Node.js/Express validation]**. **[paste your code]**

3. Convert **[PHP MySQL queries]** to **[Node.js MySQL queries]** using **[MySQL npm package]. [paste your code]**

C++ to Rust

1. Translate **[C++ pointers and memory management]** to **[Rust ownership and borrowing]. [paste your code]**
2. Convert **[C++ classes and inheritance]** to **[Rust structs and traits]. [paste your code]**
3. Translate **[C++ STL algorithms]** to **[Rust standard library algorithms]. [paste your code]**

Ruby to Python

1. Convert **[Ruby blocks and iterators]** to **[Python generators and comprehensions]. [paste your code]**
2. Translate **[Ruby on Rails controllers]** to **[Python Django views]. [paste your code]**
3. Translate **[Ruby instance variables]** to **[Python instance variables]. [paste your code]**

Swift to Kotlin

1. Translate **[Swift optionals]** to **[Kotlin nullables]**. **[paste your code]**
2. Convert **[Swift closures]** to **[Kotlin lambdas]**. **[paste your code]**
3. Translate **[Swift protocols]** to **[Kotlin interfaces]**. **[paste your code]**

R to Python

1. Convert **[R data frames]** to **[Python Pandas data frames]**. **[paste your code]**
2. Translate **[R ggplot2 visualizations]** to **[Python Matplotlib or Seaborn]**. **[paste your code]**
3. Convert **[R statistical tests]** to **[Python SciPy tests]**. **[paste your code]**

Perl to Python

1. Convert **[Perl regular expressions]** to **[Python re module]**. **[paste your code]**
2. Translate **[Perl hashes]** to **[Python dictionaries]**. **[paste your code]**

3. Convert **[Perl file handling]** to **[Python file I/O]**. **[paste your code]**

Twenty Table Output Generation Prompts

Here are some **example prompts** that can be customised for getting **tabular output**:

1. Depict the noteworthy **[number]** nations in **[datapoint 1]** and **[datapoint 2]** in a tabulated manner.
2. Specify the major **[number]** countries in **[datapoint 1]** and **[datapoint 2]** using a table layout.
3. Summarise the pivotal **[number]** nations in **[datapoint 1]** and **[datapoint 2]** through a table.
4. Feature the leading **[number]** countries for **[datapoint 1]** and **[datapoint 2]** in a well-organised table.

5. Report the exceptional **[number]** countries based on **[datapoint 1]** and **[datapoint 2]** in a structured tabulation.
6. Exhibit the influential **[number]** countries in terms of **[datapoint 1]** and **[datapoint 2]** in a tabular view.
7. Reveal the significant **[number]** nations excelling in **[datapoint 1]** and **[datapoint 2]** in a table format.
8. Arrange the top **[number]** nations by **[datapoint 1]** and **[datapoint 2]** in a tabular format.
9. Profile the remarkable **[number]** nations for **[datapoint 1]** and **[datapoint 2]** in a table.
10. Arrange the distinguished **[number]** countries according to **[datapoint 1]** and **[datapoint 2]** in a table.
11. List the leading **[number]** nations in terms of **[datapoint 1]**, **[datapoint 2]**, **[datapoint 3]**, and **[datapoint 4]** in a tabular representation.
12. Showcase the primary **[number]** countries by **[datapoint 1]**, **[datapoint 2]**, **[datapoint 3]**, and **[datapoint 4]** in a table layout.
13. Display the foremost **[number]** nations ranking for **[datapoint 1]**, **[datapoint 2]**, **[datapoint 3]**, and **[datapoint 4]** in table form.

14. Present the top-ranking **[number]** countries based on **[datapoint 1]**, **[datapoint 2]**, **[datapoint 3]**, and **[datapoint 4]** in a structured table.

15. Put the key **[number]** nations excelling in **[datapoint 1]**, **[datapoint 2]**, **[datapoint 3]**, and **[datapoint 4]** within a table.

16. Enumerate the dominant **[number]** countries in **[datapoint 1]**, **[datapoint 2]**, **[datapoint 3]**, and **[datapoint 4]** using a tabulated format.

17. List the top **[number]** nations regarding **[datapoint 1]**, **[datapoint 2]**, **[datapoint 3]**, and **[datapoint 4]** in a simple table.

18. Represent the principal **[number]** countries measured by **[datapoint 1]**, **[datapoint 2]**, **[datapoint 3]**, and **[datapoint 4]** in a laid-out table.

19. Tabulate the premier **[number]** nations considering **[datapoint 1]**, **[datapoint 2]**, **[datapoint 3]**, and **[datapoint 4]**.

20. Outline the standout **[number]** countries in relation to **[datapoint 1]**, **[datapoint 2]**, **[datapoint 3]**, and **[datapoint 4]** in a systematic table.

A table format can make complex information easier to understand by organising it into rows and columns. This layout helps the user quickly locate specific pieces of information.

Twenty PowerPoint Presentation Outline Prompts

Here are some **more prompts** that can be adapted for creating a **PowerPoint presentation outline** that can further be used to create a **PowerPoint presentation**:

1. Generate an outline for a PowerPoint presentation with **[number of slides]** slides focused on **[topic]**, detailing each slide's content.

2. Create an outline for **[number of slides]** slides on **[topic]** for a PowerPoint presentation, specifying content for each slide.
3. I'd like an outline for a **[number of slides]** slide PowerPoint presentation on **[topic]**. Please provide a content breakdown for each slide.
4. Please sketch an overview for a PowerPoint deck comprising **[number of slides]** slides about **[topic]**, indicating the content for each.
5. I'd appreciate a blueprint for a **[number of slides]** slide presentation on **[topic]** in PowerPoint format, with descriptions for each slide.
6. Could you devise a structure for a **[number of slides]** slide PowerPoint on **[topic]**, enumerating content for each?
7. Please design a framework for a PowerPoint presentation having **[number of slides]** slides concerning **[topic]**, detailing the subject matter for each slide.
8. I need a plan for a **[number of slides]** slide PowerPoint on **[topic]**. Can you outline what each slide should cover?
9. Kindly put together an outline suitable for a **[number of slides]** slide PowerPoint presentation centred on **[topic]**, elaborating on the content for every slide.

10. I'd like to see a layout for a **[number of slides]** slide presentation on **[topic]** in PowerPoint. Please indicate the proposed content for each slide.

11. Draft a schematic for a PowerPoint presentation consisting of **[number of slides]** slides that delve into **[educational topic]** for **[grade level]** students, specifying the content for each slide.

12. Could you formulate an outline for a **[number of slides]** slide PowerPoint presentation centred around **[educational topic]** for **[grade level]** students, with a detailed breakdown for each slide?

13. I'm interested in a roadmap for a **[number of slides]** slide PowerPoint presentation on **[educational topic]** aimed at **[grade level]** students. Please delineate the content for each slide.

14. Please construct a guide for a **[number of slides]** slide PowerPoint presentation focusing on **[educational topic]** for **[grade level]** students, outlining the subject matter for each slide.

15. I'd appreciate a content plan for a **[number of slides]** slide PowerPoint presentation related to **[educational topic]** for **[grade level]** students, specifying what each slide should contain.

16. Could you sketch a blueprint for a **[number of slides]** slide PowerPoint presentation in the area of

[educational topic] for **[grade level]** students, detailing the content for each slide?

17. Please develop a content strategy for a **[number of slides]** slide PowerPoint presentation on **[educational topic]** for **[grade level]** students, indicating what should be covered in each slide.

18. I'd like an agenda for a **[number of slides]** slide PowerPoint presentation about **[educational topic]** for **[grade level]** students, elaborating on the content for each slide.

19. Could you create a content matrix for a **[number of slides]** slide PowerPoint presentation that focuses on **[educational topic]** for **[grade level]** students, specifying the subject matter for each slide?

20. I'm looking for a content map for a **[number of slides]** slide PowerPoint presentation on **[educational topic]** for **[grade level]** students. Please provide a detailed outline for each slide.

Fifty-Five Simplify or Adapt Prompts

Here are some **example prompts** that can be customised to simplify or **change the difficulty level** of resources:

1. Could you reframe the following lesson plan to be more interactive for **[teaching level or age group]** on the topic of **[educational topic]**? **[paste the content]**.
2. Please adapt the content below to incorporate more hands-on activities suitable for **[teaching level or age group]** in **[educational topic]**. **[paste the content]**.
3. Reformat the following material to include multimedia elements that will engage **[teaching level or age group]** in **[educational topic]**. **[paste the content]**.
4. Could you enrich the content below with real-world examples relevant to **[teaching level or age group]** studying **[educational topic]**? **[paste the content]**.
5. Please restructure the following lesson to include more collaborative learning for **[teaching level or age group]** in **[educational topic]**. **[paste the content]**.

6. Rewrite the content below to include gamification elements for **[teaching level or age group]** focused on **[educational topic]**. **[paste the content]**.

7. Could you redevelop the following content to include more problem-solving exercises for **[teaching level or age group]** in **[educational topic]**? **[paste the content]**.

8. Please reorient the material below to focus on experiential learning for **[teaching level or age group]** in **[educational topic]**. **[paste the content]**.

9. Could you repurpose the content below to include more self-assessment tools for **[teaching level or age group]** studying **[educational topic]**? **[paste the content]**.

10. Please reinvigorate the following lesson plan to include more storytelling elements for **[teaching level or age group]** in **[educational topic]**. **[paste the content]**.

11. Could you resequence the content below to include more flipped classroom elements for **[teaching level or age group]** focused on **[educational topic]**? **[paste the content]**.

12. Please retool the following material to include more inquiry-based learning for **[teaching level or age group]** in **[educational topic]**. **[paste the content]**.

13. Could you retrofit the content below to include more peer teaching opportunities for **[teaching level or age group]** studying **[educational topic]**? **[paste the content]**.
14. Please redevelop the following lesson plan to focus more on social-emotional learning for **[teaching level or age group]** in **[educational topic]**. **[paste the content]**.
15. Could you re-energise the content below to include more project-based learning for **[teaching level or age group]** focused on **[educational topic]**? **[paste the content]**.
16. Please reorganise the following material to include more case studies relevant to **[teaching level or age group]** in **[educational topic]**. **[paste the content]**.
17. Could you improve and optimise the content below to include more blended learning elements for **[teaching level or age group]** studying **[educational topic]**? **[paste the content]**.
18. Please redevelop the following lesson plan to include more cultural diversity elements for **[teaching level or age group]** in **[educational topic]**. **[paste the content]**.
19. Could you rewrite the provided content to focus more on critical thinking skills for **[teaching level or age**

group] focused on **[educational topic]**? **[paste the content]**.

20. Please recontextualise the following material to include more ethical discussions for **[teaching level or age group]** in **[educational topic]**. **[paste the content]**.
21. Rewrite the material below to better suit the learning environment of **[teaching level or age group]**: **[paste the content]**.
22. Re-craft the content below to be more in line with the educational standards of **[teaching level or age group]**: **[paste the content]**.
23. Re-arrange the following content to make it more relevant for **[teaching level or age group]**: **[paste the content]**.
24. Rewrite the following content to better resonate with **[teaching level or age group]**: **[paste the content]**.
25. Could you re-orient the following content to better match the learning pace of **[teaching level or age group]**? **[paste the content]**.
26. Please re-contextualise the following material to make it more suitable for **[teaching level or age group]**: **[paste the content]**.
27. Could you rework the below content to suit **[teaching level or age group]**? **[paste the content]**.

28. Rework and improve the following content to make it more effective for **[teaching level or age group]**: **[paste the content]**.
29. Please recreate the content below to make it more engaging for **[teaching level or age group]**: **[paste the content]**.
30. Could you rewrite the content below to better serve the learning needs of **[teaching level or age group]**? **[paste the content]**.
31. Adapt the following resource to better align with the educational objectives of **[teaching level or age group]**: **[paste the content]**.
32. Please re-engineer the following content to better fit the learning styles of **[teaching level or age group]**: **[paste the content]**.
33. Could you rework the content below to better align with the curriculum for **[teaching level or age group]**? **[paste the content]**.
34. Could you rewrite the following material to be more in tune with the cognitive abilities of **[teaching level or age group]**? **[paste the content]**.
35. Please recreate the material below to make it more appealing for **[teaching level or age group]**: **[paste the content]**.

36. Could you rewrite the content below to be more in sync with the educational goals of **[teaching level or age group]**? **[paste the content]**.
37. Please re-synthesise the following content to make it more applicable for **[teaching level or age group]**. **[paste the content]**.
38. Could you please customise the following content to align with the educational needs of **[teaching level or age group]**? **[paste the content]**.
39. Revise the material below to make it more relatable for **[teaching level or age group]**: **[paste the content]**.
40. Transform the content below to be more age-appropriate for **[teaching level or age group]**: **[paste the content]**.
41. Rewrite the content below to include more mindfulness activities for **[teaching level or age group]** in **[educational topic] [paste the content]**.
42. Please rearticulate the following material to focus on sustainability for **[teaching level or age group]** studying **[educational topic]**. **[paste the content]**.
43. Redevelop the content below to include more STEM activities suitable for **[teaching level or age group]** in **[educational topic]**. **[paste the content]**.
44. Could you restructure the following lesson plan to include more debate and discussion elements for

[teaching level or age group] focused on **[educational topic]**? **[paste the content]**.

45. Please reengineer the material below to focus on digital literacy for **[teaching level or age group]** in **[educational topic]**. **[paste the content]**.
46. Adapt the content below to include more visual aids and infographics for **[teaching level or age group]** studying **[educational topic]**. **[paste the content]**.
47. Could you reconstitute the following lesson plan to focus on civic education for **[teaching level or age group]** in **[educational topic]**? **[paste the content]**.
48. Please recreate the content below to include more role-playing activities for **[teaching level or age group]** focused on **[educational topic]**. **[paste the content]**.
49. Reconceptualise and improve the following material to include more interactive quizzes for **[teaching level or age group]** in **[educational topic]**. **[paste the content]**.
50. Could you repurpose the content below to focus on financial literacy for **[teaching level or age group]** studying **[educational topic]**? **[paste the content]**.
51. Please reuse the following lesson plan to include more virtual field trips for **[teaching level or age group]** in **[educational topic]**. **[paste the content]**.

52. Recreate the content below to include more guest speakers relevant to **[teaching level or age group]** focused on **[educational topic]**. **[paste the content]**.

53. Could you redevelop the following material to focus on conflict resolution for **[teaching level or age group]** in **[educational topic]**? **[paste the content]**.

54. Please rewrite the content below to include more coding activities for **[teaching level or age group]** studying **[educational topic]**. **[paste the content]**.

55. Reorient the following lesson plan to focus on creative writing exercises for **[teaching level or age group]** in **[educational topic]**. **[paste the content]**.

ChatGPT can help make complex topics more accessible to people who might struggle with technical jargon or dense academic language. This can be particularly useful for younger audiences or those new to a subject matter.

Fifty Resource Creation for Multiple Cohorts Prompts

Here are some additional **example prompts** that can be customised for creating a **resource for multiple cohorts** in one go:

1. Create a **[number of words]**-word educational material focusing on **[topic]** specifically tailored for students in **[grade/level]**, **[grade/level]**, and **[grade/level]**.
2. Produce a **[number of words]**-word learning guide on **[topic]**, individually designed for **[grade/level]**, **[grade/level]**, and **[grade/level]** students.
3. Develop a **[number of words]**-word instructional resource on **[topic]**, distinctively for **[grade/level]**, **[grade/level]**, and **[grade/level]** students.
4. Craft a **[number of words]**-word educational content on **[topic]**, separately aimed at **[grade/level]**, **[grade/level]**, and **[grade/level]** students.
5. Compose a **[number of words]**-word teaching aid on **[topic]**, uniquely for **[grade/level]**, **[grade/level]**, and **[grade/level]** students.

6. Assemble a **[number of words]**-word study material on **[topic]**, respectively for **[grade/level]**, **[grade/level]**, and **[grade/level]** students.
7. Construct a **[number of words]**-word lesson plan on **[topic]**, individually suited for **[grade/level]**, **[grade/level]**, and **[grade/level]** students.
8. Formulate a **[number of words]**-word educational toolkit on **[topic]**, distinctly for **[grade/level]**, **[grade/level]**, and **[grade/level]** students.
9. Design a **[number of words]**-word learning module on **[topic]**, specifically for **[grade/level]**, **[grade/level]**, and **[grade/level]** students.
10. Draft a **[number of words]**-word educational outline on **[topic]**, respectively targeting **[grade/level]**, **[grade/level]**, and **[grade/level]** students.
11. Author a **[number of words]**-word educational syllabus on **[topic]**, each section tailored for **[grade/level]**, **[grade/level]**, and **[grade/level]** students.
12. Generate a **[number of words]**-word teaching blueprint on **[topic]**, distinctly crafted for **[grade/level]**, **[grade/level]**, and **[grade/level]** students.

13. Prepare a **[number of words]**-word study guide on **[topic]**, each part aimed at **[grade/level]**, **[grade/level]**, and **[grade/level]** students.
14. Compile a **[number of words]**-word educational article on **[topic]**, separately for **[grade/level]**, **[grade/level]**, and **[grade/level]** students.
15. Curate a **[number of words]**-word learning resource on **[topic]**, individually intended for **[grade/level]**, **[grade/level]**, and **[grade/level]** students.
16. Author a **[number of words]**-word educational workbook on **[topic]**, specifically for **[grade/level]**, **[grade/level]**, and **[grade/level]** students.
17. Create a **[number of words]**-word teaching manual on **[topic]**, each chapter for **[grade/level]**, **[grade/level]**, and **[grade/level]** students.
18. Write a **[number of words]**-word study outline on **[topic]**, distinctly for **[grade/level]**, **[grade/level]**, and **[grade/level]** students.
19. Create a **[number of words]**-word educational brief on **[topic]**, each section designed for **[grade/level]**, **[grade/level]**, and **[grade/level]** students.
20. Develop a **[number of words]**-word learning pamphlet on **[topic]**, respectively for **[grade/level]**, **[grade/level]**, and **[grade/level]** students.

21. Develop a **[number of words]**-word instructional manual on **[topic]**, selectively aimed at **[grade/level]**, **[grade/level]**, and **[grade/level]** students.
22. Compose a **[number of words]**-word educational roadmap on **[topic]**, specifically developed for **[grade/level]**, **[grade/level]**, and **[grade/level]** students.
23. Produce a **[number of words]**-word scholastic outline on **[topic]**, singularly crafted for **[grade/level]**, **[grade/level]**, and **[grade/level]** students.
24. Prepare a **[number of words]**-word learning dossier on **[topic]**, targeted uniquely at **[grade/level]**, **[grade/level]**, and **[grade/level]** students.
25. Write a **[number of words]**-word instructional compendium on **[topic]**, distinctly prepared for **[grade/level]**, **[grade/level]**, and **[grade/level]** students.
26. Produce a **[number of words]**-word teaching protocol on **[topic]**, individually optimised for **[grade/level]**, **[grade/level]**, and **[grade/level]** students.
27. Develop a **[number of words]**-word pedagogic series on **[topic]**, exclusively customised for **[grade/level]**, **[grade/level]**, and **[grade/level]** students.

28. Create a **[number of words]**-word study regimen on **[topic]**, distinctly beneficial for **[grade/level]**, **[grade/level]**, and **[grade/level]** students.
29. Compose a **[number of words]**-word educational rubric on **[topic]**, particularly refined for **[grade/level]**, **[grade/level]**, and **[grade/level]** students.
30. Manifest a **[number of words]**-word teaching schema on **[topic]**, set specifically for **[grade/level]** and **[grade/level]** students.
31. Compile a **[number of words]**-word learning narrative on **[topic]**, individually streamlined for **[grade/level]** and **[grade/level]** students.
32. Craft a **[number of words]**-word academic anthology on **[topic]**, exclusively oriented for **[grade/level]** and **[grade/level]** students.
33. Create a **[number of words]**-word scholarly itinerary on **[topic]**, uniquely mapped out for **[grade/level]**, and **[grade/level]** students.
34. Write a **[number of words]**-word study guide on **[topic]**, distinctively aligned for **[grade/level]** and **[grade/level]** students.
35. Create a **[number of words]**-word educational exemplar on **[topic]**, specifically adjusted for **[grade/level]** and **[grade/level]** students.

36. Produce a **[number of words]**-word knowledge package on **[topic]**, expressly for students in **[grade/level]**, and **[grade/level]**.
37. Generate a **[number of words]**-word curriculum supplement on **[topic]**, particularly catering to **[grade/level]** and **[grade/level]** students.
38. Build a **[number of words]**-word academic syllabus on **[topic]**, exclusively intended for **[grade/level]** students.
39. Produce a **[number of words]**-word pedagogical resource on **[topic]**, singularly for **[grade/level]** students.
40. Develop a **[number of words]**-word scholarly guide on **[topic]**, uniquely assembled for **[grade/level]**, **[grade/level]**, and **[grade/level]** students.
41. Create a **[number of words]**-word instructional kit on **[topic]**, specifically created for **[grade/level]** and **[grade/level]** students.
42. Piece together a **[number of words]**-word academic manual on **[topic]**, tailored distinctively for **[grade/level]**, **[grade/level]**, and **[grade/level]** students.
43. Synthesise a **[number of words]**-word learning framework on **[topic]**, individually planned for

[grade/level], **[grade/level]**, and **[grade/level]** students.

44. Compose a **[number of words]**-word supplementary resources on **[topic]**, set apart for **[grade/level].**

45. Compile a **[number of words]**-word scholastic portfolio on **[topic]**, aimed uniquely at **[grade/level]**, **[grade/level]**, and **[grade/level]** students.

46. Write a **[number of words]**-word teaching curriculum on **[topic]**, specifically structured for **[grade/level]** students.

47. Compile a **[number of words]**-word academic digest on **[topic]**, singularly focused on **[grade/level]**, **[grade/level]**, and **[grade/level]** students.

48. Create a **[number of words]**-word learning pathway on **[topic]**, distinctly conceptualised for **[grade/level]**, **[grade/level]**, and **[grade/level]** students.

49. Produce a **[number of words]**-word pedagogical framework on **[topic]**, specially adapted for **[grade/level]**, **[grade/level]**, and **[grade/level]** students.

50. Author a **[number of words]**-word scholastic template on **[topic]**, dedicated particularly to **[grade/level]**, **[grade/level]**, and **[grade/level]** students.

Utilising ChatGPT to create resources for multiple cohorts provides numerous benefits, particularly for educators, researchers, and organisations. Among the key advantages are its scalability and adaptability.

Twenty Merge and Remove Duplicate Prompts

Here are some **example prompts** that can be customised for **merging and removing duplicate content** from the resources:

*Note: Please follow the ChatGPT instructions after you have **entered the prompt** asking to **merge documents**. ChatGPT will ask you for a "**text version of each document**" that requires **merging and removal of duplicate content**.*

1. Would you be able to synthesise **[number of files]** documents, making sure to filter out any recurring elements?
2. Could you join **[number of files]** files, ensuring that no overlapping content remains?
3. Is it feasible to coalesce **[number of files]** documents while purging any repetitive segments?
4. Can you fuse **[number of files]** files, taking care to omit any redundant sections?
5. Blend **[number of files]** documents and remove any duplicate passages.
6. Would you mind integrating **[number of files]** files into a singular document, devoid of any repetitive text?
7. Could you merge **[number of files]** documents, ensuring that no duplicate entries are included?
8. Is it possible to intermingle **[number of files]** files, while eradicating any repetitive elements?
9. Can you assimilate **[number of files]** documents, making sure to exclude any redundant data?
10. Are you able to concatenate **[number of files]** files, ensuring the removal of any duplicate content?

11. Would you be able to join **[number of files]** documents, ensuring that no repetitive elements are left?

12. Could you merge **[number of files]** files into one, while filtering out any overlapping content?

13. Is it feasible to amalgamate **[number of files]** documents together, purging any redundant segments in the process?

14. Can you unify **[number of files]** files into a single document, omitting any repetitive sections?

15. Are you capable of combining **[number of files]** documents together, while removing any duplicate elements?

16. Would you mind combining **[number of files]** files into a unified document, devoid of any repetitive text?

17. Could you integrate **[number of files]** documents into one, ensuring that no duplicate entries are included?

18. Is it possible to unify **[number of files]** files into a single composite, while eradicating any repetitive elements?

19. Can you unify **[number of files]** documents into one, making sure to exclude any redundant data?

20. Are you able to join **[number of files]** files, ensuring the removal of any duplicate content?

Thirty Flashcard Prompts

Here are some **example prompts** that can be **adapted** for **creating flashcards** using ChatGPT on the topic of your choice:

1. Synthesize **[number]** flashcards to explain the complexities of **[topic]**, targeting students at the **[educational level]** who are enrolled in the **[subject/unit]** course.
2. Construct **[number]** pedagogically sound flashcards to deepen the scholarly understanding of **[topic]** among **[educational level]** students. Content to be incorporated: **[paste the content]**.
3. Innovatively curate **[number]** flashcards to empower students at the **[educational level]** in their academic mastery of **[topic]** within the **[subject/unit]** curriculum.
4. Compose **[number]** flashcards that methodically dissect **[topic]**, specifically designed to align with the learning objectives of the **[subject/unit]** program at the **[educational level]**.
5. Develop **[number]** flashcards to facilitate cognitive engagement with **[topic]**, thereby enhancing the

academic performance of **[educational level]** students in the **[subject/unit]** syllabus.

6. Compose **[number]** flashcards to reinforce the academic rigour of **[topic]** among **[educational level]** students. Reference content: **[paste the content]**.
7. Generate **[number]** flashcards that encapsulate the key academic tenets of **[topic]**, tailored to meet the educational needs of **[educational level]** students in the **[subject/unit]** program.
8. Produce **[number]** flashcards with a pedagogical focus on **[topic]**, intended to resonate with the academic goals of **[educational level]** students studying **[subject/unit]**.
9. Create **[number]** flashcards to cultivate scholarly expertise in **[topic]** among **[educational level]** students. Content to be included: **[paste the content]**.
10. Develop **[number]** flashcards to accelerate the academic proficiency of **[topic]** among **[educational level]** students, as part of their **[subject/unit]** curriculum.
11. Formulate **[number]** flashcards centred on **[topic]** to bolster the learning experience for students in the **[subject/unit]** course at **[educational level]**.

12. Curate **[number]** flashcards to facilitate **[educational level]** students' grasp of **[topic]** in their **[subject/unit]** studies. Content to use: **[paste the content]**.
13. Produce **[number]** flashcards to enrich **[educational level]** students' understanding of **[topic]** as part of their **[subject/unit]** syllabus.
14. Develop **[number]** flashcards that delve into **[topic]**, specifically for pupils in the **[subject/unit]** program at **[educational level]**.
15. Make **[number]** flashcards to augment **[educational level]** students' knowledge in **[topic]**, aligned with their **[subject/unit]** curriculum.
16. Compose **[number]** flashcards to fortify **[educational level]** students' grasp of **[topic]** in their **[subject/unit]** studies. Content for reference: **[paste the content]**.
17. Generate **[number]** flashcards that encapsulate **[topic]**, in line with the **[subject/unit]** curriculum for **[educational level]** students.
18. Develop **[number]** flashcards honing in on **[topic]**, tailored to meet the needs of **[educational level]** students in the **[subject/unit]** program.
19. Compile **[number]** flashcards to enhance **[educational level]** students' proficiency in **[topic]** within their **[subject/unit]** coursework. Content to include: **[paste the content]**.

20. Make **[number]** flashcards to expedite **[educational level]** students' mastery of **[topic]** in their **[subject/unit]** program.

21. Create **[number]** flashcards to augment the scholastic comprehension of **[topic]** for students at the **[educational level]**, as part of their **[subject/unit]** curriculum.

22. Compose **[number]** flashcards to bolster the academic acumen of **[topic]** among **[educational level]** students. Content for inclusion: **[paste the content]**.

23. Formulate **[number]** flashcards to enrich the pedagogical depth of **[topic]**, specifically for students enrolled in the **[subject/unit]** program at the **[educational level]**.

24. Develop **[number]** flashcards to enhance the scholarly discourse on **[topic]** among **[educational level]** students, as part of their **[subject/unit]** studies.

25. Generate **[number]** flashcards to foster academic inquiry into **[topic]**, tailored for **[educational level]** students in the **[subject/unit]** program.

26. Produce **[number]** flashcards to facilitate the intellectual exploration of **[topic]** for **[educational level]** students. Content to be used: **[paste the content]**.

27. Develop **[number]** flashcards to nurture academic mastery of **[topic]** among **[educational level]** students, aligned with the **[subject/unit]** curriculum.
28. Create **[number]** flashcards to stimulate intellectual engagement with **[topic]**, aimed at **[educational level]** students in the **[subject/unit]** program.
29. Produce **[number]** flashcards to advance the academic understanding of **[topic]** among **[educational level]** students. Content for reference: **[paste the content]**.
30. Create **[number]** flashcards to elevate the scholastic rigour of **[topic]**, intended for students at the **[educational level]** who are part of the **[subject/unit]** program.

One Hundred Classroom and Student Management Prompts

Here are some **example prompts** that can be **adapted** for **classroom and student management** related tasks:

1. Propose **[number]** strategies for fostering **[positive attitudes towards learning]** among **[students]**.
2. Elaborate on **[number]** techniques for leveraging **[educational technology]** without causing **[classroom distractions]**.
3. Provide **[number]** measures to create an inclusive and diverse **[classroom environment]**.
4. Identify **[number]** methods to help students alleviate **[test anxiety]**.
5. Describe **[number]** approaches to promote **[self-regulation and time management skills]** in students.
6. Offer **[number]** solutions for helping students mitigate **[test anxiety]**.
7. Recommend **[number]** initiatives to achieve **[classroom environment]** diversity and inclusion.
8. Suggest **[number]** ways to cultivate **[positive attitudes towards learning]** in your **[students]**.

9. Share **[number]** techniques for advancing **[self-regulation and time management skills]** among students.
10. Detail **[number]** tactics for guiding students through **[test anxiety]** management.
11. Enumerate **[number]** methods to enhance **[self-regulation and time management skills]** in your classroom.
12. Present **[number]** effective practices for implementing **[educational technology]** without disrupting the **[classroom]**.
13. Discuss **[number]** strategies to inspire **[positive attitudes towards learning]** in your **[students]**.
14. Outline **[number]** methods for harnessing **[educational technology]** while reducing **[classroom distractions]**.
15. Provide **[number]** concrete steps for building a **[classroom environment]** that commemorates diversity.
16. Share **[number]** tips for establishing a strong connection with your **[students]**.
17. Recommend **[number]** strategies to make students feel appreciated and secure in the **[classroom]**.
18. Discuss **[number]** methods for promoting transparent dialogue between **[teachers and students]**.
19. Detail **[number]** techniques for assisting students in defining and reaching their **[personal objectives]**.

20. Write an essay on the role of **[empathy and understanding]** in enhancing **[teacher-student relationships]**.
21. List **[number]** ways to cultivate trust and mutual respect with your **[students]**.
22. Propose **[number]** actions to create an emotionally safe **[classroom environment]**.
23. Enumerate **[number]** approaches for facilitating open discussions between **[educators and learners]**.
24. Provide **[number]** plans for guiding students towards **[personal goal completion]**.
25. Reflect on the significance of **[empathetic interactions]** in sustaining lasting **[teacher-student bonds]**.
26. Recommend **[number]** best practices for fostering **[positive attitudes towards learning]** in your **[students]**.
27. Discuss **[number]** effective ways to maximize the use of **[educational technology]** while minimising **[classroom distractions]**.
28. Outline **[number]** principles to create a diverse and inclusive **[classroom environment]**.
29. Identify **[number]** strategies to help students overcome their **[lack of confidence]**.
30. Describe **[number]** methods for nurturing **[self-regulation and time management skills]** in students.
31. Provide **[number]** solutions to assist students in tackling their **[lack of confidence]**.

32. Support **[number]** policies aimed at achieving diversity and inclusion in the **[classroom environment]**.
33. Encourage **[number]** techniques to elevate **[positive attitudes towards learning]** in your **[students]**.
34. Share **[number]** approaches for boosting **[self-regulation and time management skills]** in students.
35. Define **[number]** pathways to help students address **[lack of confidence]** challenges.
36. List **[number]** strategies to improve **[self-regulation and time management skills]** in your educational setting.
37. Elaborate on **[number]** best practices for integrating **[educational technology]** seamlessly into the **[classroom]**.
38. Explore **[number]** innovative ideas to enhance **[positive attitudes towards learning]** among your **[students]**.
39. Illustrate **[number]** measures for optimising **[educational technology]** without causing **[classroom distractions]**.
40. Present **[number]** concrete steps for creating a diverse **[classroom environment]**.
41. Offer **[number]** tips for forming strong relationships with your **[students]**.
42. Confirm **[number]** ways to make students feel valued and supported in the **[classroom]**.

43. Examine **[number]** avenues for open and effective communication between **[teachers and students]**.
44. Highlight **[number]** tactics to guide students in setting and achieving **[personal objectives]**.
45. Write a reflection on the crucial role of **[empathy and understanding]** in strengthening **[teacher-student relationships]**.
46. Suggest **[number]** methods for building trust and mutual respect with your **[students]**.
47. Promote **[number]** actions for maintaining emotional well-being in the **[classroom environment]**.
48. Report **[number]** techniques for fostering open dialogue between **[educators and learners]**.
49. Propose **[number]** guidelines for directing students toward **[personal goal completion]**.
50. Reflect on the long-term benefits of **[empathetic interactions]** in sustaining **[teacher-student bonds]**.
51. Craft a parent-facing communique detailing the advantages of participating in parent-teacher conferences. **[specify date and time]**
52. Write a thoughtful reply to a parent expressing concerns over a sudden decline in their child's academic performance. **[paste parent's email]**
53. Author a tailored note to a parent suggesting a face-to-face conversation about their child's unsettling conduct in class. **[mention student name]**

54. Formulate a comprehensive answer to a parent challenging the rationale behind your homework guidelines. **[paste parent's email]**
55. Articulate the critical role of consistent school attendance in a message to a parent whose child has been habitually missing classes. **[paste student name]**
56. Develop a persuasive email aimed at parents to highlight the value of face-to-face interactions between teachers and parents. **[insert meeting details]**
57. Respond to a parent's apprehensions about their child's dwindling grades with a solution-oriented email. **[paste parent's email]**
58. Initiate a dialogue with a parent regarding their child's disruptive tendencies in a carefully crafted message. **[state student name]**
59. Clarify your stance on homework assignments in a detailed email response to a parent's query. **[paste parent's email]**
60. Address the issue of frequent absences in a message to a parent, stressing the long-term academic consequences. **[identify student name]**
61. Create a parent-focused email introducing the school's newly adopted **[positive behaviour reinforcement initiative]**.
62. Write a considerate email reply to a parent seeking guidance on resources available for their child with **[learning challenges]**. **[mention student name]**

63. Construct an informative letter to parents discussing imminent **[standardised tests]** and strategies for **[effective preparation]**.
64. Generate a thoughtful message to address a parent's worries about their child's **[social interactions]** in school. **[cite student name]**
65. Compose an announcement email to parents detailing an upcoming **[school function or fundraising activity]**.
66. Compose an email to parents unveiling a new school-wide initiative aimed at promoting **[positive behaviour and values]**.
67. Write a responsive email to a parent who is inquiring about available support for their child's **[learning difficulties]**. **[include student name]**
68. Create an advisory notice to parents concerning future **[standardised assessments]** and tips to aid in their child's **[preparation]**.
69. Respond to a parent concerned about their child's ability to **[socialise effectively]** in the educational environment. **[state student name]**
70. Draft an engaging email to parents outlining the highlights of an impending **[school gala or charity drive]**.
71. Write an email directed at parents to introduce the school's innovative program focused on **[encouraging positive behaviour]**.

72. Compose a compassionate reply to a parent seeking assistance on resources tailored for children experiencing **[educational challenges]**. **[note student name]**
73. Develop an informational memo to parents outlining the upcoming **[standardised assessments]** and best practices for **[successful preparation]**.
74. Provide a comprehensive response to a parent expressing concern over their child's **[social adaptability]** at school. **[identify student name]**
75. Write an inviting email to parents spotlighting an upcoming **[school-sponsored event or fundraiser]**.
76. Design an introductory email to parents to unveil a freshly implemented, school-wide **[well-being and behaviour initiative]**.
77. Create a tactful response for a parent inquiring about available accommodations for their child with **[learning barriers]**. **[specify student name]**
78. Issue an advisory bulletin to parents highlighting **[forthcoming standardised tests]** and effective **[study strategies]**.
79. Formulate a targeted message to a parent who is concerned about their child's **[social integration]** at school. **[reference student name]**
80. Pen an attention-grabbing email to parents detailing the key attractions of an upcoming **[school event or charitable initiative]**.

81. Share **[number]** practical strategies for fostering a **[classroom environment]** that thrives on **[positive energy]**.
82. Provide **[number]** effective methods for achieving optimal **[acoustic conditions]** in the **[classroom]**.
83. Advocate for **[number]** creative techniques to heighten **[student engagement]** during **[classroom discussions]**.
84. Explore **[number]** impactful solutions to mitigate the challenge of **[chronic tardiness]** among **[students]**.
85. Enumerate **[number]** robust **[anti-fraud measures]** to safeguard **[exam integrity]**.
86. Suggest **[number]** proven approaches for cultivating an **[inspiring and inclusive learning space]**.
87. Discuss **[number]** innovative **[noise-control methods]** to create a peaceful **[classroom atmosphere]**.
88. Recommend **[number]** tactics for **[encouraging active participation]** during **[interactive educational activities]**.
89. Detail **[number]** proactive interventions for managing **[consistent late arrivals]** in **[students]**.
90. Provide **[number]** best practices for **[preventing dishonesty]** during **[academic evaluations]**.
91. Offer **[number]** insights to maintain a **[positive and collaborative classroom setting]**.
92. Provide **[number]** **[sound-management techniques]** to establish a focused **[learning environment]**.

93. Suggest **[number]** ways to ignite **[student involvement]** in **[academic conversations]**.
94. Examine **[number]** strategies for assisting **[students]** who exhibit **[persistent lateness]**.
95. Describe **[number]** methods to **[counter academic dishonesty]** during **[key assessments]**.
96. Share **[number]** effective strategies for nurturing a **[positive learning environment]** within the **[classroom]**.
97. Explain **[number]** practical methods for managing **[ambient noise levels]** in the **[classroom]**.
98. Recommend **[number]** creative approaches for boosting **[active participation]** during **[classroom discussions]**.
99. Discuss **[number]** constructive solutions for handling **[chronic tardiness]** among **[students]**.
100. Draft a comprehensive strategy for eliciting and implementing **[student feedback]** to optimise **[teaching practice]**.

Both classroom and student management are intricately linked and play a significant role in shaping the overall educational experience. By utilising the ChatGPT prompts provided, you can delve into a range of strategies and methods that are effective for managing both the classroom environment and individual students. These prompts offer a starting point for educators to consider how best to foster a positive, productive space for learning, while also attending to the unique needs and strengths of each student.

One Hundred Educational Research Prompts

The prompts included in this section are for **various types of educational research** that can be **customised** for various **topics** of **interest.**

1. Conduct a comprehensive literature review to identify and synthesize the key **[neuroscientific theories]** related to **[memory formation]** and **[recall processes]**.
2. Undertake a 2000 word meta-analysis of the existing **[psychological studies]** on the effects of **[mindfulness meditation]** in reducing **[anxiety symptoms]** among **[adolescent populations]**.
3. Carry out a 2000 word systematic review of **[neuroimaging studies]** to examine the neural correlates of **[language acquisition]** in **[bilingual children]**.
4. Perform a meta-analysis of **[educational interventions]** aimed at enhancing **[mathematical proficiency]** in **[elementary school students]**.

5. Conduct a 1500 word literature review on the **[historical evolution]** of **[educational technology]** and its impact on **[learning outcomes]**.
6. Undertake a meta-analysis of the **[pedagogical effectiveness]** of **[active learning strategies]** in **[higher education]**.
7. Carry out a systematic review of **[neuroscientific research]** to identify the **[neural pathways]** associated with **[creative thinking]**.
8. Perform a meta-analysis of studies examining the **[impact of socio-economic factors]** on **[educational achievement]** across **[diverse student populations]**.
9. Conduct a comprehensive literature review to assess the **[evolutionary theories]** explaining **[adolescent risk-taking behaviour]**.
10. Undertake a meta-analysis of **[quantitative research]** studies on the relationship between **[educational attainment]** and **[career success]**.
11. Carry out a literature review focusing on the **[historical development]** of **[learning theories]** in the context of **[online education]**.
12. Perform a meta-analysis of **[cognitive psychology studies]** investigating the **[effectiveness of memory techniques]** in **[improving information retention]**.

13. Conduct a 1800 word systematic review of **[neuroscientific literature]** to explore the **[neural substrates]** of **[decision-making processes]** in **[adolescents]**.

14. Undertake a comprehensive literature review to identify **[emerging trends]** in **[education technology adoption]** in **[K-12 education]**.

15. Carry out a meta-analysis of **[quantitative studies]** examining the **[impact of parental involvement]** on **[early childhood literacy]**.

16. Perform a literature review on the **[historical context]** and **[theoretical frameworks]** underpinning **[cultural competence]** in **[teacher education]**.

17. Conduct a systematic review of **[neuropsychological research]** to explore the **[neurocognitive processes]** involved in **[learning disabilities]**.

18. Undertake a 2000 word meta-analysis of **[psychological studies]** investigating the **[relationship between motivation]** and **[academic achievement]** in **[adolescent students]**.

19. Carry out a comprehensive literature review to examine the **[theoretical foundations]** and **[research methodologies]** employed in **[STEM education]**.

20. Perform a meta-analysis of **[studies on educational interventions]** to determine the overall **[effect size]**

of **[inclusive classroom practices]** on **[student learning outcomes]**.

21. Write a 1200 word report about the impact of **remote learning** on the academic performance of **[primary school students]**.

22. How do different **[teaching styles]** affect student engagement in a **[high school]** setting?

23. To what extent do **[extracurricular activities]** contribute to the overall development of a **[university student]**?

24. How does the integration of **[technology]** in the classroom affect the learning outcomes of **[students with special needs]**?

25. What role does **[parental involvement]** play in a child's academic success in **[early education]**?

26. How do **[school nutrition programmes]** influence the cognitive abilities and concentration levels of **[students]**?

27. What are the long-term effects of **[standardised testing]** on student motivation and self-esteem?

28. How does a **[culturally inclusive curriculum]** impact the social dynamics and relationships among **[students]**?

29. What are the psychological effects of **[grade retention]** on **[primary school students]**?

30. How do different **[classroom layouts]** and designs impact student engagement and focus?

31. Write a 1200 word report on the benefits and drawbacks of implementing a **[flipped classroom model]** in **[higher education]**.

32. How does **[peer tutoring]** influence academic performance and social skills among **[middle school students]**?

33. What impact do **[school-based mental health services]** have on student well-being and academic performance?

34. How effective are **[game-based learning strategies]** in enhancing mathematical skills among **[primary school students]**?

35. What are the factors that contribute to **[academic burnout]** among **[postgraduate students]**?

36. How does the use of **[open educational resources (OER)]** affect the quality of education in **[underfunded schools]**?

37. What role does **[emotional intelligence]** play in academic success among **[high school students]**?

38. How do different **[assessment methods]** influence student engagement and learning outcomes in **[online courses]**?
39. What are the ethical considerations in using **[AI and machine learning tools]** for an educational assessment?
40. How does the incorporation of **[real-world problems]** in the curriculum influence problem-solving skills among **[university students]**?
41. How does **[neuroplasticity]** influence **[learning outcomes]** in **[adult education]**?
42. What are the implications of **[machine learning algorithms]** in **[adaptive learning systems]** for **[higher education]**?
43. How does **[socioeconomic status]** intersect with **[educational attainment]** in **[urban and rural settings]**?
44. To what extent do **[implicit biases]** in **[educational materials]** affect **[student perceptions]** of **[gender and race]**?
45. How do **[cognitive load theories]** apply to the design of **[online educational interfaces]**?
46. What impact do **[blockchain technologies]** have on the **[academic credential verification process]**?

47. How does **[interdisciplinary collaboration]** in **[academic research]** influence **[innovation and knowledge transfer]**?
48. What are the **[psychometric properties]** of **[standardised assessments]** in measuring **[emotional and social competencies]**?
49. How do **[fluctuations in political climate]** affect **[educational policy reform]** and **[curriculum development]**?
50. What role does **[quantum computing]** play in the future of **[educational data analysis]**?
51. How does **[cultural capital]** influence **[academic success]** among **[first-generation university students]**?
52. What are the ethical implications of **[biometric surveillance]** in **[educational settings]**?
53. How does **[constructivist pedagogy]** influence **[student autonomy]** in **[project-based learning environments]**?
54. What impact does **[virtual reality]** have on **[spatial awareness and problem-solving skills]** in **[STEM education]**?
55. How do **[ethical considerations]** in **[educational research]** influence **[methodological choices]** and **[data interpretation]**?

56. What are the **[cognitive and emotional impacts]** of **[long-term exposure to screen-based learning]**?
57. How does **[metacognitive training]** influence **[academic performance]** in **[complex subjects like quantum physics]**?
58. What role does **[emotional resilience]** play in **[academic persistence]** among **[PhD candidates]**?
59. How do **[institutional policies]** influence **[faculty diversity]** and what is its impact on **[student success]**?
60. What are the **[psychological and physiological effects]** of **[chronic academic stress]** on **[mental health]** among **[graduate students]**?
61. Investigate the **[neurobiological mechanisms]** underlying **[cognitive development]** in **[early childhood education]**.
62. Examine the **[algorithmic efficacy]** of **[machine learning]** in **[personalised educational pathways]** within **[tertiary institutions]**.
63. Conduct a **[longitudinal study]** on the **[socioeconomic determinants]** affecting **[educational attainment]** across **[geographically diverse populations]**.

64. Evaluate the **[psychological impact]** of **[implicit biases]** present in **[educational curricula]** on **[self-identity formation]** among **[adolescents]**.

65. Assess the **[cognitive load]** imposed by **[user interface design]** in **[e-learning platforms]** and its effect on **[information retention]**.

66. Explore the **[cryptographic integrity]** of **[blockchain technologies]** in **[academic credentialing]**.

67. Investigate the **[synergistic effects]** of **[interdisciplinary research]** on **[scholarly innovation]** and **[knowledge dissemination]**.

68. Analyse the **[psychometric validity]** and **[reliability]** of **[standardised assessments]** in gauging **[non-cognitive skills]**.

69. Examine the **[sociopolitical factors]** influencing **[educational policy]** and **[curricular adaptation]**.

70. Assess the **[computational capabilities]** of **[quantum computing]** in **[big data analytics]** for **[educational research]**.

71. Investigate the role of **[cultural capital]** as a **[moderating variable]** in **[academic achievement]** among **[first-generation tertiary students]**.

72. Examine the **[ethical ramifications]** of **[biometric data collection]** in **[educational surveillance]**.

73. Evaluate the **[pedagogical efficacy]** of **[constructivist approaches]** in fostering **[learner autonomy]** within **[problem-based learning environments]**.

74. Investigate the **[spatial-cognitive benefits]** of **[virtual reality simulations]** in **[STEM pedagogy]**.

75. Conduct a **[meta-analysis]** on the **[ethical considerations]** shaping **[methodological paradigms]** in **[educational research]**.

76. Assess the **[neurocognitive consequences]** of **[prolonged screen exposure]** in **[digital learning environments]**.

77. Examine the **[metacognitive strategies]** employed in **[high-level academic performance]** in **[quantum physics coursework]**.

78. Investigate the **[psychological resilience factors]** contributing to **[academic persistence]** among **[doctoral candidates]**.

79. Evaluate the **[institutional policies]** that either facilitate or hinder **[faculty diversity]** and their subsequent impact on **[student academic outcomes]**.

80. Conduct a **[cross-sectional study]** on the **[psychophysiological stress responses]** to **[academic pressures]** among **[postgraduate students]**.

81. Conduct an extensive literature review to analyse the prevailing **[social policies]** addressing **[poverty**

alleviation] and their impact on **[vulnerable communities]**.

82. Undertake a meta-analysis of existing **[sociological studies]** on the **[causes and consequences]** of **[income inequality]** in **[urban settings]**.
83. Carry out a systematic review of **[criminological research]** to examine the **[factors contributing to juvenile delinquency]** and their implications for **[youth rehabilitation]** programs.
84. Perform a literature review on the **[historical evolution]** of **[gender equality movements]** and their effects on **[women's empowerment]**.
85. Conduct a meta-analysis of **[psychosocial studies]** investigating the **[impact of social isolation]** on **[mental health]** among **[elderly populations]**.
86. Undertake a comprehensive review of **[public health initiatives]** aimed at addressing **[substance abuse]** and their effectiveness in **[reducing addiction rates]**.
87. Carry out a systematic review of **[societal attitudes]** towards **[racial diversity]** and their influence on **[racial harmony]** in multicultural societies.
88. Perform a meta-analysis of **[studies on community development]** to assess the **[socioeconomic outcomes]** of **[neighbourhood revitalisation]** projects.

89. Conduct a literature review on the **[policy frameworks]** and **[social implications]** of **[immigration]** in **[contemporary societies]**.
90. Undertake an in-depth analysis of **[sociological theories]** explaining the **[phenomenon of homelessness]**.
91. Carry out a systematic review of **[social work research]** to explore the **[efficacy of trauma-informed care]** in **[supporting survivors of domestic violence]**.
92. Perform a literature review on the **[historical context]** surrounding **[human rights advocacy]**.
93. Conduct a meta-analysis of **[studies on educational disparities]** to examine the **[achievement gap]** among students from **[disadvantaged backgrounds]**.
94. Undertake a comprehensive review of **[social policies and healthcare access]** for **[marginalised populations]** and their implications for **[health equity]**.
95. Carry out a systematic analysis of **[societal perceptions]** of **[mental illness]** and their influence on **[stigma reduction]** campaigns.
96. Perform a meta-analysis of **[research on social justice]** to determine the overall **[impact]** of **[activist movements]** on **[policy changes]**.

97. Conduct a literature review on the **[evolution of family dynamics]** and their implications for **[child development]** in modern **[society]**.
98. Do a critical analysis of **[social media platforms]** as vehicles for **[social activism]** and their role in **[promoting social change]**.
99. Conduct a systematic review of **[social science research]** to assess the **[effectiveness]** of **[restorative justice]** programs in **[reducing recidivism]**.
100. Perform a meta-analysis of **[studies on political polarisation]** to examine the **[impact of media consumption]**.

ChatGPT can assist researchers in brainstorming ideas for experiments, surveys, or research questions. The platform is capable of generating a list of potential research angles or methodologies that researchers might consider for their studies. Whether you're in the initial stages of forming a research question or looking for innovative approaches to data collection and analysis, ChatGPT can serve as a valuable resource for sparking creativity and offering diverse perspectives.

One Hundred and Ten Professional Development Prompts

The prompts included in this section are **universal** types that would suit most **professionals** for common tasks such as preparing for **job interviews**, creating and updating **resumes**, and **writing job application cover letters**:

INTERVIEW

1. Generate practice interview questions for a **[job title]** job and give me pointers on my performance. **[Paste your resume here]**
2. I tend to get anxious in **[interview situation or type]**. Provide some techniques to overcome job-related anxiety.
3. What are some out-of-the-box questions I can ask my interviewer for a **[job title]** position?
4. I've got an interview lined up at **[company]**. What queries could give me insights into their **[organisation aspects]**?

5. I have a video interview on the horizon. What tech prep should I undertake in advance for the **[position**]?
6. What non-verbal cues should I be mindful of during a **[type of interview**]?
7. How should I tackle the 'Introduce yourself' query in a video interview for a **[job title**] role?
8. I'm uneasy about video interviews. Could you offer some morale-boosting **[pointers/advice/tips**]?
9. I'm keen on joining **[Company**]. How can I capture their attention during my job interview?
10. In a video interview for a **[job title]** role, how should I go about presenting myself when asked to introduce myself?
11. How can I effectively address the 'Introduce yourself' question during a video interview for a **[job title]** role?
12. During a **[type of interview]**, what are some non-verbal signals I should pay attention to?
13. What body language cues should I be conscious of throughout my **[type of interview]**?
14. In the course of a **[type of interview]**, what non-verbal indicators should I keep an eye out for?

15. Before my upcoming video interview for the **[position]**, what tech essentials should I sort out?
16. I have a video interview scheduled for the **[position]**. What tech checklist should I follow to be fully prepared?
17. What probing questions should I ask to better understand **[company]**'s **[organisation aspects]** during my upcoming interview?
18. I'm set for an interview with **[company]**; what should I inquire about to get a deeper understanding of their **[organisation aspects]**?
19. My interview with **[company]** is coming up. What questions can help me unravel the intricacies of their **[organisation aspects]**?
20. I'm prone to feeling jittery during **[interview situation or type]**. What are some coping strategies to alleviate career-focused stress?

COVER LETTERS

21. **[Draft a persuasive and relatable cover letter**] in 180 words **[that brings to light my qualifications, experiences, and skills**] for the **[Science teacher role at XYZ College**] using my resume. **[Paste your resume here**]

22. **[Write an amicable and objective-focused cover letter**] in 170 words **[accentuating my qualifications, experiences, and skills**] for the **[Senior lecturer position at ABC University**] using my resume. **[Paste your resume here**] **[Author a succinct and resolute cover letter**] in 160 words **[featuring my qualifications, experiences, and skills**] for the **[Program Director role at TUV Consulting**] using my resume. **[Paste your resume here**]
23. **[Write a forward-thinking cover letter**] in 190 words **[explaining my qualifications, experiences, and skills**] for the **[Maths teacher position at University**] using my resume. **[Paste your resume here**]
24. **[Generate a captivating cover letter**] in 180 words **[exhibiting my qualifications, experiences, and skills**] for the **[Job position]** at **[Organisation name**] using my resume. **[Paste your resume here**]
25. **[Write a genuine sounding cover letter**] in 150 words **[stressing my qualifications, experiences, and skills**] for the **[Job position]** at **[Organisation name**] using my resume. **[Paste your resume here**]
26. **[Create an enthusiastic cover letter**] in 170 words **[spotlighting my qualifications, experiences, and skills**] for the **[Job position]** position at

[Organisation name] using my resume. **[Paste your resume here**]

27. **[Compose an outcome-oriented cover letter**] in 190 words **[displaying my qualifications, experiences, and skills**] for the **[Job position]** position at **[Organisation name]** using my resume. **[Paste your resume here**]

28. Put together a spirited **[170]** word cover letter that shines a spotlight on my abilities, qualifications, and experiences relevant to the **[Job position]** at **[Organisation name]**. **[Paste your resume here**]

29. Write a **[200]** word **[high-energy]** cover letter illuminating my qualifications and experiences for the **[Job position]** post at **[Organisation name]**. **[Paste your resume here**]

30. Draft a **[150]** word **[sincere cover]** cover letter accentuating my skills and experiences for the **[Job position]** role at **[Organisation name]. [Paste your resume here**]

GENERAL CAREER QUERIES

31. Assist me in crafting an email to request an exploratory chat with a professional in **[industry or role**].

32. Provide me with a **[strategy]** for a post-application follow-up email.
33. Recommend inquiries that will project my **[emotion type]** for sustained career advancement within the organisation.
34. What should I inquire about to determine the work-life balance at **[company]**?
35. Provide me with questions that will help me understand the group dynamics at **[company]**.
36. What's the most courteous way to turn down a job proposition through **[communication type]**?
37. I've been on the job hunt for a while without success. Suggest some search approach for **[job position]**
38. Are there any niche job search websites suitable for **[industry type]**?
39. Discuss **[number]** methods for effectively juggling **[career responsibilities]** and **[personal well-being]** as a teacher.
40. Write a **[personal vision statement]** outlining **[career goals]** in education and steps to achieve them.

TEACHING AND PEDAGOGICAL REFLECTIONS

41. Summarise **[number]** key takeaways from a recent **[educational research study/paper]** that could improve **[classroom management/teaching methods]**.

42. Describe **[number]** challenges and solutions for teachers adapting to **[new educational technologies/digital classrooms]**.

43. Compile **[number]** best practices for enhancing **[student engagement/participation]** in a **[remote/in-person]** setting.

44. Create a **[plan/strategy]** for fostering a **[collaborative/competitive]** learning environment in **[classroom/online platform]**.

45. Explain **[number]** ways to assess **[student performance/learning outcomes]** without traditional exams.

46. Suggest **[number]** innovative techniques to encourage **[critical thinking/problem-solving]** skills in students.

47. Reflect on the role of **[teacher autonomy/administrative guidance]** in shaping **[curriculum/teaching style]**.

48. Pinpoint **[number]** resources for improving **[emotional intelligence/social skills]** in students.

49. Identify **[number]** steps for implementing **[sustainability practices/eco-friendly methods]** in the **[classroom/school]**.

50. Assess **[number]** strategies for addressing **[bullying/harassment]** issues within the educational setting.

51. Formulate a plan for **[peer reviews/teacher evaluations]** to enhance **[educational quality/teaching efficacy]**.

52. Discuss **[number]** approaches for effectively communicating with **[parents/guardians]** regarding **[student progress/behavioural issues]**.

53. Analyse **[number]** techniques for **[differentiated instruction/personalised learning]** in a diverse classroom.

54. Share **[number]** tips for successfully managing **[classroom disruptions/online class participation]**.

55. Examine **[number]** aspects of **[cross-disciplinary/interdisciplinary]** teaching and their impact on **[student learning/engagement]**.

56. Recommend **[number]** key sources for integrating **[socio-emotional development]** in the **[classroom/educational setting]**.

57. Compose an analysis of a recent **[team-teaching experience/cooperative project**] and its effects on **[instructional approaches/classroom dynamics**].

58. Develop a strategy for leveraging **[student critiques/feedback**] as a means for **[pedagogical improvement/teaching enhancement**].

59. Illustrate **[number**] life hacks for achieving **[work-life balance**] in the **[educational sector/teaching profession**].

60. Point out **[number**] digital platforms or apps beneficial for infusing **[social-emotional aspects**] into **[classroom management/teaching methods**].

61. Share insights from a recent **[partnership**] with another education provider and its ramifications on **[teaching style**].

62. Develop a framework for actively gathering and assimilating **[feedback/opinions**] from students for **[pedagogical refinement/teaching improvement**].

63. Reflect on a **[co-teaching scenario/joint teaching experience**] and how it altered **[classroom dynamics/teaching methods**].

64. Propose a methodical approach for collecting and integrating **[student opinions/feedback**] to elevate **[teaching standards/educational quality**].

65. Propose **[number]** avenues for mastering **[new educational technologies]** as part of ongoing **[professional development]**.

66. Draft a self-assessment checklist for evaluating one's own **[teaching methodologies]** and **[classroom management skills]**.

67. Compile **[number]** resources that offer **[cutting-edge pedagogical research]** that could be implemented in the **[classroom]**.

68. Share **[number]** ways to engage in **[peer review]** within **[educational institutions]** for mutual professional development.

69. Describe **[number]** unconventional methods for collecting **[student feedback]** that could lead to **[pedagogical innovations]**.

70. Detail **[number]** strategies for integrating **[interdisciplinary learning]** into **[teaching practice]**.

71. Identify **[number]** activities for enhancing **[cultural competency]** to better teach a **[diverse student body]**.

72. Examine **[number]** ways to apply **[data analytics]** in tracking and improving **[student performance]**.

73. Create a plan for **[leadership development]** within the **[educational setting]**, outlining **[number]** key milestones.
74. Discuss **[number]** peer-reviewed articles that have significantly influenced **[teaching philosophy]**.
75. Develop a guide with itemised for conducting **[self-reflective teaching audits]** at the end of each **[academic term]**.
76. Establish **[number]** criteria for selecting **[educational conferences]** that align with **[professional objectives]**.
77. Offer **[number]** tips for **[self-care]** that also contribute to **[better teaching performance]**.
78. Propose **[number]** avenues for mastering **[new educational technologies]** as part of ongoing **[professional development]**.
79. Discuss **[number]** peer-reviewed articles that have significantly influenced a **[teaching philosophy]**.
80. Develop a concise guide for conducting **[self-reflective teaching audits]** at the end of each **[academic term]**.
81. Establish **[number]** criteria for selecting **[educational conferences]** that align with **[professional objectives]**.

82. Offer **[number]** tips for **[self-care]** that also contribute to **[better teaching performance]**.

83. Advocate for **[number]** pedagogical tools that can aid in **[remote learning/in-person instruction]**.

84. Mention **[number]** dedicated organisations that focus on **[continual professional development]** in **[field/subject area]**.

85. Outline **[number]** practices for maintaining **[work-life balance/mental wellbeing]** as an educator.

86. Provide **[number]** principles for a **[balanced lifestyle]** that accommodates both **[teaching commitments]** and **[personal life]**.

87. Suggest **[number]** non-traditional approaches to harvesting **[learner insights]** that could fuel **[cutting-edge teaching methods]**.

88. Investigate **[number]** methodologies for employing **[big data]** to refine and elevate **[scholastic outcomes]**.

89. Architect a comprehensive blueprint for **[instructional leadership growth]** within an **[academia-focused environment]**, demarcating **[number]** pivotal stages.

90. Suggest **[number]** scholarly publications that have been game-changers in shaping your **[pedagogic stance]**.

SOCIAL MEDIA-DRIVEN NETWORKING STRATEGIES

91. Uncover **[number]** untapped strategies for leveraging **[LinkedIn]** to build **[professional teaching networks]**.

92. Investigate **[number]** cutting-edge ways to use **[Twitter chats]** for **[educational thought leadership]**.

93. Craft **[number]** ingenious methods for employing **[Instagram Stories]** to showcase **[classroom innovations]**.

94. Develop **[number]** unique approaches for utilizing **[Facebook Groups]** to foster **[collaborative educational projects]**.

95. Pinpoint **[number]** original techniques for navigating **[Clubhouse]** to engage in **[real-time pedagogical discussions]**.

96. Analyse **[number]** modern tactics for using **[Pinterest boards]** to collect and share **[educational resources]**.

97. Formulate **[number]** breakthrough ideas for maximizing **[Reddit AMAs (Ask Me Anything)]** to discuss **[teaching philosophies]**.

98. Design **[number]** state-of-the-art methods for employing **[YouTube channels]** to disseminate **[teaching best practices]**.

99. Conceptualise **[number]** visionary strategies to reach **[a broader educational community]**.

100. Explore **[number]** audacious ways to use **[Snapchat filters]** for **[virtual classroom engagement]**.

101. Devise **[number]** cutting-edge strategies for leveraging **[LinkedIn]** to expand your **[educational network]**.

102. Uncover **[number]** inventive tactics for using **[Twitter chats]** to engage with **[thought leaders in education]**.

103. Outline **[number]** ways to curate **[educational content]** on **[Pinterest]** for professional growth.

104. Enumerate **[number]** ingenious methods for hosting **[virtual networking events]** on platforms like **[Facebook]**.

105. Elucidate **[number]** state-of-the-art techniques for using **[Instagram Stories]** to share **[classroom innovations]** with peers.

106. Investigate **[number]** creative approaches for utilizing **[YouTube]** to showcase **[teaching methodologies]**.

107. Illustrate **[number]** breakthrough practices for leveraging **[Substack newsletters]** to share **[academic research]**.

108. Clarify **[number]** modern strategies for using **[Reddit forums]** to gather **[peer reviews on teaching materials]**.

109. Examine **[number]** advanced ways to use **[Snapchat]** for **[informal educational discussions]**.

110. Suggest **[number]** dynamic techniques for utilising **[Slack channels]** to collaborate on **[curriculum development]**.

CHAPTER 18

FIFTY-TWO VIDEO OUTPUTS OF CHATGPT PROMPTS FOR TEACHING, LEARNING AND PROFESSIONAL DEVELOPMENT

18. Fifty-Two Video Outputs of ChatGPT Prompts for Teaching, Learning and Professional Development

The **video output** of different prompts can help you **visualise** the likely ChatGPT **outputs you may expect to see** when you use **similar prompts**.

Seeing the ChatGPT outputs for **specific prompts** may spark new prompt ideas for the **common teaching and learning tasks** you may want **to accomplish using ChatGPT.**

This section has **fifty-two ChatGPT** prompts with **video output** that you can access using the provided **link or OR code.**

PROMPT 01 – DEVELOPING A LESSON PLAN

Create a lively and stimulating **[5]**-week educational lesson plan that scrutinises **[10]** elements of **[Human Anatomy]** for **[undergraduate]** students. Enumerate **[3]** participatory tasks and **[2]** weekly milestones to track and ensure student advancement.

ChatGPT Video Output URL and QR Code:

https://tinyurl.com/AnatomyLessonPlan

PROMPT 02 – DEVELOPING A LESSON PLAN

Design a lesson plan for **[undergraduate]** students on **[sustainability]**, outlining **[10]** lessons and activities that build upon one another over **[12]** weeks.

ChatGPT Video Output URL and QR Code:

https://tinyurl.com/Sustainability-LessonPlan

PROMPT 03 – CREATING QUIZ

Produce a quiz that includes **25 Likert scale questions** to gauge students' attitudes or perceptions about **[Investigating the Factors Affecting Urbanization in a Region]**.

ChatGPT Video Output URL and QR Code:

https://tinyurl.com/LikertScaleQuiz

PROMPT 04 – CREATING QUIZ

Create a quiz featuring **25 debate questions** that ask students to argue for or against a statement related to **[Examining the Impact of Social Media on Mental Health]**.

ChatGPT Video Output URL and QR Code:

https://tinyurl.com/GPTDebateQuiz

PROMPT 05 - BRAINSTORMING

Can you formulate a set of questions that delve into the **[socio-economic impacts]** of **[poverty]** on **[vulnerable communities]**?

ChatGPT Video Output URL and QR Code:

https://tinyurl.com/FormulateQuestions

Prompt 06 – BRAINSTORMING

Could you suggest some **[subtopics]** that explore the **[limitations and challenges]** of implementing **[artificial intelligence]** in **[legal systems]**?

ChatGPT Video Output URL and QR Code:

https://tinyurl.com/SubtopicIdeas

PROMPT 07 – ENGAGING IN CONVERSATION

What's your perspective on **[online learning or e-learning platforms]**? Have you had any standout experiences? How do you think **[this mode of education]** is reshaping traditional classrooms?

ChatGPT Video Output URL and QR Code:

https://tinyurl.com/ConvExample01

PROMPT 08 – ENGAGING IN CONVERSATION

What **[educational technology or tool]** do you wish was more widely used? How would it address a current **[educational gap or challenge]**? What steps could schools take to implement it?

ChatGPT Video Output URL and QR Code:

https://tinyurl.com/ConvExample02

PROMPT 09 – LANGUAGE TRANSLATION

[Convert] this **[English Language]** philosophical text into **[Spanish Language]**, preserving its complex ideas: **[Everything we hear is an opinion, not a fact. Everything we see is a perspective, not the truth.]**

ChatGPT Video Output URL and QR Code:

https://tinyurl.com/EngToSpan

PROMPT 10 – MULTILINGUAL TRANSLATION

Reinterpret the following sentence from **[English]** to **[Polish]** and **[Mandarin]**: **[Throughout history, many philosophers and scholars have examined courage from different perspectives, discussing its ethical, psychological, and moral dimensions.]**

ChatGPT Video Output URL and QR Code:

https://tinyurl.com/EngToPolMand

PROMPT 11 – SUMMARISING

[Summarise] the **[causes and consequences]** of the **[First World War]**.

ChatGPT Video Output URL and QR Code:

https://tinyurl.com/WWI-Summary

PROMPT 12 – SUMMARISING

[Compile] a **[summary]** of the **[major theories and principles]** in **[criminology]**.

ChatGPT Video Output URL and QR Code:

https://tinyurl.com/CriminologyTheories

PROMPT 13 – PROOFREADING AND OPTIMISATION

Proofread and optimise [*Mars, often referred to as the "Red Planet," holds a special place in our solar system as the fourth planet from the Sun. Its distinctive reddish hue is attributed to the abundant iron oxide (rust) covering its surface. Throughout history, Mars has captured the imaginations of astronomers and stargazers with its enigmatic presence. Despite its similarity to Earth in terms of day length (about 24.6 hours), a Martian year is considerably longer, lasting approximately 687 Earth days. Mars boasts remarkable geographical features, including Olympus Mons, the largest volcano in our solar system, and Valles Marineris, a colossal canyon system dwarfing Earth's Grand Canyon. The planet's atmosphere, though thin, consists primarily of carbon dioxide, rendering it inhospitable for human life without significant life support systems. Mars is known for its polar ice caps, composed of both water and dry ice, offering valuable insights into its climate history. Over the years, NASA and other space agencies have launched numerous robotic missions to explore Mars, seeking clues about the possibility of past or present life. One such mission is the Curiosity rover, tirelessly examining the Martian surface since its arrival in 2012.*

] for clarity and coherence.

52.

ChatGPT Video Output URL and QR Code:

https://tinyurl.com/ProofreadOptimise

PROMPT 14 – PROVIDING FEEDBACK

Provide feedback on **[Structural Integrity]**, recommending paragraph divisions or reordering for better flow in [*Homo sapiens, also known as modern humans, stand as the lone survivors within the Homo genus. This intriguing tale of evolution showcases our adaptability and ingenuity. For millennia, Indigenous Australians have been inhabitants of this continent, demonstrating an extraordinary connection to the land and a profound understanding of its distinct ecosystems, illustrating the enduring nature of Homo sapiens' ability to flourish in diverse surroundings. In contemporary times, Homo sapiens have harnessed their intellectual and technological capabilities to accomplish astounding achievements, from inventing the wheel to venturing into the depths of space. Our intricate societies, diverse cultures, and shared languages mirror the depth of human existence, distinguishing us from the animal kingdom. Nevertheless, with our success comes significant challenges, including environmental concerns and moral dilemmas.*

ChatGPT Video Output URL and QR Code:

https://tinyurl.com/LearningResourceIntegrity

PROMPT 15 – WRITING ESSAY

Explore the impact of [**Social Media Usage**] on digital privacy. Discuss how it affects individual rights and data security.

ChatGPT Video Output URL and QR Code:

https://tinyurl.com/GPTSocialMediaPrivacy

PROMPT 16 – WRITING ESSAY

Examine the role of [**Brain Computer Interface**] in the development of artificial intelligence. Discuss its ethical, practical, and technological implications.

ChatGPT Video Output URL and QR Code:

https://tinyurl.com/BrainComputerEssay

PROMPT 17 – PERFORMING SENTIMENT ANALYSIS

Assign an emotional score ranging from 1 to 10 for the sentiment expressed in the following article [*The future of humanity in 2050 holds great promise, as we embark on a path of remarkable technological advancements, societal progress, and increased global collaboration. With technology as a driving force, our lives are set to become more convenient, sustainable, and interconnected than ever before.*

Firstly, the world of healthcare is poised for a revolution. By 2050, we anticipate breakthroughs in medical science that will extend human lifespans and enhance our overall well-being. Personalized medicine, driven by genetics and precision therapies, will become the norm, ensuring that treatments are tailored to individual needs. Aging will be redefined as we maintain healthier and more active lives well into our golden years.] **(1 = deeply cynical, 10 = highly sanguine)**

ChatGPT Video Output URL and QR Code:

https://tinyurl.com/LearningResourceSentiment

PROMPT 18 – PERFORMING SENTIMENT ANALYSIS

Critically evaluate the sentiment conveyed in this story [*Topic: Devastation caused by climate change*

In the year 2080, the world bore the heavy burden of climate change's relentless march. Sarah, an elderly woman, sat on the porch of her family's coastal home, now perilously close to the encroaching sea. Her gaze drifted toward the horizon, where once vibrant beaches had surrendered to the relentless waves.

As a child, Sarah had played on these shores, the soft sand beneath her feet and the sound of laughter filling the air. But now, she watched in despair as her beloved childhood memories were swallowed by the rising tides.

Sarah's heart ached for the generations to come, knowing that they would never experience the beauty and tranquillity of the world she had known. The impact of climate change has taken its toll, leaving a legacy of sorrow and loss. In 2080, the world stood witness to the devastating consequences of its actions, a stark reminder of the irreversible changes that had reshaped the planet, leaving Sarah and countless others with a deep sadness that no words could console.

]. Is it congruent with the topic?

ChatGPT Video Output URL and QR Code:

https://tinyurl.com/StorySentiment

PROMPT 19 – WRITING JAVA PROGRAM

Compose a **[JAVA method]** that reverses a **[linked list]** without using any additional memory.

ChatGPT Video Output URL and QR Code:

https://tinyurl.com/JavaReverseList

PROMPT 20 – WRITING JAVA PROGRAM

Create **[JAVA]** code that performs **[file compression and decompression]** using **[ZIP algorithms]**.

ChatGPT Video Output URL and QR Code:

https://tinyurl.com/JavaFileCompress

PROMPT 21 – WRITING JAVASCRIPT CODE

Generate **[JavaScript]** code that uses **[Drag and Drop API]** to allow users to **[rearrange items]** on a web page.

ChatGPT Video Output URL and QR Code:

https://tinyurl.com/JS-DragDrop

PROMPT 22 – WRITING JAVASCRIPT FUNCTION

Develop a **[JavaScript]** function that uses **[CSS Variables]** to dynamically change the **[theme]** of a web page.

ChatGPT Video Output URL and QR Code:

https://tinyurl.com/JS-CSSTheme

PROMPT 23 – WRITING PHP CODE

Compose **[PHP]** code to **[establish a connection]** with a **[MySQL data source]** and **[fetch]** all **[MODEL]** from a **[CAR]**.

ChatGPT Video Output URL and QR Code:

https://tinyurl.com/PHPMySQLConnect

PROMPT 24 – WRITING PHP SCRIPT

Generate **[PHP]** script to **[handle]** an **[image upload]** and **[store]** it in a **[images folder]**.

ChatGPT Video Output URL and QR Code:

https://tinyurl.com/PHPImageUpload

PROMPT 25 – WRITING SQL QUERY

Generate an SQL query to **[merge]** the **['Staff']** and **[Divisions]** tables to **[reveal]** the **[employee names]** and their **[respective department titles]**.

ChatGPT Video Output URL and QR Code:

https://tinyurl.com/GPTSQLMergeRecords

PROMPT 26 – WRITING SQL QUERY

Construct an SQL query to **[aggregate]** **[customer names]** and their **[lifetime purchase values]** from the **[Customers]** table, grouping them by **[membership status]**.

ChatGPT Video Output URL and QR Code:

https://tinyurl.com/SQLAggregateGroup

PROMPT 27 – DEBUGGING CODE

Debug and fix errors in the provided Java code

```
[import java.util.InputMismatchException;

import java.util.Scanner;

public class TwelveDigitCalculator {

  public static void main(String[] args) {

    scanner = new Scanner(System.in);

    try {

      System.out.println("Enter the first 12-digit number: ");

      long num1 = scanner.nextLong();

      System.out.println("Enter the second 12-digit number: ");

      long num2 = scanner.nextLong();

      // Check if the numbers are 12-digit

      if (String.valueOf(Math.abs(num1)).length() > 12 || String.valueOf(Math.abs(num2)).length() > 12) {

        throw new Exception("Numbers should be 12 digits or less.");

      }

      System.out.println("Enter an operator (+, -, *, /): ");

      char operator = scanner.next().charAt(0);
```

```
        long result = 0;
        switch (operator) {
            case '+':
                result = num1 + num2;
                break;
            case '-':
                result = num1 - num2;
                break;
            case '*':
                result = num1 * num2;
                break;
            case '/':
                if (num2 == 0) {
                    throw new ArithmeticException("Cannot divide by zero.");
                }
                result = num1 / num2;
                break;
            default:
                throw new Exception("Invalid operator.");
        }
```

```
            System.out.println("Result: " + result);
        } catch (InputMismatchException e) {
            System.out.println("Invalid input. Please enter a valid 12-digit number.");
        } catch (ArithmeticException e) {
            System.out.println(e.getMessage());
        } catch (Exception e) {
            System.out.println(e.getMessage());
        }
    }
}]
```

ChatGPT Video Output URL and QR Code:

https://tinyurl.com/Debug-Code

PROMPT 28 – CONVERTING JAVA TO PYTHON

Convert this Java code into Python *[import java.util.Calendar;*

import java.util.GregorianCalendar;

public class SimpleCalendar {

public static void main(String[] args) {

// Define the month and year to display

int month = 10; // October (Note: January is 0, February is 1, etc.)

int year = 2023;

// Create a new GregorianCalendar object

Calendar cal = new GregorianCalendar(year, month, 1);

// Get the number of days in that month

int daysInMonth = cal.getActualMaximum(Calendar.DAY_OF_MONTH);

// Get the day of the week for the 1st day of the month

int startDay = cal.get(Calendar.DAY_OF_WEEK);

// Print the header

System.out.println("Sun Mon Tue Wed Thu Fri Sat");

// Print leading spaces for the first day of the month

```
        for (int i = 1; i < startDay; i++) {
            System.out.print("    ");
        }
        // Print the days of the month
        for (int i = 1; i <= daysInMonth; i++) {
            System.out.printf("%3d ", i);
            // Move to the next line if it's the end of the week
            if ((i - 1 + startDay) % 7 == 0) {
                System.out.println();
            }
        }
    }
}]
```

ChatGPT Video Output URL and QR Code:

https://tinyurl.com/JavaToPython

PROMPT 29 – TABULAR OUTPUT

Arrange the top **[10]** nations by **[population]** and **[GDP]** in a tabular format.

ChatGPT Video Output URL and QR Code:

https://tinyurl.com/TabularOut2Data

PROMPT 30 – TABULAR OUTPUT

List the top **[20]** sustainable cities by **[population]**, **[country]**, **[area]**, and **[carbon footprint]** in a simple table.

ChatGPT Video Output URL and QR Code:

https://tinyurl.com/TabularOut4Data

PROMPT 31 – POWERPOINT OUTLINE

Generate an outline for a PowerPoint presentation with **[20]** slides focused on **[Roman Empire]**, detailing each slide's content.

ChatGPT Video Output URL and QR Code:

https://tinyurl.com/RomanPPTOutline

PROMPT 32 – POWERPOINT OUTLINE

Generate a detailed PowerPoint presentation outline containing **[15]** slides on **[Mayan]** for **[Year 10]** students, specifying what each slide should contain.

ChatGPT Video Output URL and QR Code:

https://tinyurl.com/MayanPPTOutline

PROMPT 33 – REPURPOSING A TEXT RESOURCE

Repurpose the following content for **postgraduate students** to be used for **undergraduate students** [*Special Theory of Relativity*

Formulated by Albert Einstein in 1905, the special theory of relativity postulates two main principles:

1. *The laws of physics are invariant (identical) in all inertial frames. That is, the laws of physics apply the same way in all frames of reference that are moving at constant velocity relative to each other.*
2. *The speed of light in a vacuum is the same for all observers, regardless of their motion or the motion of the light source.*

One of the most famous equations to come out of the special theory of relativity is E=mc2, which demonstrates the equivalence of mass and energy. This equation has had numerous applications, including in the development of nuclear technology.

General Theory of Relativity

Published in 1915, Einstein's general theory of relativity is a theory of gravitation that extends the special theory to include accelerated frames of reference and thus describes gravity as a curvature of space-time. In the general theory, Einstein proposed that what we perceive as gravity arises from the curvature of space-time. Massive objects like the Earth or the Sun warp the geometry of the surrounding space-time, and this warped space-time dictates the motion of other objects, which we perceive as gravitational attraction.

Implications and Experimental Verifications

The theories of relativity have been confirmed through numerous experiments and observations. Some of the critical confirmations for general relativity came with the accurate prediction of the bending of light around massive objects (gravitational lensing), the precise motion of planets, and the expansion of the universe.

In the realm of special relativity, time dilation has been confirmed through experiments involving particles moving close to the speed of light. GPS technology also needs to take into account both special and general relativistic effects to maintain accurate timekeeping across its satellite network.

Applications

Beyond the realm of theoretical physics, the theory of relativity has many practical applications. These include but are not limited to, the development of nuclear energy (and weaponry), GPS technology, and the understanding of black holes and cosmic phenomena.

Ongoing Research

Research in the field of relativity continues to be a hot topic in modern physics. Scientists are currently investigating phenomena like black holes, gravitational waves, and the nature of dark energy, all of which involve aspects of relativity.

*The theories of relativity not only revolutionized our understanding of space, time, and gravity but also led to a deeper understanding of the universe at both the cosmic and subatomic scales.***]**

ChatGPT Video Output URL and QR Code:

https://tinyurl.com/RepurposePGtoUG

PROMPT 34 – RESOURCES CREATION FOR MULTIPLE COHORTS

Develop **[800]**-word educational content on **[Sustainable Living]**, separately aimed at **[undergraduate]**, **[postgraduate]**, and **[doctoral]** students.

ChatGPT Video Output URL and QR Code:

https://tinyurl.com/SustainTeaching

PROMPT 35 – CREATING FLASHCARDS

Compose **[25]** flashcards that teach about **[CPR]**, specifically designed to align with the learning objectives of the **[Bachelor of Nursing]** program at the **[University of Tasmania]**.

ChatGPT Video Output URL and QR Code:

https://tinyurl.com/CPR-Flashcards

PROMPT 36 – CREATING FLASHCARDS

Produce **[10]** flashcards with a pedagogical focus on **[early childhood]**, intended to resonate with the academic goals of **[diploma level]** students studying **[childcare]**.

ChatGPT Video Output URL and QR Code:

https://tinyurl.com/EarlyChildFlashcards

PROMPT 37 – STUDENT MANAGEMENT

Propose **[5]** strategies for fostering **[positive attitudes towards learning]** among **[students]**.

ChatGPT Video Output URL and QR Code:

https://tinyurl.com/PositiveLearnAttitude

PROMPT 38 – STUDENT MANAGEMENT

Identify **[10]** methods to help students alleviate **[exam anxiety]**.

ChatGPT Video Output URL and QR Code:

https://tinyurl.com/ExamAnxietyMethods

PROMPT 39 – STUDENT MANAGEMENT

Describe top **[5]** approaches to promote **[self-regulation and time management skills]** in students based on research.

ChatGPT Video Output URL and QR Code:

https://tinyurl.com/SelfRegulateSkills

PROMPT 40 – CLASSROOM MANAGEMENT

Recommend **[6]** strategies to achieve **[classroom environment]** diversity and inclusion.

ChatGPT Video Output URL and QR Code:

https://tinyurl.com/ClassroomDiversity

PROMPT 41 – CLASSROOM MANAGEMENT

Outline **[5]** methods for harnessing **[educational technology]** to reduce **[classroom distractions]**.

ChatGPT Video Output URL and QR Code:

https://tinyurl.com/EdTechDistractions

PROMPT 42 – CLASSROOM MANAGEMENT

Recommend **[4]** strategies to make students feel appreciated and secure in the **[classroom]**.

ChatGPT Video Output URL and QR Code:

https://tinyurl.com/Student-Appreciation

PROMPT 43 – LITERATURE REVIEW

Conduct 2000 word literature review on the **[historical evolution]** of **[educational technologies]** and its impact on **[learning outcomes]**. Include relevant references in Harvard style.

ChatGPT Video Output URL and QR Code:

https://tinyurl.com/EdTechHistoryReview

PROMPT 44 – META-ANALYSIS

Undertake a 2000 word meta-analysis of the existing **[psychological studies]** on the effects of **[mindfulness meditation]** in reducing **[anxiety symptoms]** among **[adolescent populations]**. Include relevant references in APA style.

ChatGPT Video Output URL and QR Code:

https://tinyurl.com/MindfulnessMeta

PROMPT 45 – SYSTEMATIC REVIEW

Create and Carry out a 2000 word systematic review of **[neuroimaging studies]** to examine the neural correlates of **[language acquisition]** in **[bilingual children]**. Include all the sections that are included in a typical systematic review. Include references in Harvard style.

ChatGPT Video Output URL and QR Code:

https://tinyurl.com/NeuroImgReview

PROMPT 46 – EDUCATIONAL RESEARCH REPORT

Write a 2500 word research report providing insights about the correlation between **[extracurricular activities]** and the overall mental development of a **[university student].** Include references in **[Harvard]** style.

ChatGPT Video Output URL and QR Code:

https://tinyurl.com/ExtraCurrMentalDev

PROMPT 47 – JOB INTERVIEW

I tend to get anxious in [**face-to-face interview**]. Provide some techniques to overcome job-related anxiety.

ChatGPT Video Output URL and QR Code:

https://tinyurl.com/JobIntervTech

PROMPT 48 – JOB INTERVIEW

I've got an interview lined up at [**company**]. What queries could give me insights into their [**organisation aspects**]?

ChatGPT Video Output URL and QR Code:

https://tinyurl.com/OrgAspectQueries

PROMPT 49 – JOB INTERVIEW

What non-verbal cues should I be mindful of during a **[zoom video interview**]?

ChatGPT Video Output URL and QR Code:

https://tinyurl.com/ZoomNonVerbal

PROMPT 50 – JOB SEARCH

I've been on the job hunt for a while without success. Suggest some search strategies for a **[Senior Lecturer Position**]

ChatGPT Video Output URL and QR Code:

https://tinyurl.com/SrLecturerSearch

PROMPT 51 – PEDAGOGICAL REFLECTIONS

Describe **[10]** challenges and solutions for teachers adapting to **[online digital classrooms]**.

ChatGPT Video Output URL and QR Code:

https://tinyurl.com/DigitalClassChallenge

PROMPT 52 – PEDAGOGICAL REFLECTIONS

Create a **[detailed plan]** for fostering a **[collaborative]** learning environment in **[classroom]**.

ChatGPT Video Output URL and QR Code:

https://tinyurl.com/GPTCollaborative-Plan

CHAPTER 19

ACCURACY OF AI GENERATED CONTENT DETECTORS

19. Accuracy of AI Generated Content Detectors

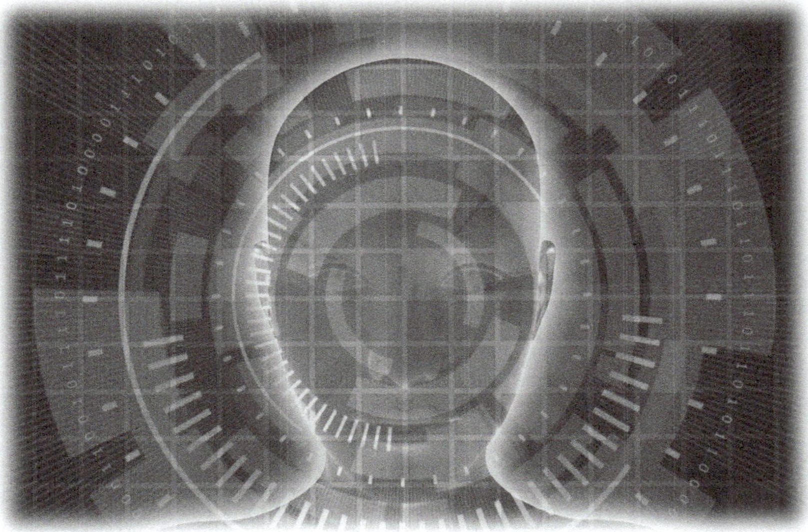

There are many companies that market software and online access to **AI Generated Content Detectors**. However, at the time of writing this book, none have achieved **100% accuracy**. There have been **numerous instances** where students were **wrongly accused** of using AI tools like **ChatGPT** to cheat on assignments.

The **widespread adoption** of AI-detecting tools by educators has led to potential pitfalls, including **false positives**, which have been reported in **various teaching institutions**.

As an **educator**, it's crucial to understand the current limitations of AI detectors and not **penalise** genuine work. **Wrongly accusing** a student of **cheating with AI** can be **more harmful** than being deceived by **AI-generated content**.

Problems with Current AI Content Detectors

Here are some **news links** that can help to understand the **severity of the problem** related to **AI content detection** worldwide.

https://tinyurl.com/AIDetectionInaccurate

https://tinyurl.com/FalsePositiveAIDetection

https://tinyurl.com/AIEducationIssue

Popular **Learning Management System (LMS)** plagiarism detection plugin **Turnitin** has introduced an **AI writing**

detection capability designed to help educators identify text that might be generated by a generative AI tool.

However, Turnitin's own detection is not 100% accurate and is **incorrectly** identifying human-generated content as AI generated content **multiple times**. Currently, the **unreliability** of AI detectors and their potential for false positives is high.

The challenges of distinguishing between **AI-generated** and **human-made content** suggest that AI detectors aren't fool-proof solution to the looming **AI-cheating issue**.

Since AI writing detection may **not always be accurate**, it should not be used as the sole basis for **academic misconduct** cases against students.

Further **scrutiny** and **human judgment** are required, in conjunction with an organisation's specific **academic policies**, to determine if any **academic misconduct** has occurred.

Five Popular AI Content Detectors

Currently, there are over **twenty AI content detectors** and the list is growing as the days pass by. To cover each of these tools is beyond the scope and focus of this book.

However, here are some **AI-generated content detection software** options that may be of interest to some readers.

1. **Winston AI – 84% Accuracy**

Winston AI which has a paid subscription **has been** a **highly accurate detection tool** among the ones tested. It has an overall accuracy score of 84%. It successfully detected every GPT-4 text and was the best tool for detecting AI content combined with human text or run through a paraphrasing tool.

2. **Originality.AI - 76% Accuracy**

Originality.AI is a **premium tool** that offers a high accuracy rate. It had a false positive during testing, but it's one of the best tools available.

3. **Sapling - 68% Accuracy**

Sapling is a **free** AI detector with an accuracy of 68%. It provides reliable results **without any cost**.

4. CopyLeaks 66% Accuracy

CopyLeaks is another tool that offers **decent accuracy** in detecting AI-generated content.

5. ZeroGPT 64% Accuracy

ZeroGPT is designed to detect content generated by models like GPT and offers a reasonable accuracy rate.

There is a discussion among AI companies about watermarking their generated content, which will make it easier to identify whether the content is **human-written or AI-generated**.

However, there is **no straightforward solution** to this issue of **successfully detecting** AI-generated content.

> Turnitin a world-renowned plagiarism detection plugin company has acknowledged a reliability problem with AI cheating-detection software used on 38 million student papers. Computer scientists warn we may never be able to reliably detect AI generated content.

Glossary

Artificial Intelligence (AI): A field of computer science focused on creating systems that can perform tasks that would normally require human intelligence, such as decision-making, visual perception, and language understanding.

Machine Learning: A subfield of AI that provides systems the ability to automatically learn and improve from experience without being explicitly programmed.

Deep Learning: A type of machine learning that involves neural networks with multiple layers, allowing for more complex learning and decision-making.

Neural Network: A computing system inspired by the human brain, consisting of interconnected nodes (neurons) that process information.

Natural Language Processing (NLP): A subfield of AI that focuses on the interaction between computers and humans through natural language, enabling machines to understand, interpret, and generate human language.

Chatbot: A software application that can conduct a conversation with users, often used in customer service or as a virtual assistant.

Bias: In the context of AI and machine learning, bias refers to the tendency of a model to make decisions that are slanted due to the data it was trained on or the way it was designed.

"Artificial intelligence is growing up fast, as are robots whose facial expressions can elicit empathy and make your mirror neurons quiver."

- Diane Ackerman

"Artificial intelligence is one of the most profound things we're working on as humanity. It's more profound than fire or electricity."

- Sundar Pichai

"Artificial intelligence is changing the way we live, work, and play, and it's just the beginning." - Jerry Yang

"The development of artificial intelligence and its impact on the way we live and work is one of the most significant and challenging technological advancements of our time."

- Demis Hassabis

Free App Offer

Download the App for Android smartphone/tablet at

https://tinyurl.com/affirmationapp

This affirmation app has inbuilt brainwaves sound and white noise which can be used for developing a positive mindset and can help you to stay focused and achieve your goals. The brainwave synchronization has been found to enhance relaxation response and positively influence cognitive abilities. There are six categories of affirmations included - happiness, health, success, wealth, relationship and weight loss. Each of these categories has 15 affirmations which can be further edited to give it a more personal touch for improved effectiveness. You can even add more categories and affirmations or edit or delete the existing ones to have a unique user experience and customization.

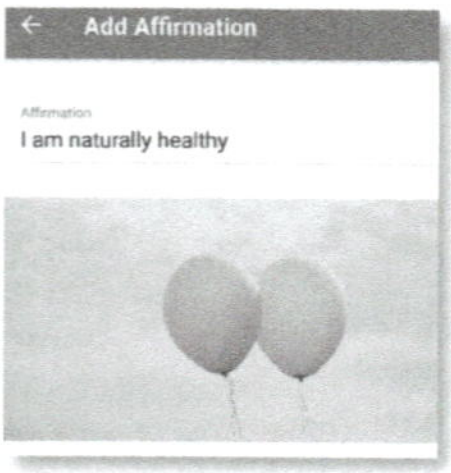

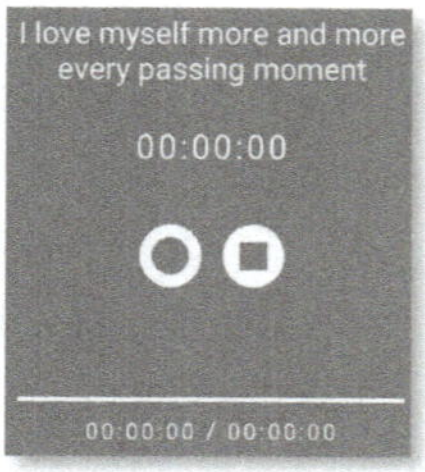

This App is compatible ONLY with Android smartphones and tablets.
This App is NOT COMPATIBLE with iOS (Apple) smartphones and tablets.

Books allow us to expand our knowledge. This knowledge expands our awareness, which in turn expands our thinking.
OUR THINKING EXPANDS OUR WORLD.

-- Quote by Keshav Jha

More Books by Keshav Jha

Visit

www.maxlifepublishing.com

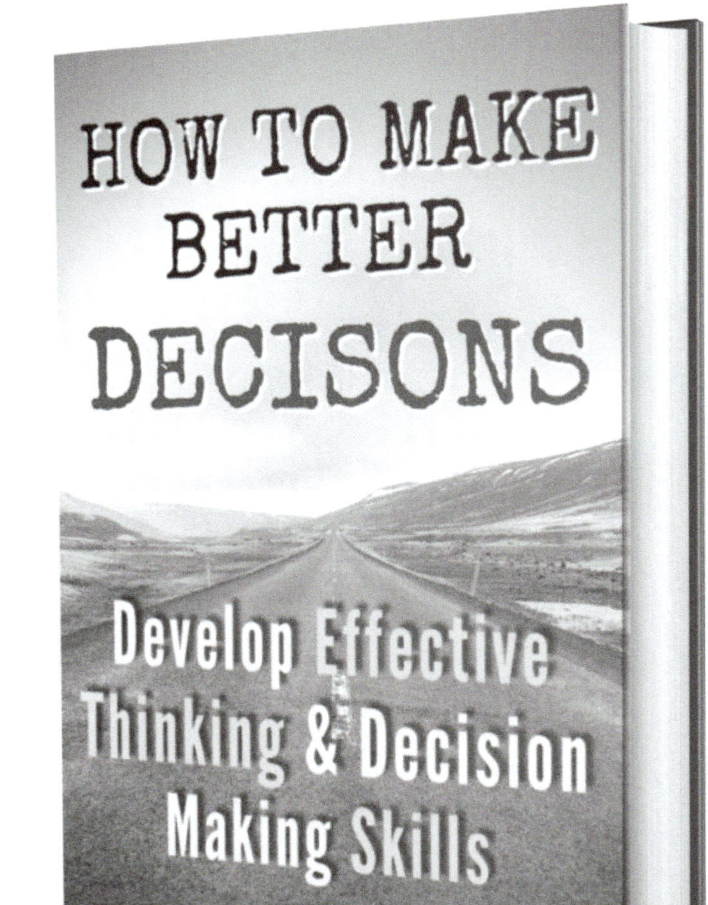
HOW TO MAKE
BETTER
DECISONS
Develop Effective
Thinking & Decision
Making Skills
KESHAV JHA

BEING
Become Happy in
as Little as
30 Seconds NOW
HAPPY
200
Proven Easy & Quick Ways
to Become More Happy
KESHAV JHA

SURESHOT
WAYS TO
ACHIEVE
GOALS
3 Steps Goal Setting
For Teenageers
KESHAV JHA

POWERFUL & EFFECTIVE
"Me Time"
STRATEGIES
HOW TO
FILL YOUR
OWN
CUP
200
SELF-LOVE IDEAS
"Learn to Love Yourself"
KESHAV JHA

STOP
PROCRASTINATION
100 SMART STRATEGIES FOR
OVERCOMING PROCRASTINATION
KESHAV JHA

USE THE POWER OF
YOUR SUBCONSCIOUS
MIND
SUBCONSCIOUS
MIND
MASTERY
EASY AND PROVEN WAYS TO
PROGRAM YOURSELF FOR
EXTRAORDINARY
SUCCESS
KESHAV JHA

YOGA
For
BETTER LIVING
CREATE
HIGH ENERGY
LIFE !
DEVELOP HEALTHY MIND AND BODY
KESHAV JHA

ANCIENT WiSDOM
for
ENGLIGHTENED LIVING
YOGA
VASISTHA
Simplified
KESHAV JHA

"This book exemplifies the principles of love, trust and gratitude toward one's partner."
FOREWORD BY DR. JOHN DEMARTINI
World-renowned Human Behaviour Specialist who featured in the international documentary movie - 'The Secret'
FIFTY THINGS I LOVE ABOUT MY WIFE
LOVE IS THE ONLY WAY
Includes
16 Principles of Love for Better Relationships
"This book humbles me and makes me look deeply again into my own relationships. Thank you for the inspiration of your life and work."
- WIM HOF, also known as 'The Iceman'
KESHAV JHA

Made in the USA
Middletown, DE
05 November 2026

36587661R00384